Lighting Design
for Commercial Portrait Photography

Jennifer Emery

Amherst Media, Inc. ■ Buffalo, NY

Acknowledgments

I want to first thank my husband Matthew Emery for never letting me go down that road of insecurity, and for being more man than me. Thanks for always making me feel intelligent.

Special thanks to Serena Montenegro for always being my built-in proofreader and my partner in photography crime. Thanks to Ford Lowcock and Craig Mohr at Santa Monica College for trusting me to develop the new college course that was the inspiration for this book. Thanks to my students for inspiring me to create great lighting demos, contributing to the book, and for just plain geeking out with me about photography. I'd also like to thank my teaching assistant Preston Perkins for getting all those setup photos and brainstorming on set with me. Thanks to the models and makeup artists who donated their time, supplies, incredible creativity, and work ethic in creating the images in this book. And thanks to everyone at Amherst Media for teaming up with me on this great venture.

Finally, thank you to my friends and family (you know who you are) for your support and always thinking my photography is pretty cool!

Published by:
Amherst Media, Inc., P.O. Box 586, Buffalo, N.Y. 14226, Fax: 716-874-4508
www.AmherstMedia.com

Publisher: Craig Alesse
Senior Editor/Production Manager: Michelle Perkins
Editors: Barbara A. Lynch-Johnt, Harvey Goldstein, Beth Alesse
Associate Publisher: Kate Neaverth
Editorial Assistance from: Carey A. Miller, Sally Jarzab, John S. Loder
Business Manager: Adam Richards
Warehouse and Fulfillment Manager: Roger Singo

ISBN-13: 978-1-60895-895-5
Library of Congress Control Number: 2015955655
Printed in The United States of America.
10 9 8 7 6 5 4 3 2 1

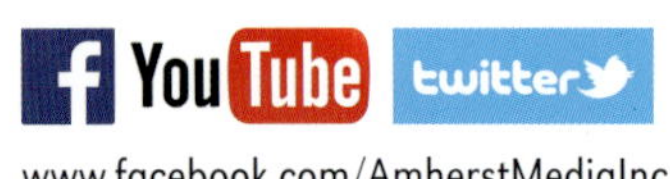

www.facebook.com/AmherstMediaInc
www.youtube.com/c/AmherstMedia
www.twitter.com/AmherstMedia

Contents

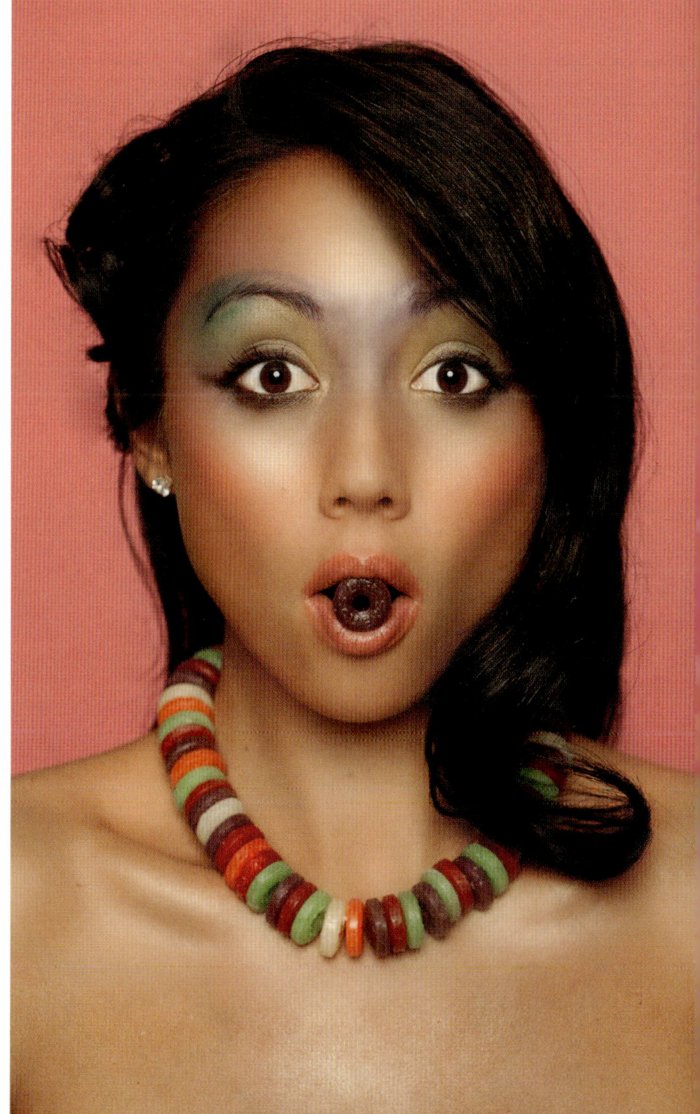

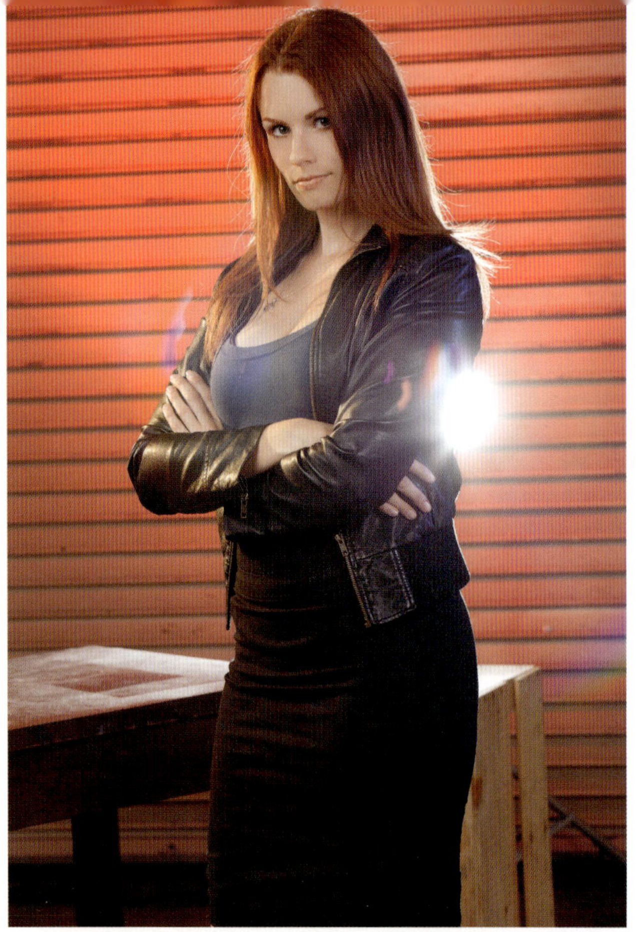

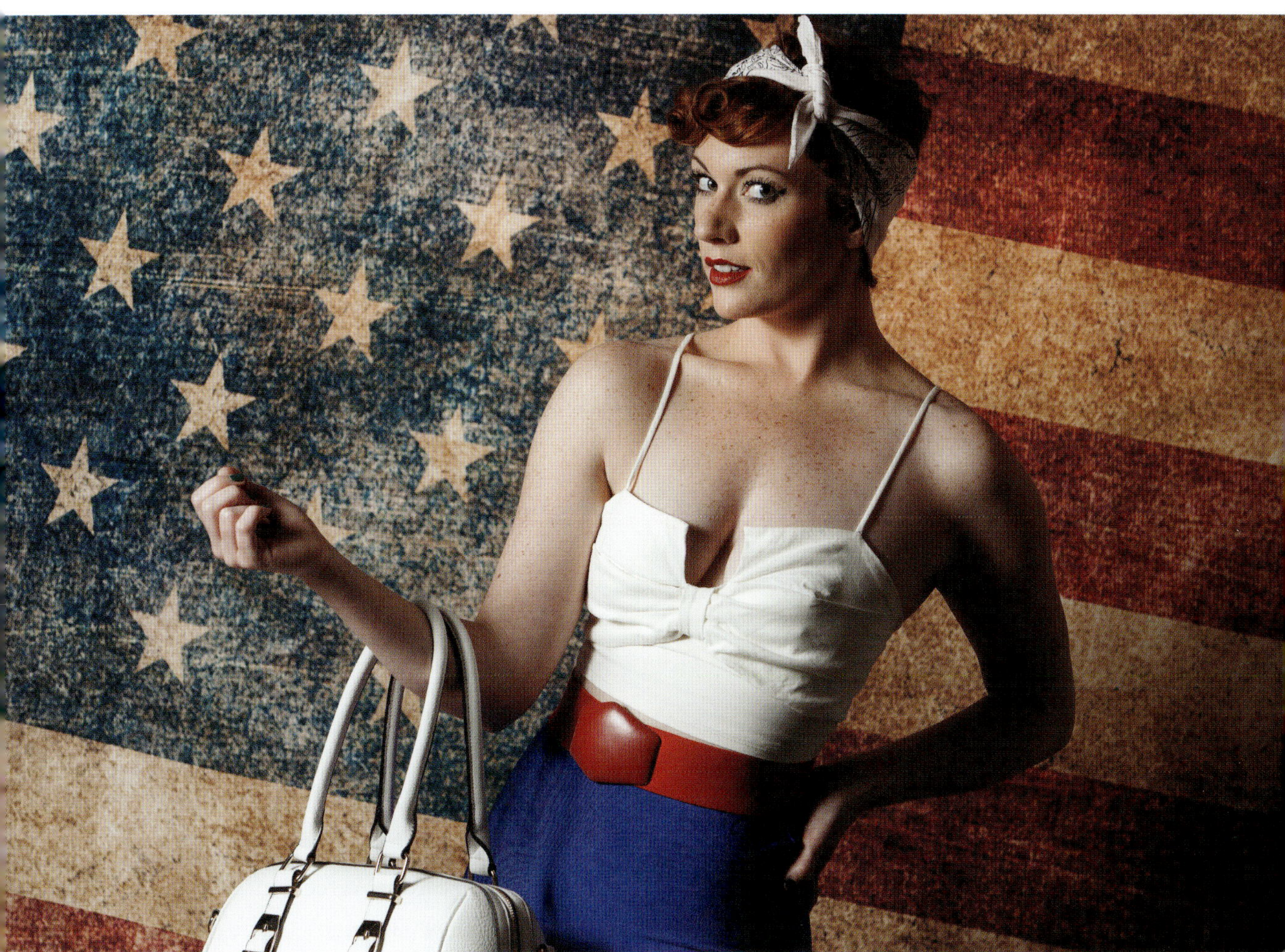

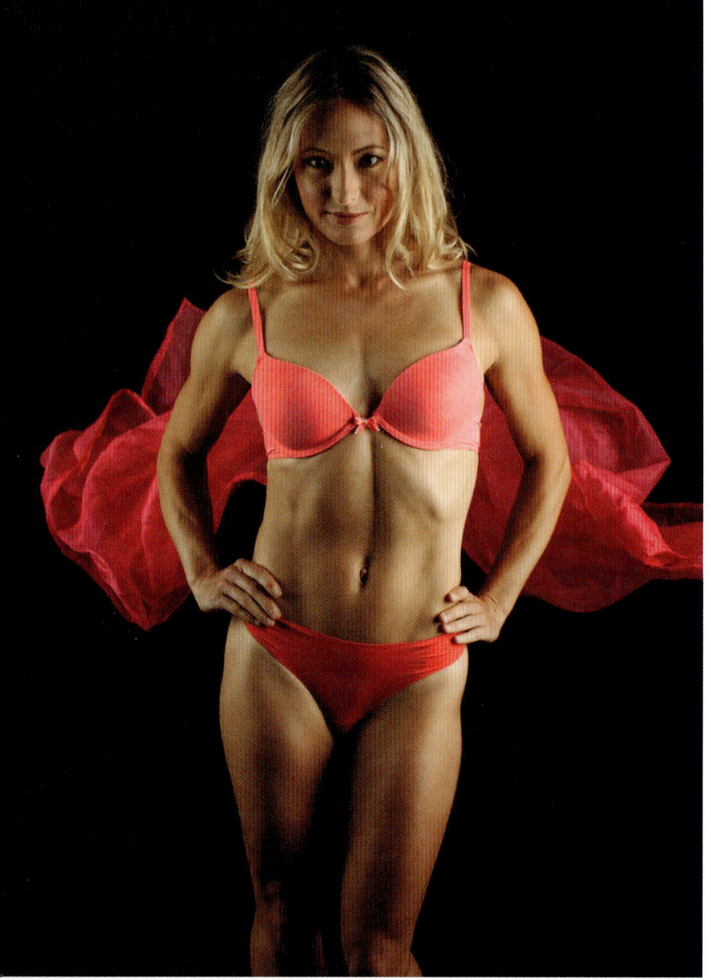

About the Author

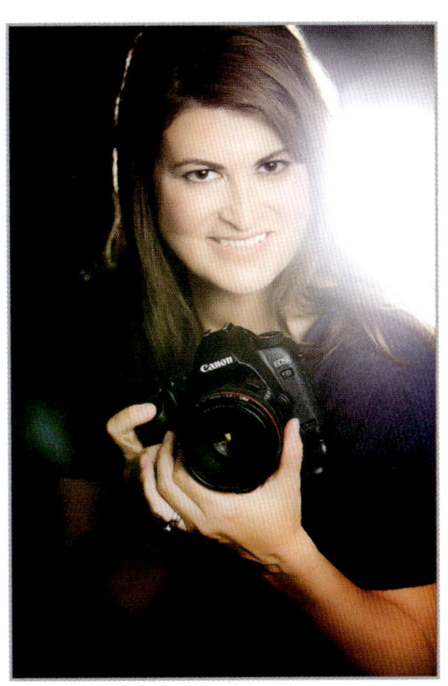

Photo by Jade Alayne (weddingsbyjade.com).
Hair and makeup by Mariah Nicole (mariahnicole.com).

Jennifer (Zivolich) Emery of PBJ Candids, based in Los Angeles, CA, has been a freelance photographer for over twenty years. She specializes in lifestyle and commercial photography and describes her work as cinematic with a fashion feel. She is also a part-time adjunct photography instructor at a community college and teaches workshops at various institutions. Her work has been published in *Pasadena Magazine*, *Inside Weddings* and *Grace Ormonde*, and her business has been featured on such television networks as the TLC Network. She has been honored with awards from WPPI Awards of Excellence and received the Creative Artistic Award for individual portraits from National Photo Awards. Jennifer is also an actor, screenwriter, and small production producer. She holds a BA in Speech Communication from Cal State Northridge. Find more about Jennifer at www.pbjcandids.com.

Introduction

My History

When I was very young, my father had a home darkroom setup and an enlarger that fascinated me. I took my first photography class in sixth grade, and at age fifteen received my first 35mm camera from my father—and I guess the path was set. In college, I ran a portrait studio at a department store; it was one of the worst jobs I ever had, but I learned the rules of basic portrait posing. I was also pursuing an acting career and occasionally did some modeling. On shoots, my interest in and knowledge of photography was obvious to the photographers, and I was often asked if I wanted to assist—pulling double duty as a model and assistant on magazine and commercial shoots. This was my introduction to the world of commercial photography. Once out of college, I started working part-time as a professional photographer, shooting actors' headshots and models' zed cards. This eventually led to wedding and portrait photography—and then back again to the commercial photography world.

My Work Today

Today, I specialize in lifestyle and editorial photography that is cinematic with a fashion feel. My work spans many genres from film and industrial production stills, campaign photography, print, and fashion, to the retail market of portraits, headshots, and events. The through-line is that most of my work is *people* photography. My work requires lighting quickly, in many different environments, and answering to clients' visual expectations.

While I studied some photography in college and continually update my skills through professional seminars, most of what I know was learned on the job. I also worked many years training photographers for large national event-photography companies. Therefore, my way of teaching is very real-world and hands-on. This book is written in that manner; it takes lighting lessons and applies them to real-world commercial photography examples.

Commercial vs. Retail Photography

Traditionally, commercial photography is thought of as advertising, magazine, fashion photography, and the like—work where you are hired by a company to photograph images to be used in a commercial context. Retail photography, on the other hand, is what would be called "direct to client." This includes jobs like weddings and portraits, where you create images of the client (or their family members) for personal use.

If you are in retail photography, chances are you will regularly cross over into commercial photography. For example, a portrait client might ask you to photograph a small advertising campaign for their company. Experienced retail photographers know how to light and pose in any situation. They can move quickly and are very adaptable. They are also used to working with real people and making them look good.

My point is, if you are a retail photographer, don't be afraid to learn to do commercial shoots. This book will help any type of photographer conquer many of the obstacles that will arise during a commercial photography shoot. But, just as with any type of photography, you have to practice, practice, practice and be honest with your clients about your experience and abilities.

Application of the Book

This book will cover actual applications in fashion and commercial photography. It will explore several advanced lighting techniques using strobes, as well as how to light using speedlights (small flashes) in artificial- and natural-light settings. In each chapter, we will look at a different lighting technique and a different commercial setting that gives the technique a real-world application—everything from editorial fashion shoots to cast photos, beauty shots, and catalog shoots. Lighting is not all it takes in commercial photography, so we will also cover a little about producing and directing photo shoots. Additionally, the book will cover items such as casting and working with your client. Good shooting!

Disclosure

I just want to mention that I talk about many different products made by several companies. Although I use and love their products, I do not endorse any of them and I was not paid by any of the companies to mention them in the

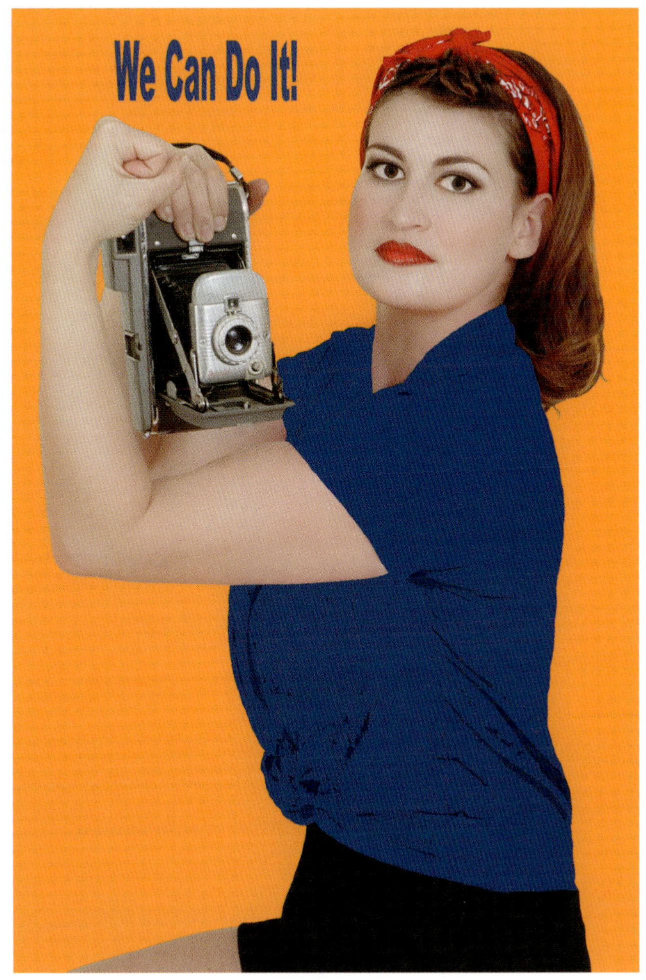

▲ Self-portrait from my *Pin Me Up* fine-art series. *Image by Jennifer Emery and Serena Montenegro.*

book. The names of the products are simply stated so that the reader has an understanding of what item I was using to produce the image.

1. Tools

Do you need to go out and buy expensive strobes and modifiers to achieve professional results? No. For the most part, the equipment you need as a commercial photographer is the same required for *any* kind of people photography. This is an advanced photography book, so I will assume you already use a lot of these items and are doing some pro-level photography.

Full-Frame Sensor DSLR Camera

I will assume you are shooting with a midrange DSLR camera, something that is at least "prosumer" level, with a full-frame sensor. I do recommend having a second camera for backup. When I upgrade my camera every few years, I use my old camera as my backup.

Plan to upgrade your camera every three to five years. Digital cameras are basically little computers. They have a shelf life, and at some point the repairs cost more than a new camera. (I also advise purchasing the extended warranty; my motherboard failed when my camera was just over a year old—and the replacement cost was *half* the price of a new camera.) Also, technology changes quickly. If you are shooting with a camera that is five years old and its largest file is 12 megapixels, but new cameras are 21 megapixels, your quality will be lacking.

You may be wondering about medium format cameras like a Hasselblad body and a digital back. But, really, how can anyone afford that? If you see one in use, it's probably rented for the job—trust me. The digital back alone costs $14,000 to $40,000 and most shoots simply do not require such high resolution.

Lenses

Commercial shoots require the sharpness and wide apertures of pro-level lenses. I shoot Canon, so that means I use the L-series lenses.

Zooms

If you are starting out, a professional zoom lens that moves between wide and standard portrait lens lengths (like a 28–105mm lens) is a good bet and enables you to change your cropping immediately, without having to move your body forward and back. This is a good all-around lens, but it's not *super* sharp because it's a zoom lens. Still, most commercial and fashion photographers have a pro-level 70–200mm f/2.8L lens in their arsenal.

▼ Here I am on location after Hurricane Katrina, heading up a photojournalist team with my Canon gear. *Image by Ian Horn.*

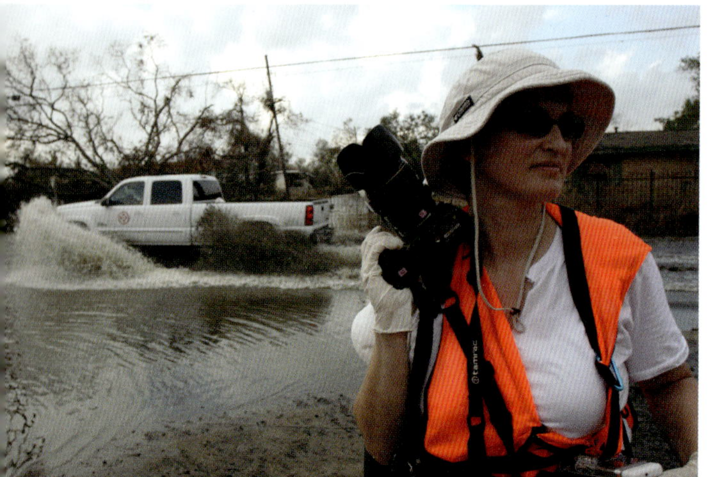

Primes

The only way to get *extremely* sharp images
is with prime (fixed focal length) lenses. For
beauty images, where this is critical, you really
want something like a 85mm or 100mm
portrait lens. Some photographers even like a
160mm. I prefer the 100mm f/2.8L Macro.
It's a super-sharp, amazing portrait lens with
great compression *and* it doubles as a macro
lens, so I can use it to shoot very close-up images. It's also good for product photography.

Other Options

It's nice to have the option to go very wide,
making the 17–35mm f/2.8 zoom another
useful addition to your arsenal. If you have
any funds left, a 50mm f/1.2L is a good lens,
too—but I have to say that it's on the bottom
of my list if you have a good 70–200mm zoom
and a 85mm or 100mm prime.

A Basic Kit

For your basic kit, the following lenses are
what I recommend. Again, all lenses should be
pro-level models, like the Canon L-series.

> 70–200mm f/2.8L
> 85mm f/1.2L (or 100mm f/2.8L Macro)
> 17–35mm f/2.8L
> 28–105mm f/4L
> 50mm f/1.2L (maybe)

Speedlights/Flashes

In this book, you will sometimes see me refer
interchangeably to "speedlights" or "flashes." These are both generic terms for a small,
external flash—the kind that has a hotshoe

Renting Equipment

High-end commercial photographers often shoot at rental studios, and
all the equipment is rented and paid for by production. The camera,
lights, C-stands, sand bags, and even the computer monitor–those
are mostly rentals. And if the photographer is using their personal
equipment, they also charge a rental fee for that. On the other hand,
the rest of us in the middle to lower range of client budgets are expected to spend money on our own equipment in order to stay in the
price range. This means a shoot actually can cost the little guy more
upfront money–it's kind of a catch-22.

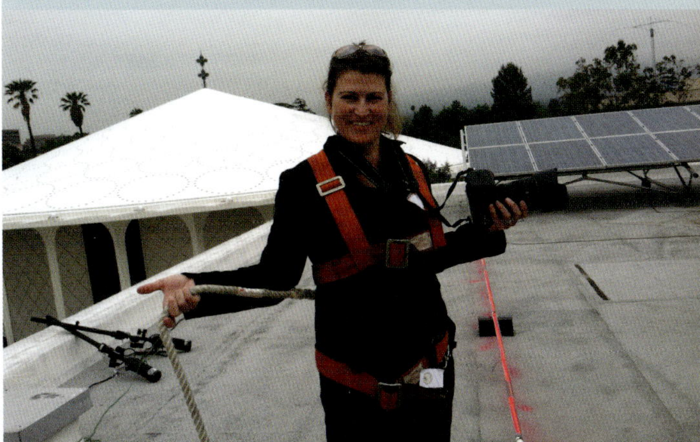

▲ This cell phone photo shows me getting ready to shoot from a building
roof with a rental camera.

mount. Nikon users may refer to those units as
"SB" flashes, while Canon users sometimes call
them "TTL" flashes. Many quality models are
also available from third-party manufacturers.

Basic Considerations

What's more important than the brand name
is making sure that the flash will (at the very
least) sync with your camera. Most flashes
made by your camera's manufacturer will com-
municate with your camera. Be sure to check
the specifications before you buy—especially
if you are buying a used flash. Do you need a

TTL flash? No, but you do need a flash that will sync with your camera. Fortunately, even the oldest flash units can usually be inexpensively adapted to sync with newer cameras.

TTL vs. Manual

Many flashes are equipped with TTL (through the lens) functionality, which means that the flash can "talk" to the camera and automatically determine the amount of light to output for the given situation. Do you have to use a TTL flash? No. In fact, if you use your flash off-camera, as most professionals do, you will typically be utilizing the manual modes, so the TTL function may not even be called upon.

Off-Camera Flash Accessories

Today, many flash units have built-in radio/infrared capabilities that allow the flashes to "talk" to each other in multi-light setups. Even if your flash units do have this feature, you will want a set of radio slaves and sync cords as backup. You will also need these for working with strobes; more on this later in the chapter.

There are many brands to choose from in radio slaves; Canon and Nikon each have their own proprietary systems, but third-party companies like Pocket Wizard and Impact provide additional options. Of course, not all systems are created equal. Cheap, off-brands work—but sometimes not for long.

My recommendation is to invest in any well-made brand. If you really don't have the money, get the cheap kind and use them until they break. I tend to split the difference. I have an expensive pair of name-brand radio slaves that are my workhorses. On occasion, however, I need to sync more than two light sources that don't have their own radio transmitters. Then, I pull out the inexpensive, off-brand units to get three or four lights all syncing to my camera. (*Note:* The problem here is that the different brands do not talk to each other, so I have to plug two transmitters into my camera to make it all work.)

We'll look at shooting with speedlights in more detail when we get to chapter 7.

Studio Strobes and Hot Lights
Strobes

A studio strobe kit with two lights will usually get the job done. If you need more lights for a specific assignment, you can rent the gear and charge the fee to your client—or sync up your speedlights to give you a three-light setup (or whatever is required). I prefer monolights, which have a built-in power pack, so you don't have to lug an external pack around with you. However, if a monolight goes down, fixing it may require more than just a bulb.

You can spend anywhere from $300 to $4000 (and much more) on studio lighting kits, and these disparate prices underscore the fact that not all lights are created equal.

▼ Heading up a photojournalist team after Hurricane Katrina, I climbed a sign pole to get a shot of a rescue base-camp. With me were my Canon 5D and a 28–105mm f/4L lens. I also had my 70–200mm f/2.8L lens on standby. *Image by Ian Horn.*

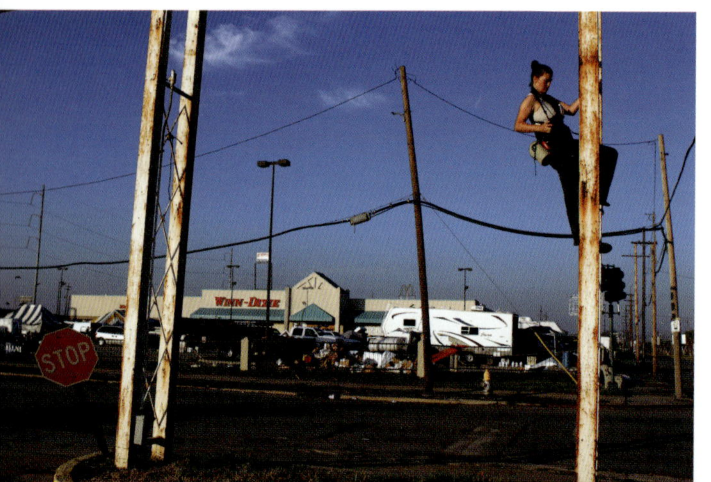

The wattage and highest sync speeds of the lights themselves vary, as do the quality of the included light stands, modifiers, etc. If you are on a budget, just about any strobe kit can do the job. I would, however, recommend getting something that has *at least* a 500-watt output.

Hot Lights

Hot lights provide continuous light and are another way to go. Again, a two-light kit is a good starting point and you'll want at least a 600-watt output. If you have to choose one, I would opt for the strobes. But if you can get both, that is what I'd recommend. Today, video is being incorporated into many still photographers' workloads and this is something you can only do with continuous light sources.

Mixing Sources

If your commercial photography is fast-paced and/or incorporates multiple locations, your best bet may be using off-camera speedlights (basically using them as you would studio strobes). This eliminates the need for a power outlet or the bulky studio-strobe battery kits that can be time-consuming to set up and break down. Of course, speedlights can burn out and they do not always have the power you may need in a large studio situation, so owning a good strobe kit is still recommended.

Light Modifiers and Other Accessories

Of course, you will need memory cards, a light meter, batteries, and other items.

To create professional images you also need to be able to manipulate light, so make sure

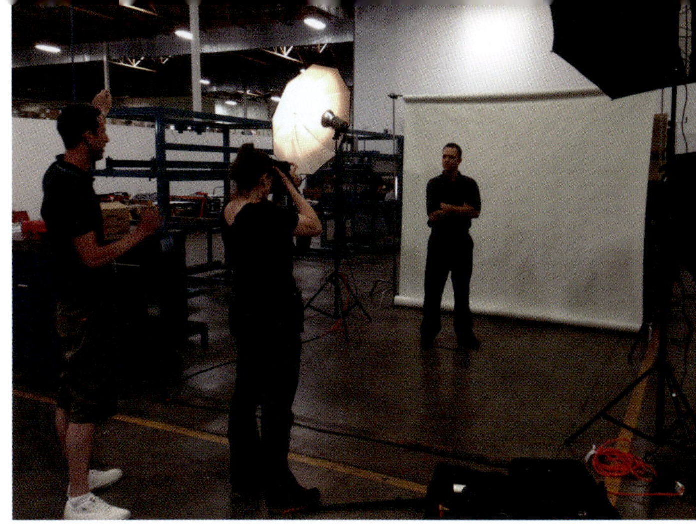

▲ A cell phone photo of me creating stills on an industrial video shoot with Take-One Productions. I'm working with the advertising agency client, while shooting with two strobes and one speedlight in an umbrella for the background light.

you invest in a few items. I recommend purchasing a few umbrellas with removable liners; these can be used as bounce-light sources for sharper lighting and reversed to a shoot-through position for softer effects. Likewise, look for reflector kits that offer the versatility of a silver and gold side along with (optimally) removable pieces that have a white and black side. (Don't forget about negative fill; black boards or flags can be very helpful—you'll see them used in many of the setups covered in this book.)

If you plan to use your modifiers with your speedlights, you will also need to purchase the appropriate adapters to hold the items. For example, a hot-shoe flash umbrella mount lets you attach the flash to a light stand but also provides a hole to position the umbrella arm in place. Alternately, there are many wonderful light modifiers designed specifically for use with speedlights—or you can even make your own.

2. Producing a Commercial Shoot

Photographers are often called on to do much more than photography. On commercial shoots, the photographer often has the added responsibility of functioning as the casting director and even the producer. This means you will need to take control of planning many, if not all, the different aspects of the production. Don't be afraid—you can do this!

How to Learn

You should never take on the production of a commercial photography shoot if you don't have any experience. A great way to learn these elements is to assist an experienced photographer or producer on some commercial photo shoots. However, I know that this opportunity may not be readily available to those in smaller cities. In that case, a good way to get used to all the elements that go into a still shoot production is to plan some test shoots. You can start by bringing together a team of other artists who want images for their portfolios— makeup artists, wardrobe stylists or designers, lighting grips or assistants, and models or actors may all be interested in creating images with you.

Planning is the key, here. If you are not organized, you'll find that the shoot usually falls short of your expectations. After one test shoot, you will begin to see what needs to be planned—and what you missed. Keep in mind that if this is a test shoot in which the participants are relatively new at commercial photography, you will definitely need to allow extra time for each step of the process. On a paying shoot, you must have a good idea of how much time you and the crew need; you do not want your clients sitting around waiting for things to happen.

Here are some things to evaluate as you are setting up test shoots and reviewing the results of your efforts.

Makeup

Did you have the makeup artist arrive early enough for them to finish and allow the shoot to start as scheduled? Before the shoot, you

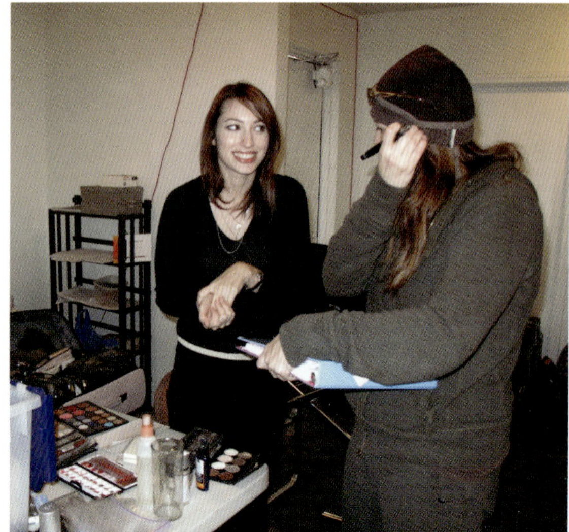

▼ Talking with key makeup artist Mariah Nicole during production images for the television pilot *30. Image by Ted Pang.*

need to ask your makeup artist how long they need to do the application, and then allow for extra time just in case they run over. (Makeup notoriously takes at least an hour longer than expected.) Remember that, in addition to the time quoted for application, the makeup artist will also need thirty to sixty minutes to park, unload, and set up their station.

Wardrobe

How long will the model be in wardrobe and how much time does the wardrobe stylist need for that? Did you do a fitting or have your model tell you her measurements for wardrobe? Did the wardrobe fit your model during the shoot?

Models

Did your models arrive on time, or were they late and did they hold up your entire shoot? Did you plan backup models just in case they didn't show up at all? Models are often late, whether it is for a test shoot or a paid job. I suggest having your models arrive at least thirty to sixty minutes before they are scheduled to go into makeup—or have them get there during the setup time. (More on casting and working with models in the next section.)

Equipment

Did you have the correct (or enough) equipment? Did you make a checklist and remember to bring everything? How long do you and your assistants need? Often, you can do your setup while the model is being prepped—but can you do the setup in one hour or do you need two? Remember that you will also need

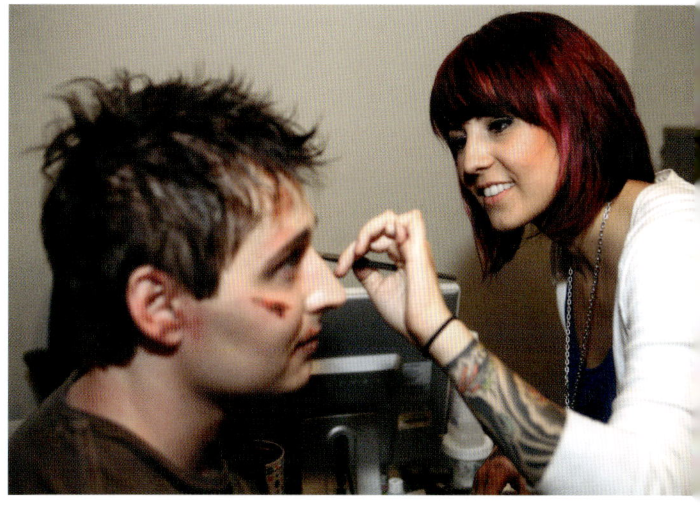

▲ Special effects makeup artist Cici Anderson during production shots for the television pilot *30. Image by Ted Pang.*

time to park, unload all the equipment, assemble it, and do lighting tests.

Craft Service

What about food or meals? Did you plan any breaks or refreshments to keep everyone on the set going? Does someone need to order lunch for everyone? Even if you are doing a test shoot that involves only a three-hour commitment, you should have some basic sustenance, like fruit and water, available to the participants.

A good example of taking care of the crew and talent is what I did during my early-morning classroom demos for a college photography class I was teaching. Everyone needed to arrive between 7:30AM and 8:00AM. The models and makeup artists committed their time in exchange for photos, so I wanted them to feel like it was worth their time and that it was a professional environment. Therefore, I always provided coffee, water, and some kind of morning snack like fruit or granola bars. Normally, the models won't eat much—but they will drink coffee and water and sometimes have a piece of fruit on the way out. It's more the point of them feeling respected. This is not a big cost to a test shoot budget; it's not a time when you need to go buy expensive cappuccinos for everyone. Just grab a bag of fruit and bring your coffee maker to brew a pot for everyone on the set.

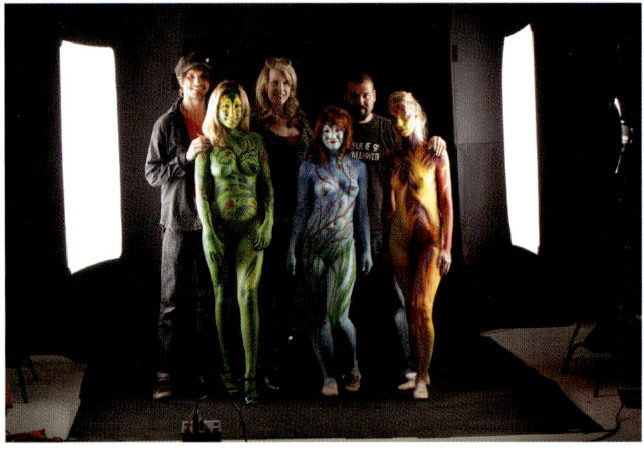

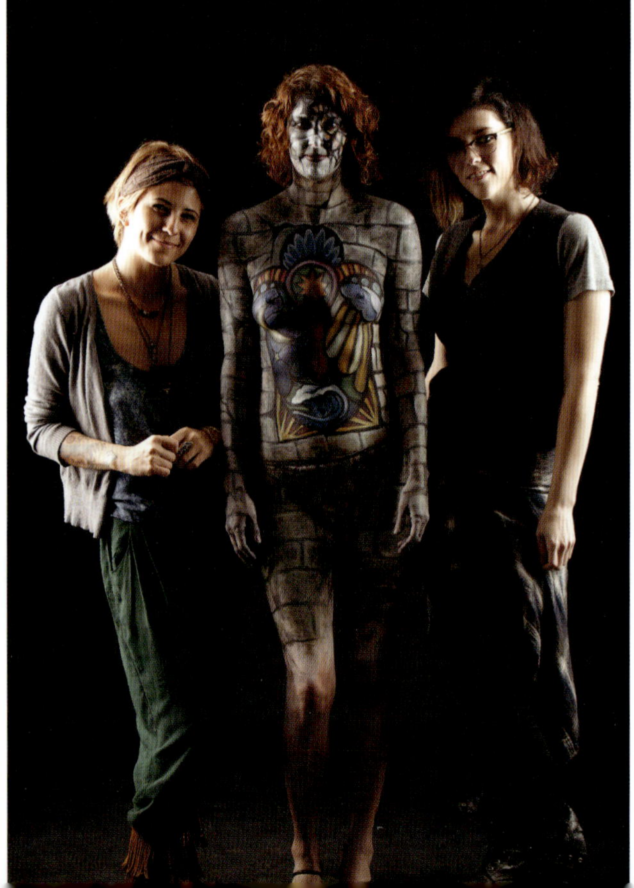

◀ Body painting makeup artist with models on my "painted ladies" set. Images from this session appear in chapter 6.

Casting and Working with Models

There are several ways to cast models for your productions, whether they are paying jobs or non-paying test shoots. You can always find models if you are professional and willing to give them nice-looking images for their portfolios.

Where to Find Models

As a photographer on smaller-budget commercial shoots, you may be required to do your own casting. For test shoots, there are always online classifieds like Craigslist and Model Mayhem. Sometimes people can be flaky when it comes to working on a trade, though—so don't just cast the model based on a photo; make sure you meet them in person for an audition. If you are in a small town, your models may be driving a long distance to your studio. In that case, consider planning a casting day that is closer to their location. This allows you to meet a number of models at the same time and at a neutral location, like a coffee shop. You can even reserve a space at a local library or college campus.

In smaller markets, putting out notices online, at local colleges, or with local agents is a good idea. If you are in a larger market, like Los Angeles or New York City, there are online casting services that work great. For example, Actors Access and LA Casting both allow you to post casting notices at no charge. However, there are a couple of things to remember about using these services for commercial pro-

◀ Body painting makeup artist with models on my "painted ladies" set. Images from this session appear in chapter 6.

duction. First, these are professional actors and models who pay to receive casting notices, so it's important not to abuse the services. Second, you have to be ready to cast. Once your notice is posted, talent will typically respond within minutes. Most of the responses will come within the first twenty-four hours after posting, so you need to check your responses quickly and start your casting process. It's best to do your post only about a week before your audition date. If it's too far out, people's schedules will change and you will have a lot of cancellations. This also applies to test shoots and posting on other public boards.

Model Compensation

If your model is receiving images in exchange for her participation in a test shoot, I don't recommend giving prints—simply because it's a cost you can avoid. Instead, deliver high-resolution images that either have a watermark or some other credit to the photographer, just for copyright safety. Keep in mind that the model may want to print or use the images on their website, so don't go overboard with a heavy watermark through the center of the image.

For test shoots, I have the models pick out one or two images and I retouch those only. I then give them all the usable (but unretouched) images as high-resolution files with a small copyright notice at the bottom of the photo. I also give them a low-res copy with a watermark for online use. I make sure every model signs a release stating that if they post the images on any public social media site, such as Facebook, they must use the *watermarked* images. In addition, I post all the

images from the shoot online for a couple of weeks for viewing.

For paying jobs, a tear sheet from the printed material is sufficient for the model's portfolio—or you can supply a high-resolution image of the final advertisement. I do not give copies of edited images to the models on these jobs, because those files belong to the client. The model only has access to the final product. The amount the model is paid really depends on the client and the type of project.

Working with Models

How you act around a model is very important. This may seem like a no-brainer, but I have been around some rather strange behavior—and I have seen the same poor behavior repeated by different people, so it seems like an important subject.

Number one: do not touch the model without her permission. Over and over again, I have seen male photographers place their hand on female models, invading their personal space and making them feel uncomfortable. This uneasiness is often detectable in the model's expression in the final images. I have even seen photographers touch or move sensitive body parts—and this is *very* inappropriate. And, for the record, this does not just apply to male photographers interacting with female models; it applies across the board to all photographers dealing with both genders of models.

For example, don't go over and move the hair out of the model's face; instead, simply ask her to move it herself. If the model can't accomplish a task based on your verbal instructions, ask permission before you go to adjust a piece of clothing, etc.—and do so sparingly. (Often, a model will say it is okay even when she is really not comfortable with it.) Likewise, when asking the model to pose differently, use your words or demonstrate the pose yourself so she can mimic it. There is very little reason

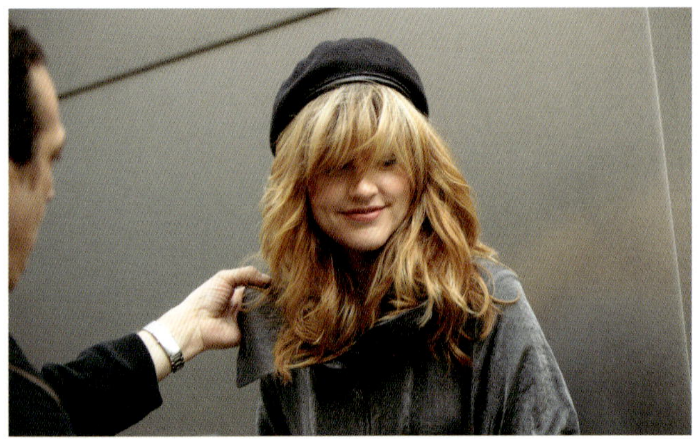

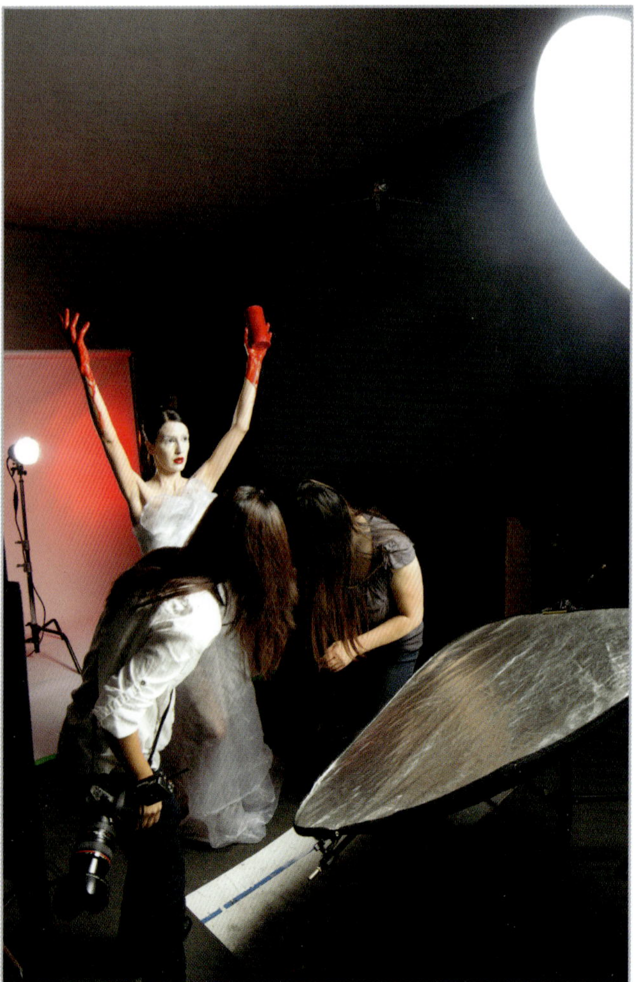

to go touch her to make her move differently into a pose. Sometimes, having a makeup artist or stylist on set can help you accomplish some of these tasks more delicately.

This is particularly important if you are shooting models who are nude or not wearing much clothing. Here, the rule of thumb is to think of this like a doctor's office where a female nurse is required to be in the room with a male doctor. If you don't have an assistant, or someone else of the same sex as your model on the set, ask the model to bring a friend to the shoot. *Anytime* you are shooting nudes, you may want to ask the model to bring a friend, just so everyone is comfortable.

Communication Is Key

Communication is very important. If you don't feel you're good at talking to people, take a public speaking class. It will help you with your directing ability on set as well as with negotiating deals for your business.

Directing is a very big part of people photography and learning this skill is very important. A student in one of my advanced photography classes specialized in product photography and expressed that she did not feel she was very good with people. I think part of this was the fact that English was not her first language. I told her to think of the models like products that she needed to talk to—to make them arrange themselves in positions. I told her to be very specific with them about where she wanted their hands, faces, and eyes, and to mold them just as she would

◀ Top: A photographer adjusts a model's clothing during one of my fashion photography workshops.

◀ Bottom: Student photographers working with a model during a classroom demo. *Image by Preston Perkins.*

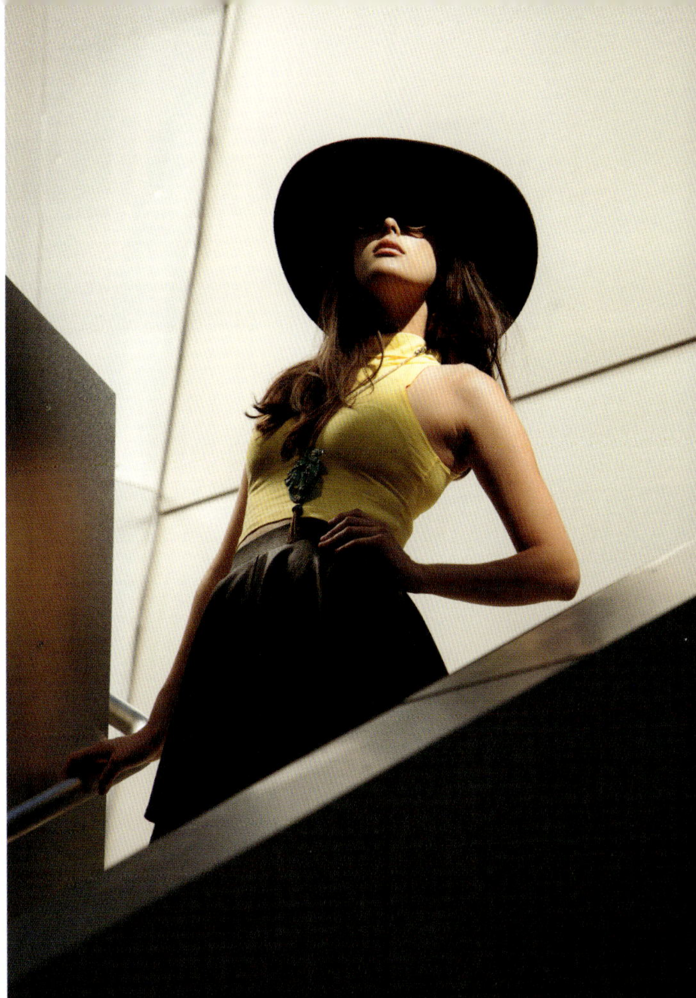

inanimate objects. She surprised herself, and her work with models was phenomenal.

Keep in mind that you can also give visual cues. Try using hand gestures, posing your body in the way you want the model to pose, or even bringing photo samples to show your models the poses you have in mind.

Finally, keep in mind that some models are naturally good at posing and others need more direction. If you are working with real people (not professional models), you need to step up and direct your subjects to make them look their best. They can't see what they look like, and poses that may *feel* right may not *look* right when captured in a still image.

Conclusion

Being a commercial photographer does not mean you just get to sit back and take photos. In many cases, it means stepping up to serve as the producer, casting director, art director, and more. Most often, it also means being a director and taking charge of everything in the image. This is what makes it exciting! You're in charge of creating your own still productions and you have a hand in all the varied elements of the artistic process. If you take charge, the images will come out exactly how you envisioned them. And when you are working with a client who has a very clear vision that you need to follow, all this experience will make you better at bringing that vision to life

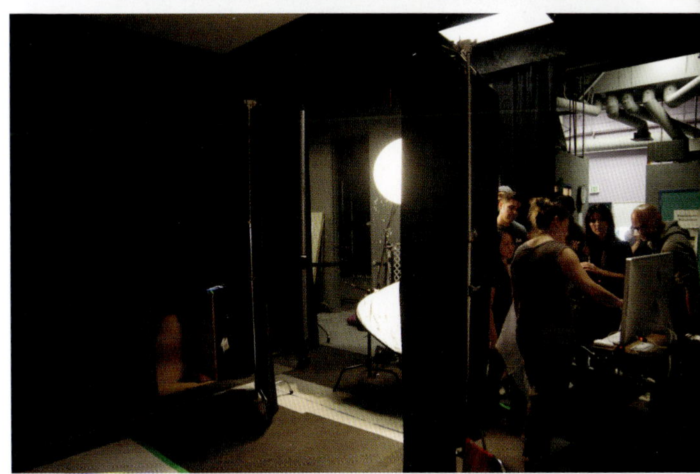

for them—meaning happier clients and, best of all, more work for you down the road. So get started now; practice and plan a test shoot!

3. Beauty Lighting

Techniques ▶ Clamshell lighting; Using a beauty dish; Controlling catchlights
Application ▶ Beauty images; Cosmetic advertising photography

Beauty lighting is essential for great fashion portraits, especially in cosmetic adverting and celebrity portraiture. You can also apply these lighting techniques to corporate and industrial commercial shoots that involve portraits of people. In this chapter, we will cover clamshell lighting, working with different beauty dish products, and a little about catchlights.

Concept and Planning

Let's apply this to a makeup advertising campaign. To do this, it is helpful for your production team to have a very clear idea of what the final product should be—some kind of theme. Once you have talked to your client about what they want to convey, you can start thinking about what this might be. Or if your client comes to you with a concept in mind, that's even better. In this case, I decided to work with a theme I chose: candy. To develop the concept, I found some sample photos online that gave me some ideas to show my makeup artist. I was then very specific about how I wanted the makeup to look. For example, I asked for the eye makeup to sweep across the face, as you see in the "lifesaver" model photo to the left.

Again, the commercial photographer may wear many hats in the production of a shoot (refer back to chapter 2 for more on produc-

◀ Candy-themed makeup by Andrea Yocky. (*Specs: f/5.6, 1/100, ISO 1250, Canon 100mm f/2.8L Macro lens*)

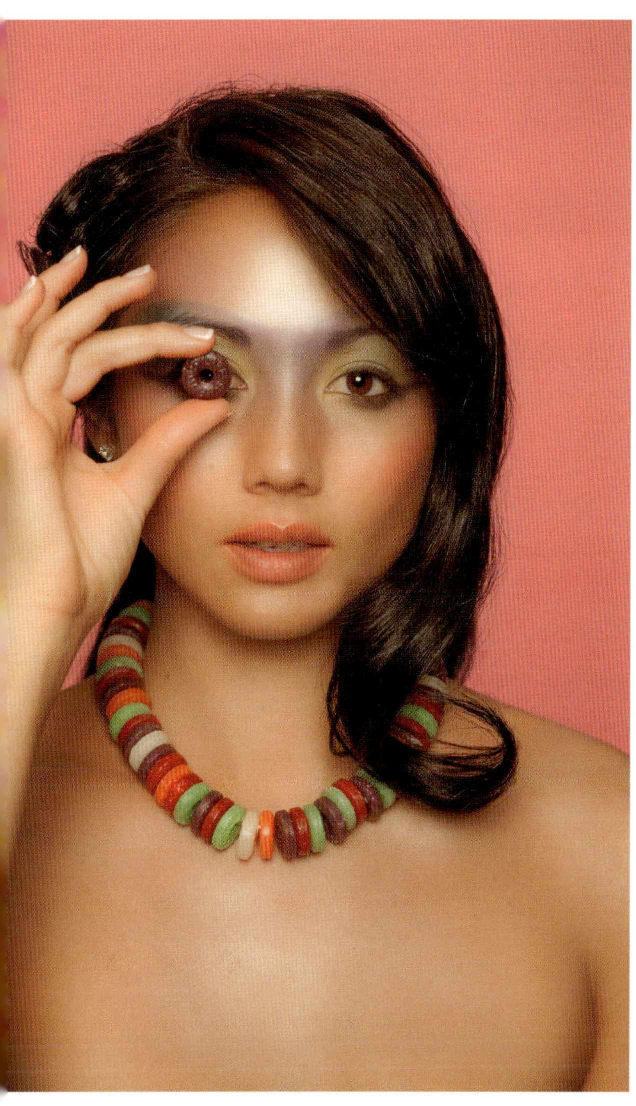

▲ Lifesaver candy makeup sub-theme. *Makeup by Andrea Yocky.* *(Specs: f/5.6, 1/100, ISO 1250, Canon 100mm f/2.8L Macro lens)*

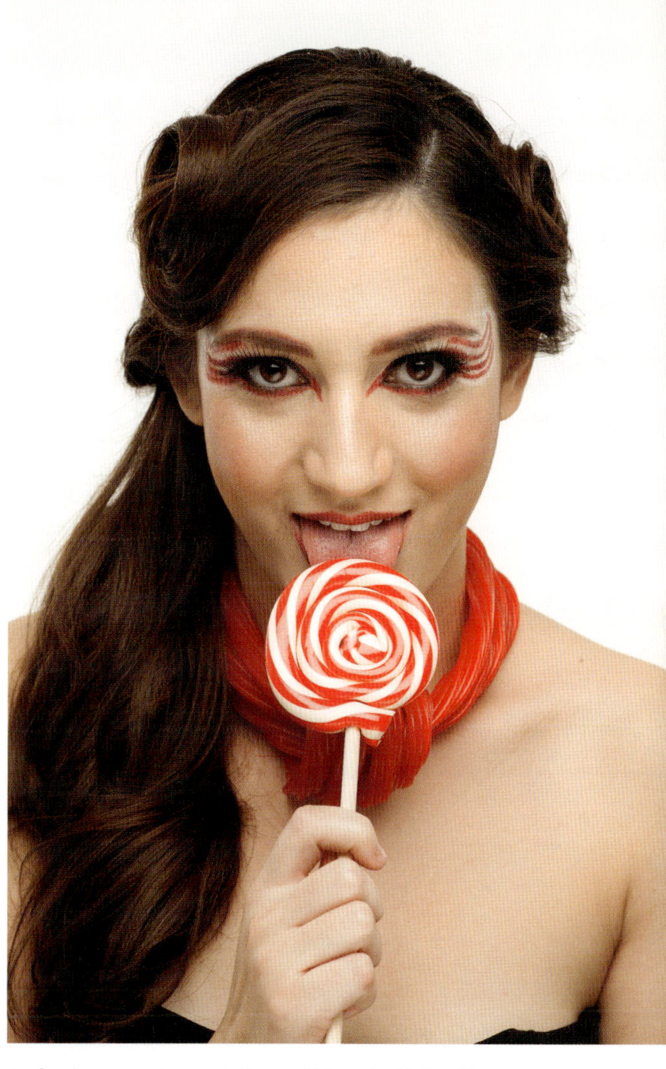

▲ Candy cane makeup sub-theme. *Makeup by Mariam Pesso.* *(Specs: f/10, 1/160, ISO 100, Canon 100mm f/2.8L Macro lens)*

tion planning). In this case, I was also the prop-master, so I went shopping for ideas and candy samples at several candy stores and large department stores, like Target. I spent only about $17.00 on candy to use as accessories and jewelry. In the examples above, you can see another "lifesaver" shot, and one from the "candy cane" sub-theme that incorporated a licorice necklace. And, yes, I made all these items myself, with the help of a sewing kit.

Lighting

There are several different kinds of beauty dish modifiers. For individual portraits, a standard small beauty dish will work fine. The large Mola is also a great choice. The larger the dish,

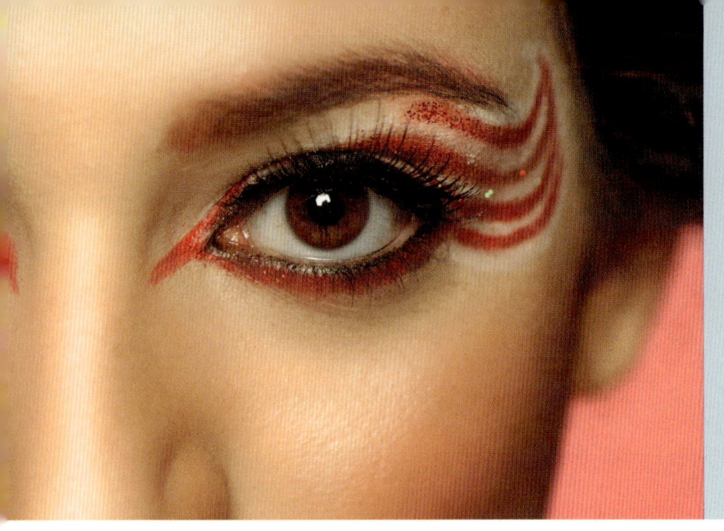

the more light will spread over the subject or an area. In the early images for this section, I was photographing only headshots, so the smaller one was sufficient. We'll graduate to larger sources later in the section.

Bare Beauty Dish

The image below, shot with a standard-size beauty dish on a strobe, works well because of the position of the dish 45 degrees to camera right and above the model's eye-line. This creates a wonderful shadow below the neck that is very flattering and dynamic. The light from a beauty dish will wrap around the face and create a small, round catchlight in the eye. Take a look at the small spot of light in the upper part of the model's eye (see the sidebar above, called "Watch the Catchlights," for a related example).

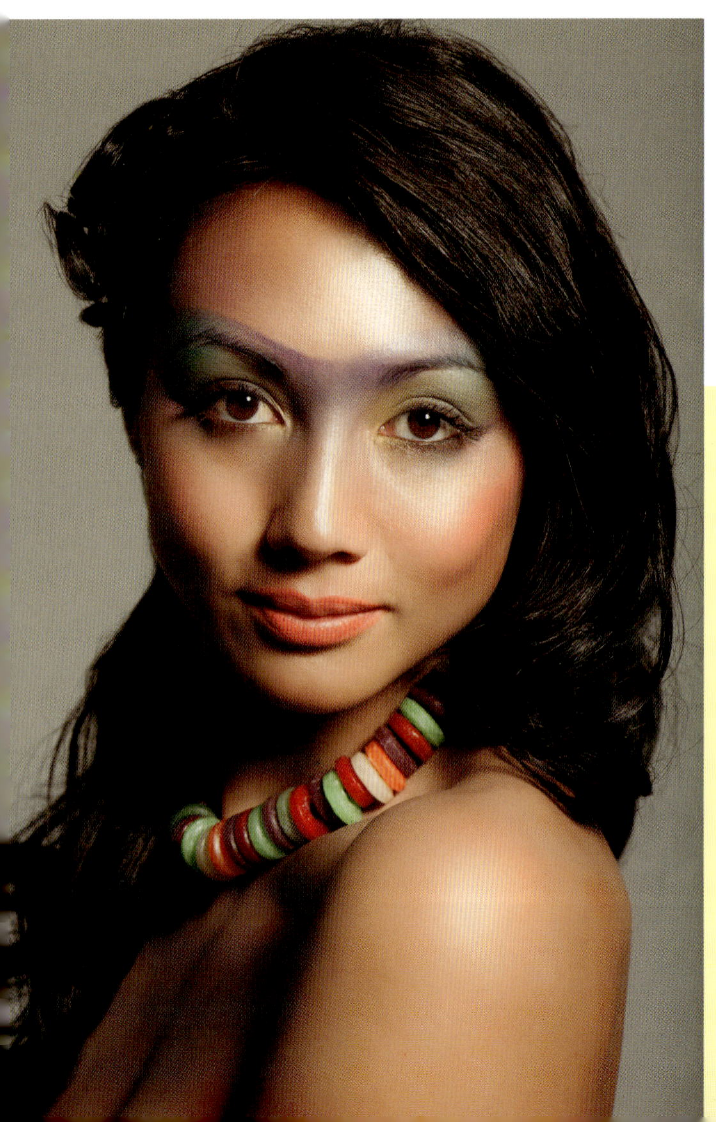

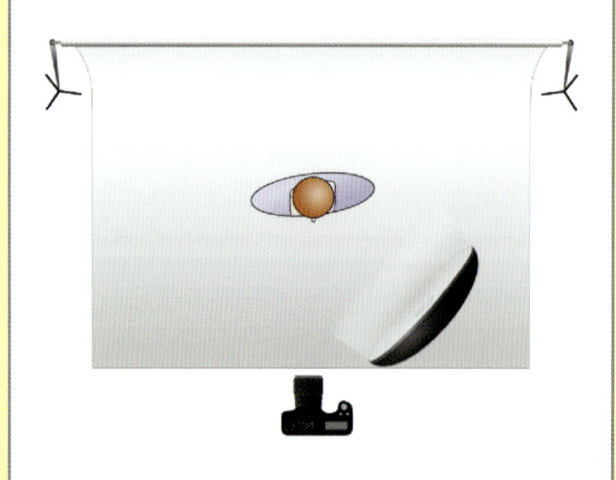

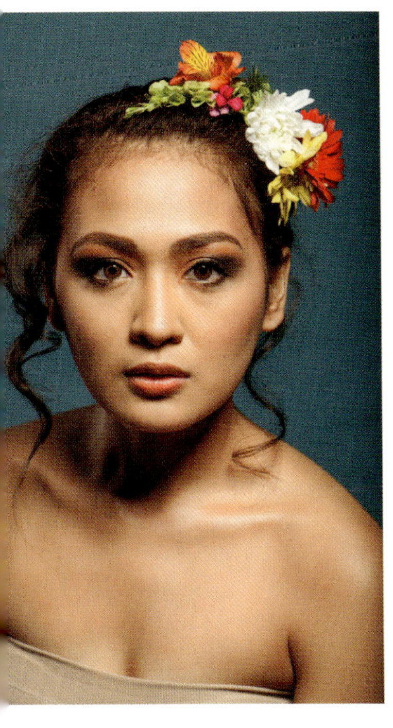 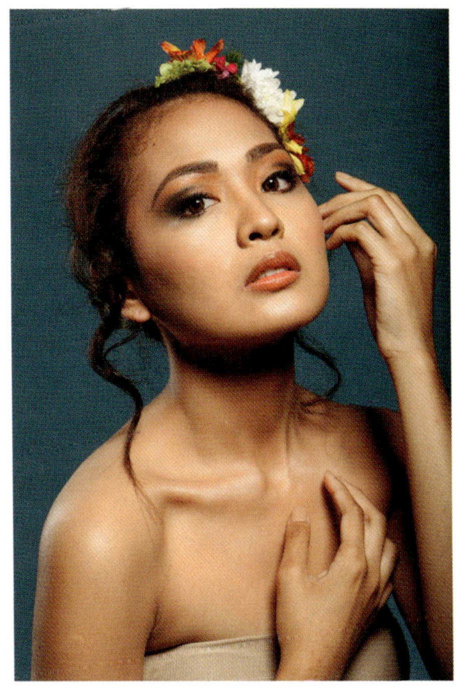 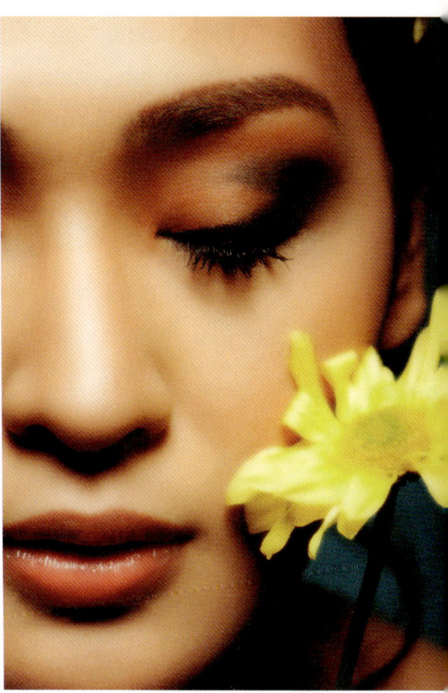

Beauty Dish Plus Diffuser

For the first image in the series above, I used a bare beauty dish. For a softer look, you can add a diffuser over the front of the beauty dish. Most beauty dishes come with a removable front diffuser—a white, translucent fabric covering that scatters and softens the light. Looking at the second image, shot with the diffuser in place, you can see that there is less shine in the hot spots on the model's face. The light is still rather directional and creates the dark shadow under the chin because of its high position (similar to the example in the previous section), but now it spreads out a bit more and is a little softer. There is no right or wrong here; it all depends on what you are going for in the look of your lighting. For example, the less harsh look of the diffused light may be a more desirable option if you are photographing someone with not-so-perfect skin.

▲ Left: The model was photographed with a bare beauty dish. *(Specs: f/9.0, 1/200, ISO 100, Canon 100mm f/2.8L Macro lens)*

▲ Center: Adding a diffuser produces less shine on the model's face in the hot spots. The light is still rather directional and creates the dark shadow under the chin. *(Specs: f/10, 1/100, ISO 100, Canon 100mm f/2.8L Macro lens)*

▲ Right: Look at how beautifully the shadows show the contours of the face. They don't call it a "beauty dish" for nothing. *(Specs: f/10, 1/200, ISO 100, Canon 100mm f/2.8L Macro lens)*

A Note on Color

In beauty and cosmetic advertising photography, you need to get the color right. For example, if you are shooting images to be used in an advertisement for a new lipstick, the photos need to convey accurately the color of the lipstick – or your client will be very unhappy. Be sure to do a custom white balance and use a color picker, like the X-Rite ColorChecker Passport.

Mola Plus a Background Light

For this image, I switched the main light to a Mola, a larger beauty dish with a diffuser. The larger dish spreads the light more; as you can see, the shadow under the model's chin is not as dark as in the previous examples. The light was positioned the same as in the previous example—above eye level and to camera right. This was the only light on the model's face. I also added a colored seamless background to the set. To illuminate it, I positioned a strobe with a snoot behind the model's head, directing it toward the backdrop to create the "halo" circle of light.

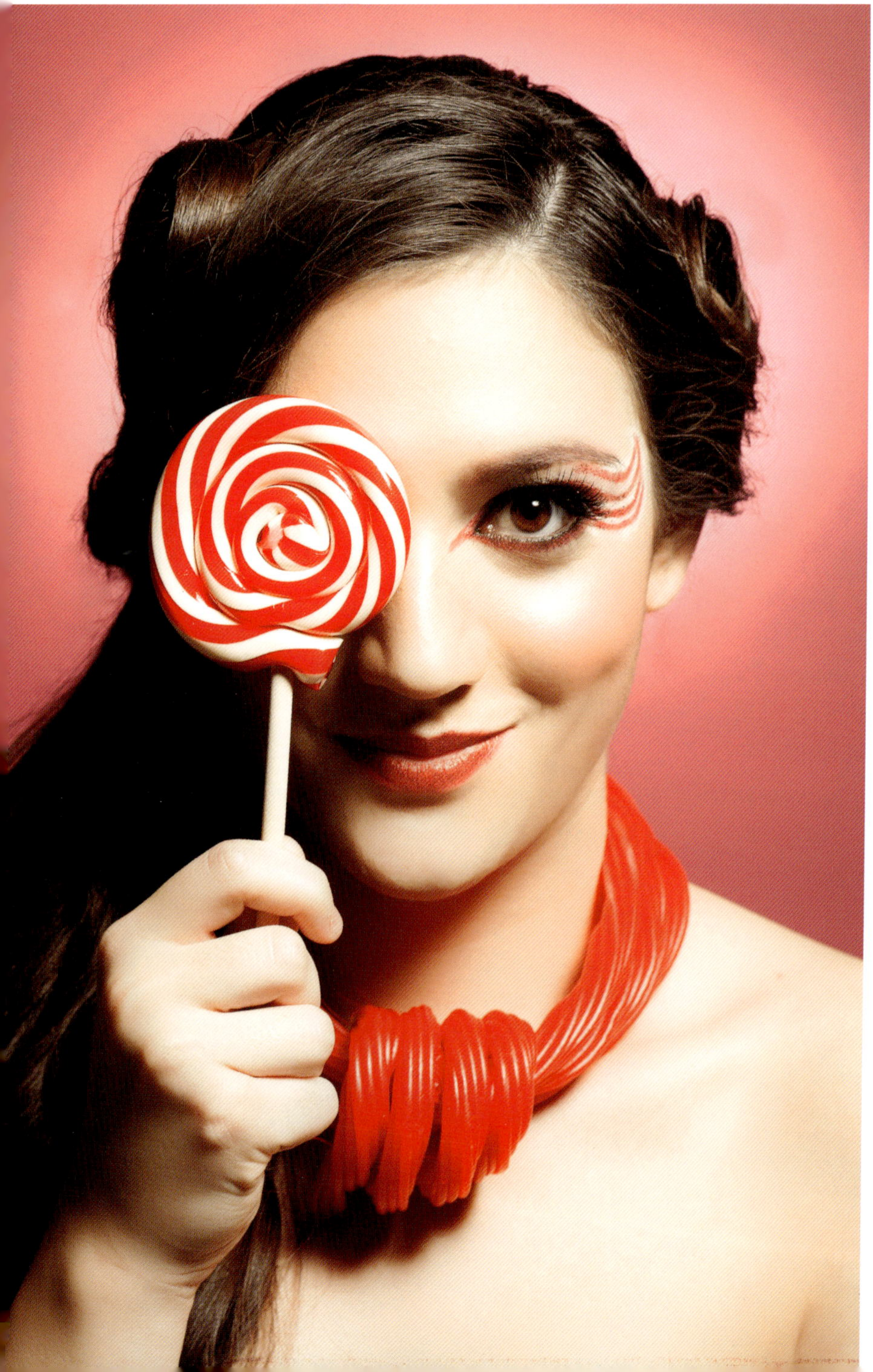

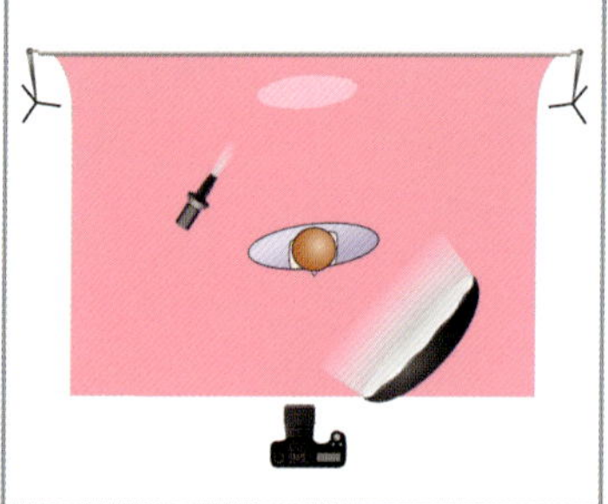

◀ I shot this using the larger Mola beauty dish with a diffuser; that is the only light illuminating the model's face. I added a colored seamless background plus a second light with a snoot. This second light was directed at the backdrop to create the "halo" of light. *(Specs: f/10, 1/200, ISO 100, Canon 100mm f/2.8L Macro lens)*

> **"** The larger dish spreads the light more; as you can see, the shadow under the model's chin is not as dark as in the previous examples. **"**

Refining the Background Light

This background lighting technique can be used a number of ways. In the image below, I set the background light (still with the snoot) off to the side. This was a great way to accent the flower in the model's hand. The photo was shot horizontally with the model's head to one side and the circle of light off to the other. Here, the only front light was a standard-size beauty dish with a diffuser. This image has some retouching, but none of the light was manipulated and the light on the background is straight out of the camera. The snoot was simply positioned to camera right behind the model and quite close to a blue seamless background. So many fun applications!

When using a snoot to create the "circle of light" look on a background, you may find it hard to make the light on the background come out just right—or to even show at all. Here is how to do it: move the light with the snoot close to the backdrop. The farther it is, the wider the circle of light will be. Take a light reading of the snoot and take a couple of test shots at that setting. Then adjust the front

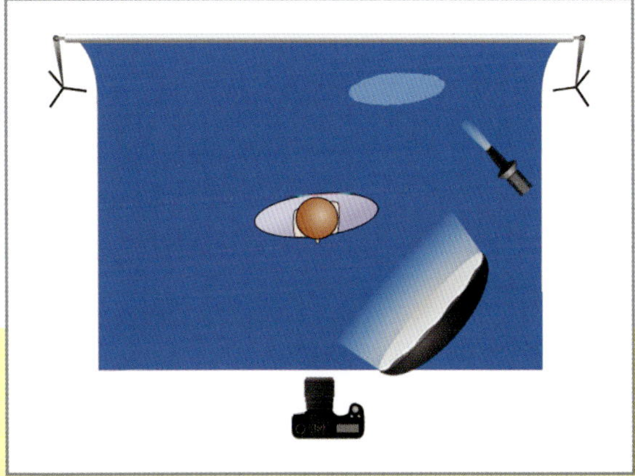

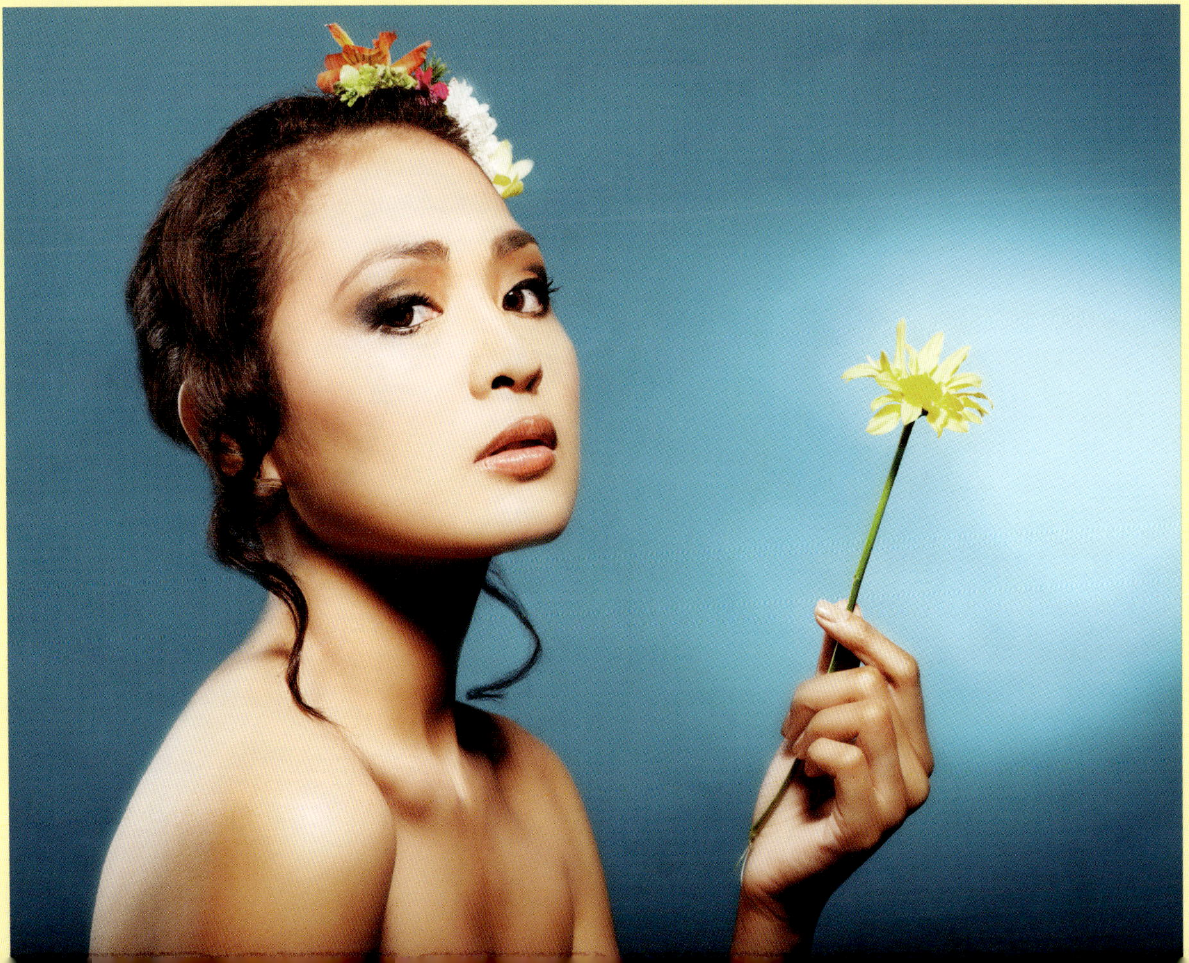

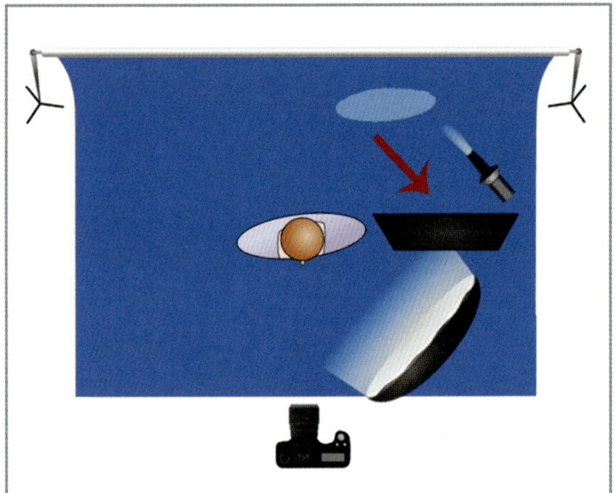

▲ A black flag or panel can be added to avoid spill from the front lights overpowering the effect of the snoot on the backdrop.

key lights up or down so your subject is lit correctly and the background lighting effect is still visible. You may want to turn off the front key light and shoot your test shots with the snoot alone, so you can see what it is doing. Also, be aware that a front light placed too close to the background will spill over past the subject and light the entire background, overpowering the light from the snoot. If you are not seeing the snoot's light, this may be your problem. If so, move the front light farther away from the background. If you don't have space, or it's not working, you may need to add a black flag (light blocker) between the front light and the background, as seen in the diagram above.

Lenses for Beauty Photography

For most of these sample images, I used a Canon 100mm f/2.8L macro lens. A longer lens like this creates really nice compression and has very sharp focus. It's best to focus right on the eyeball when using a lens with such a wide aperture, especially when shooting with a shallow depth of field. If you focus on the nose, the eyes may not be in focus – and viewers will naturally look at the eyes to determine sharpness. Check your focus on the eyes repeatedly throughout the shoot.

Sideways Clamshell Lighting

Traditional clamshell lighting (more on this in the next section) involves sandwiching the face between two horizontal front-light sources, usually a softbox above the model's face and a softbox or reflector below it. For sideways clamshell lighting, I still use two light sources—in this case, two large softboxes—but I place them vertically to either side of the model's face, about 4 feet away and slightly feathered back toward the backdrop. The lights are set at equal outputs. As you can see in the images below and on the facing page, this is a more high-key effect and very flattering. Notice the slight dark shadow line down the center of the face. In the closeup image, you can clearly see the catchlights on either side of her pupil from the softboxes.

▼▶ Below and facing page: For sideways clamshell lighting, two large softboxes flank the model and are slightly feathered back toward the backdrop. The lights are set at the same output settings (500 watts, in this case). In the closeup, the catchlights on either side of the pupils reveal the positions of the softboxes. (Specs: f/10, 1/160, ISO 100, Canon 100mm f/2.8L Macro lens)

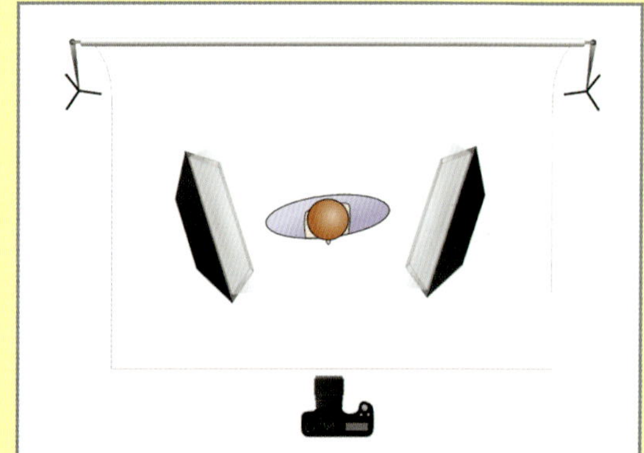

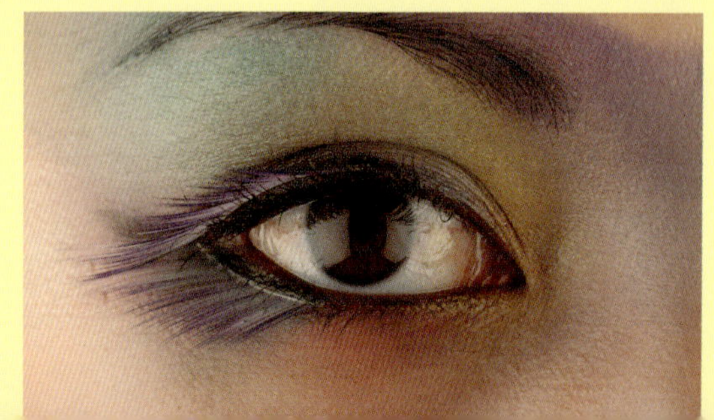

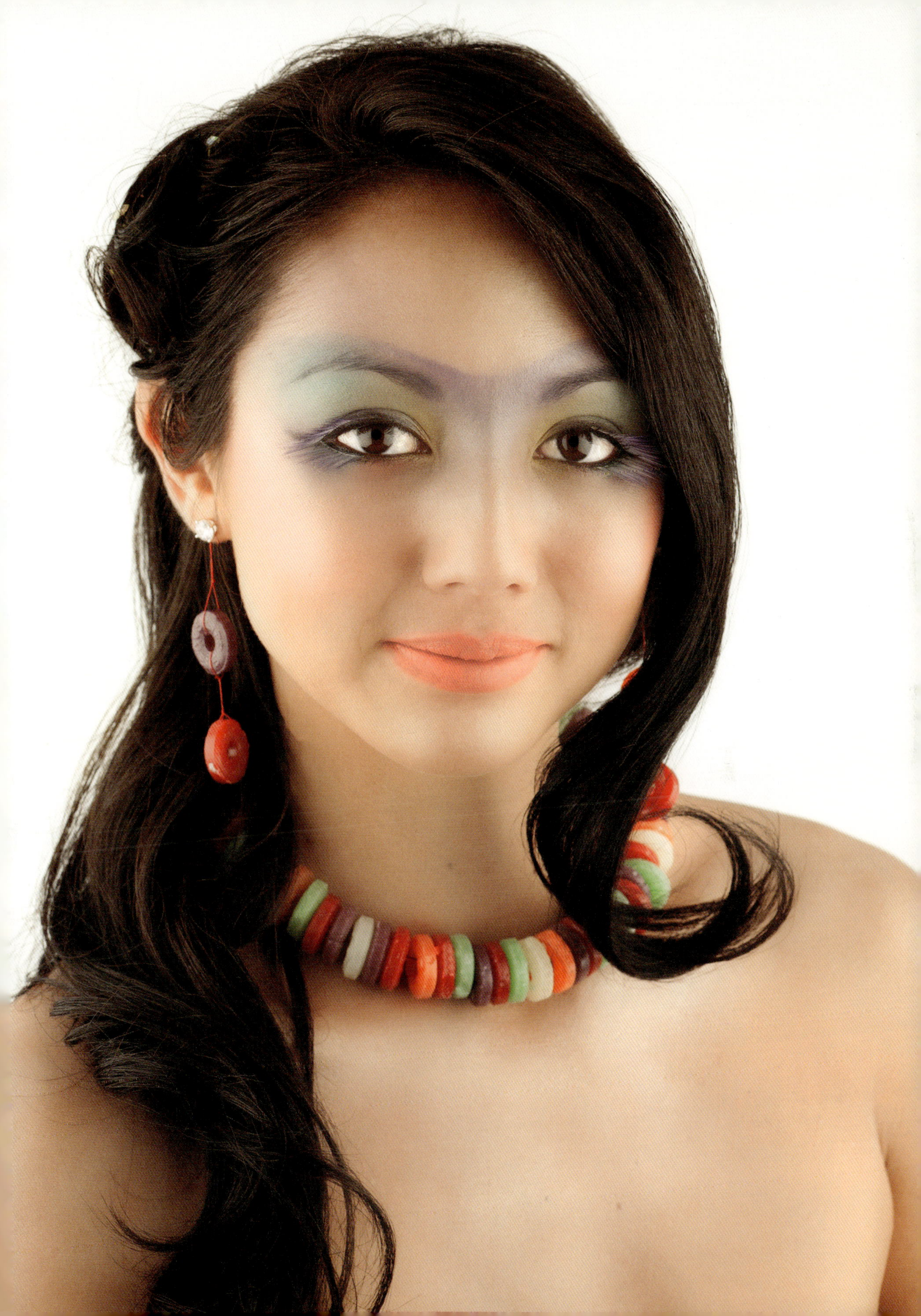

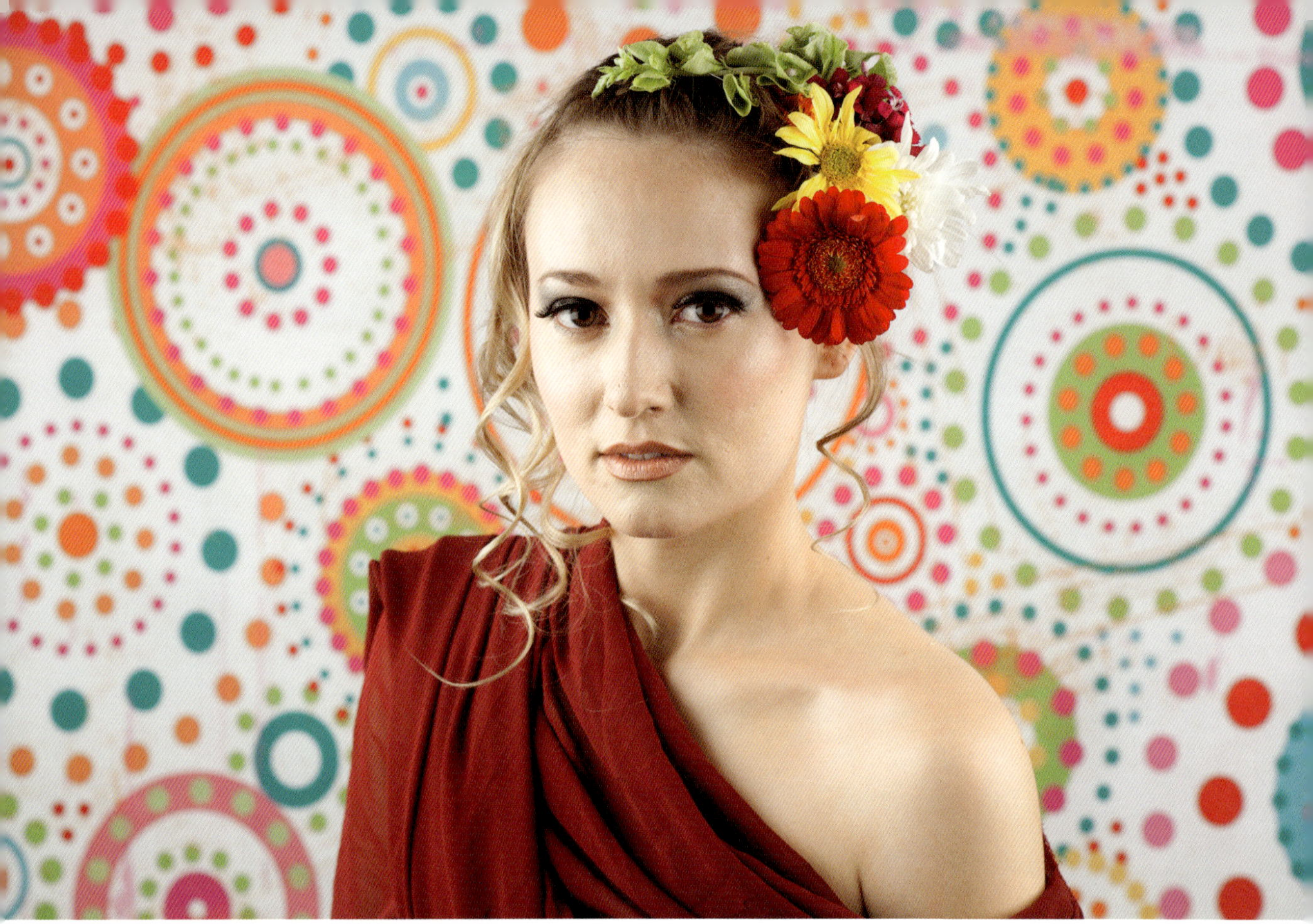

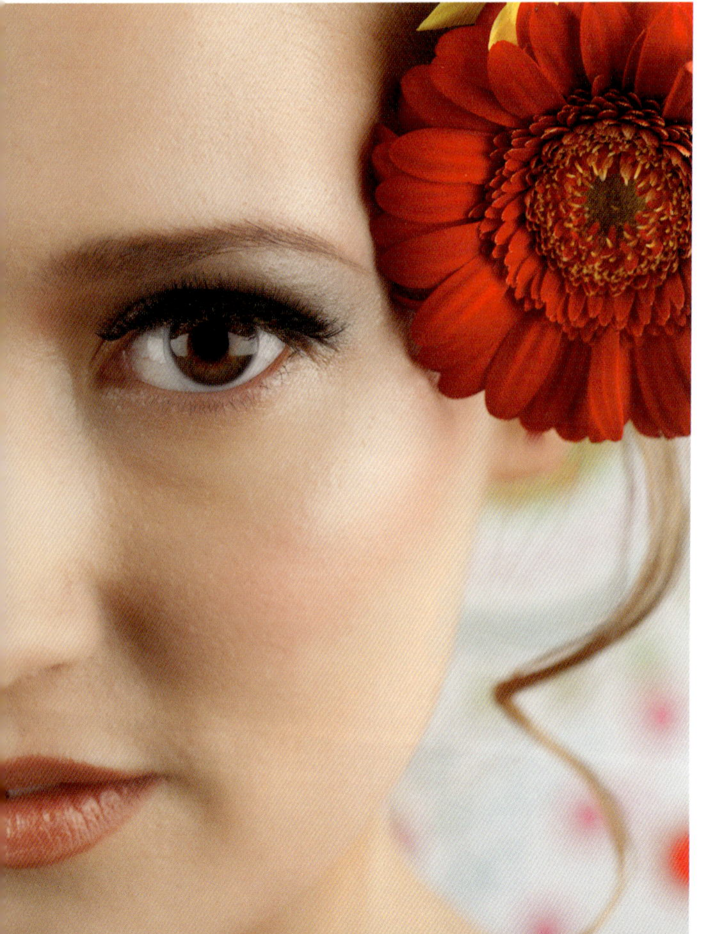

Our next image (above) shows another version of the sideways-clamshell setup with a more interesting background. The lighting setup is the same, with the model and lights very close to the background so the two lights on the model are also lighting the background. You really don't need to worry about the subject casting a shadow on the background when you have two lights on either side of them. Again, be sure to check the detail shot to see how the catchlights reveal the lights' positions.

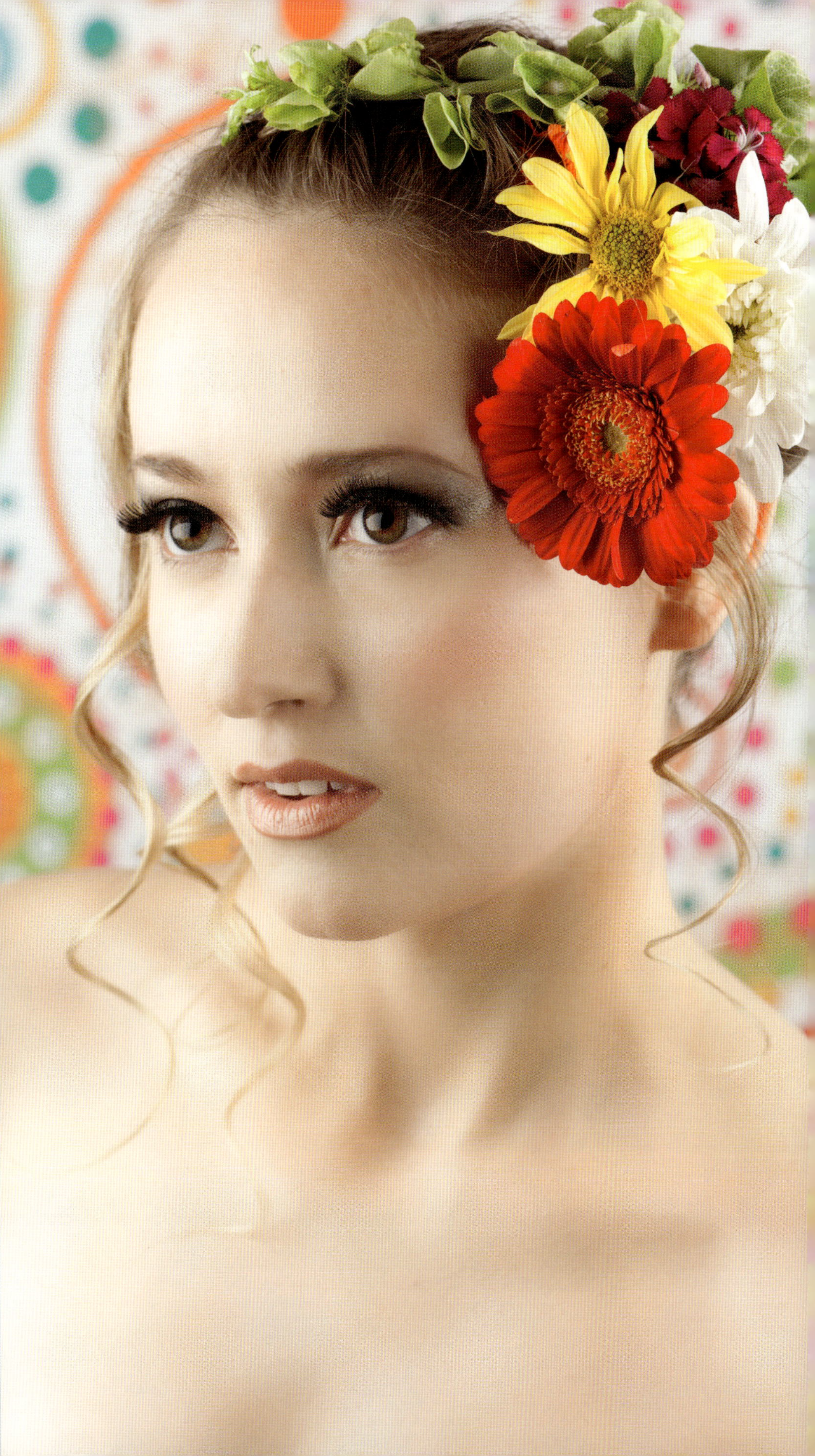

Turning the Model's Face

In this image, notice how the light is affected when the model is turned a different direction. The lights were not moved from the sideways clamshell setup described; the model was simply turned toward the camera-left softbox. You can see a slight shadow that falls down the side of the face at the center of the image. This shadow gives nice definition to the face and is caused by the softboxes being slightly feathered back toward the background.

▶ Notice how the light is affected when the model is turned in a different direction. The lights were not moved from the previously described sideways clamshell setup; only the model's position was adjusted. (Specs: f/9.0, 1/160, ISO 100, Canon 100mm f/2.8L Macro lens)

Traditional Clamshell Lighting

Clamshell lighting is Portrait 101, but it's also the best way to make any subject—even real people in such things as corporate headshots—look great. Think of the head as the pearl inside the two halves of an open clamshell. One light source (usually a softbox) is above the subject and angled down toward the face and a second light source (usually a softbox or a reflector) is positioned below the face. To create the image below, I placed a softbox above the subject's head, pointing it down toward the face at an angle. To fill under the face, I placed a flat reflector at about the model's waist height. (*Note:* Doing this the opposite way, with the main light on the bottom and fill from the top, usually does not work. It creates that unflattering Halloween look—like when someone puts a flashlight under their chin to tell a ghost story.)

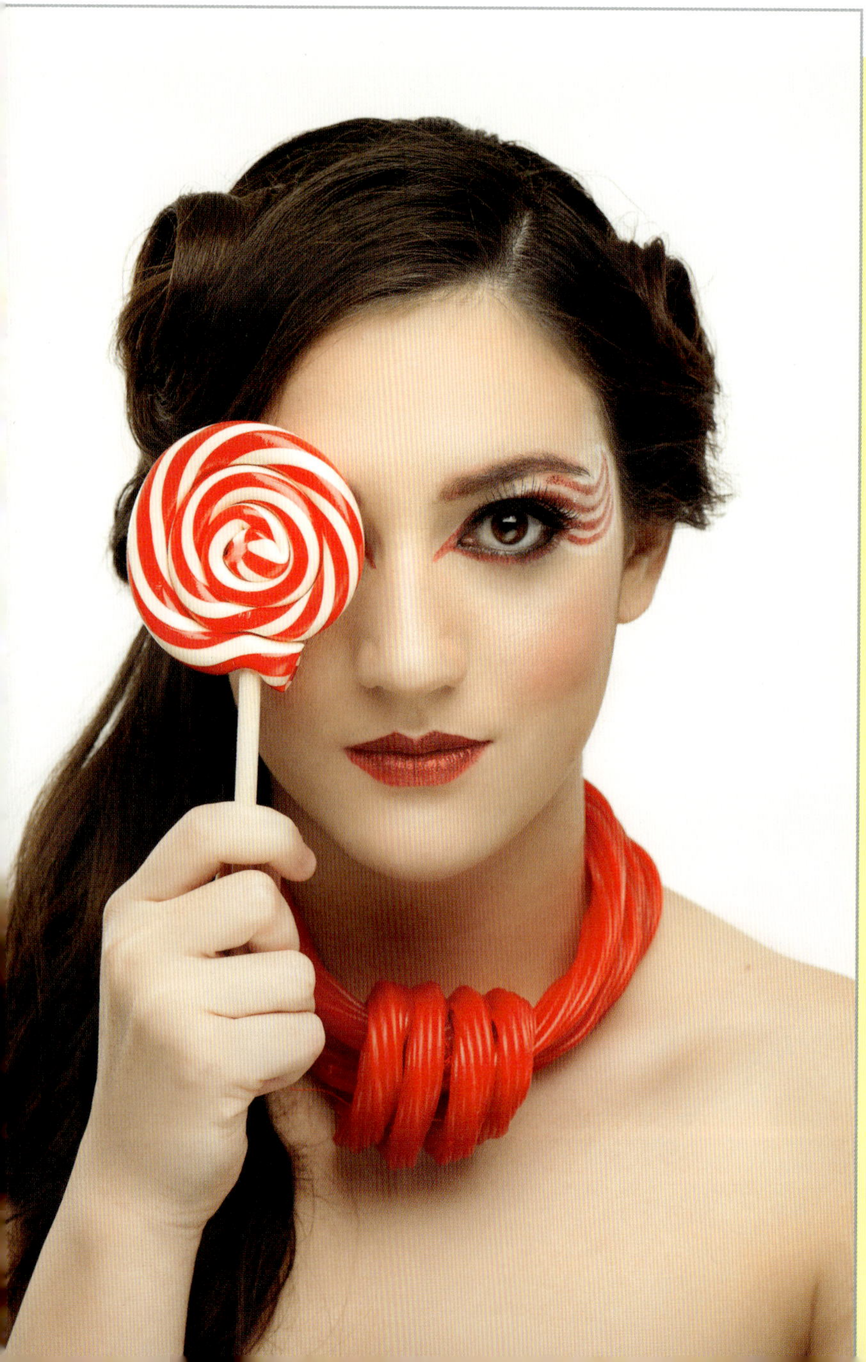

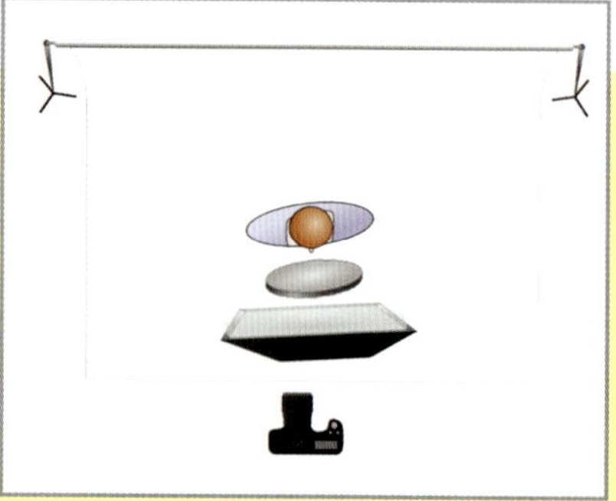

◄◄ ▲ I created traditional clamshell lighting with a softbox above the face and angled down, plus a reflector below the face for fill. Think of the head as the pearl inside the two halves of an open clamshell. *(Specs: f/10.0, 1/160, ISO 100, Canon 100mm f/2.8L Macro lens)*

► Facing page: In this traditional clamshell-light portrait, notice that the face is very evenly lit with just a little shadow under the chin. *(Specs: f/8.0, 1/200, ISO 100, Canon 100mm f/2.8L Macro lens)*

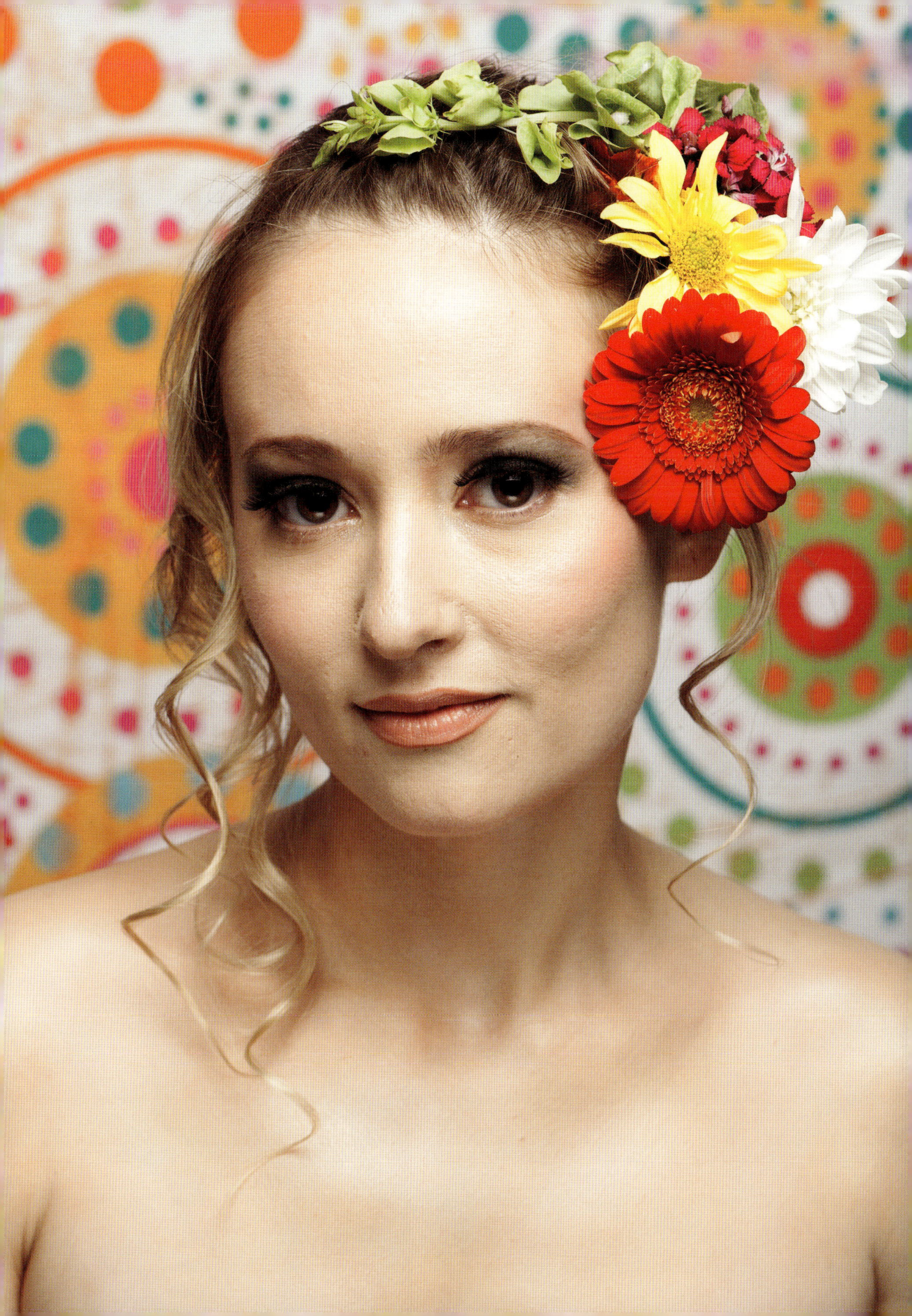

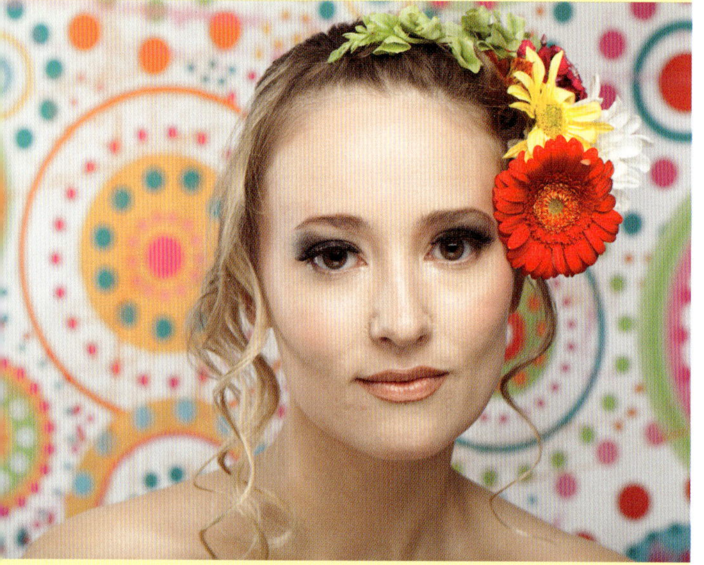

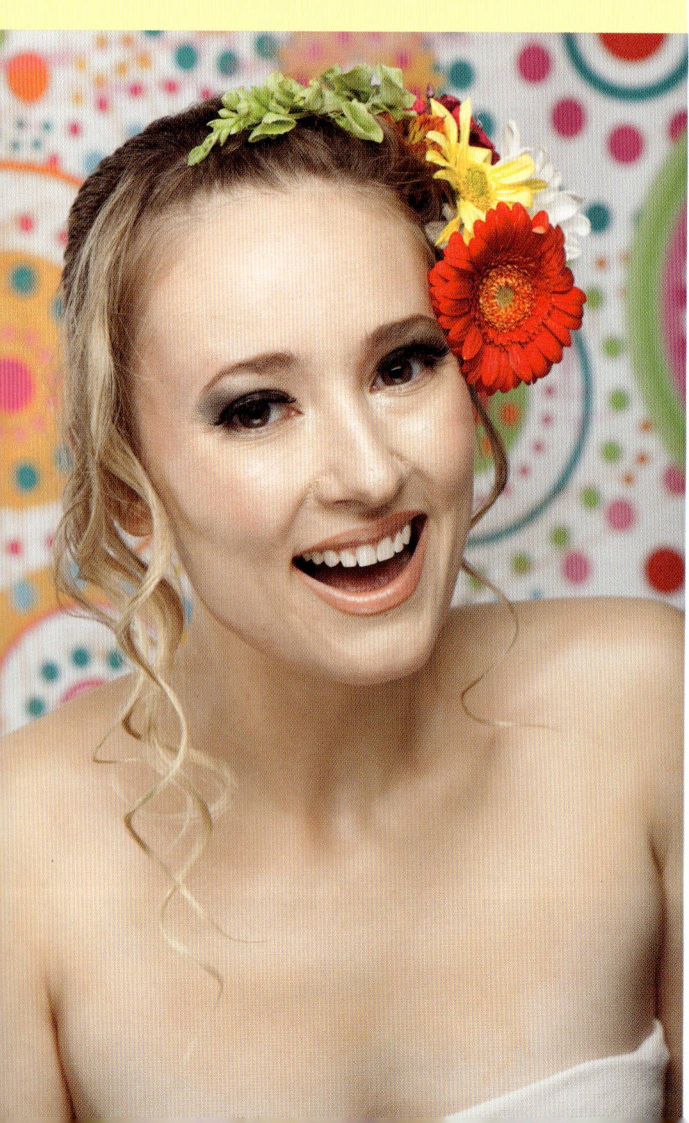

Why use a reflector instead of another softbox? It leaves more shadow under the chin, which can be more flattering if your subject has any flaws on the neck or jowl area. What you are doing is bouncing fill from your upper light source, so the fill light from below naturally loses some intensity. You can use a piece of white foam core for a softer quality to the bounce light, or opt for a silver or gold reflector to create sharper looks. Notice that the face is very evenly lit with only a little shadow under the chin. Again, check out the catchlights in the eyes, as well.

Try It for Three-Quarter Shots

Don't reserve this lighting setup for headshots alone. In the image below you can see how wonderful and flattering the light is for an actor's three-quarter-length promo shot.

▼ Try clamshell lighting for three-quarter portraits, too—not just headshots. (Specs: f/5.6, 1/160, ISO 250, 70–200mm lens at 80mm)

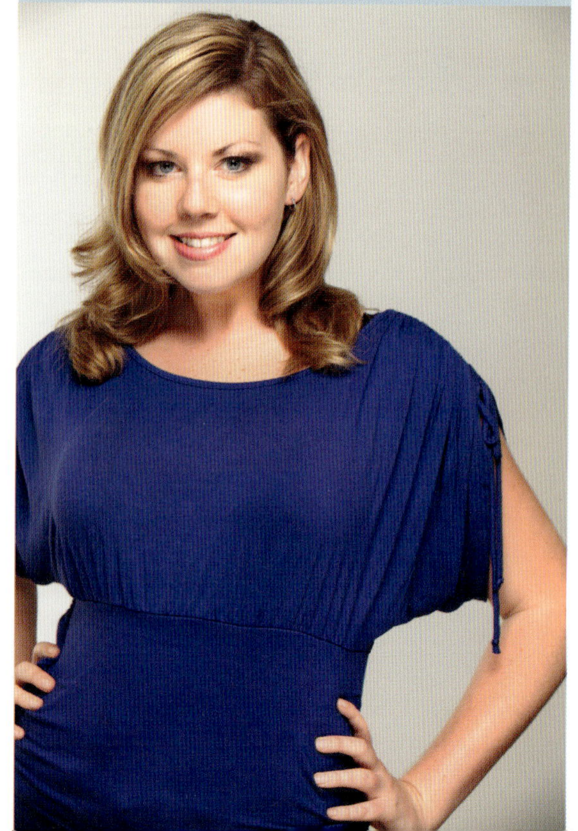

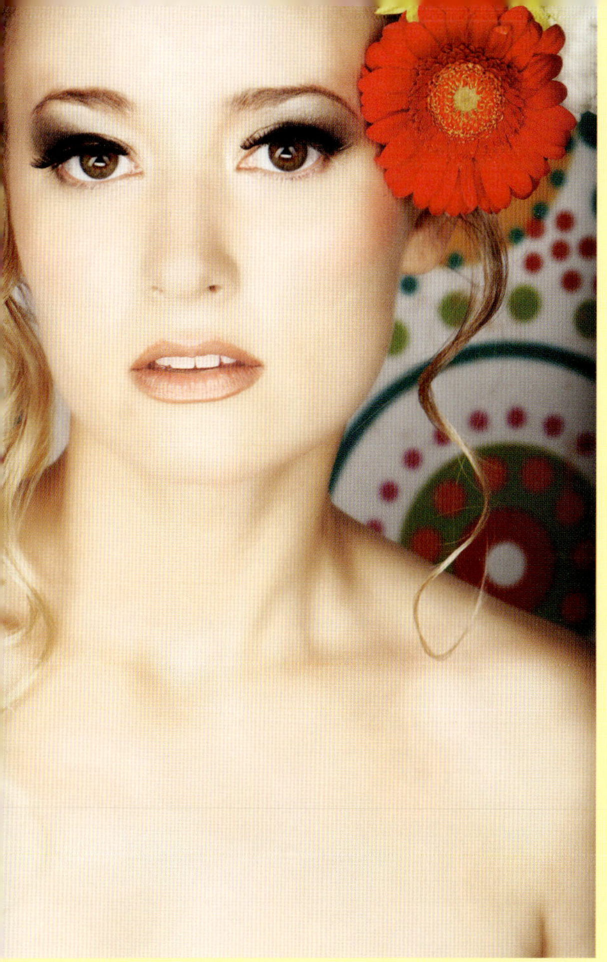

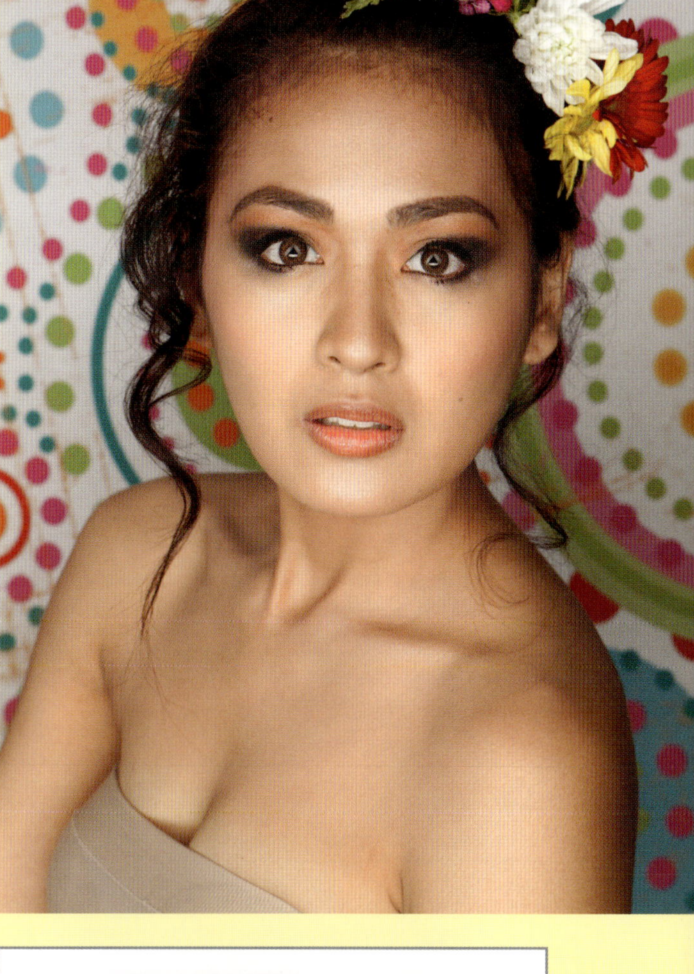

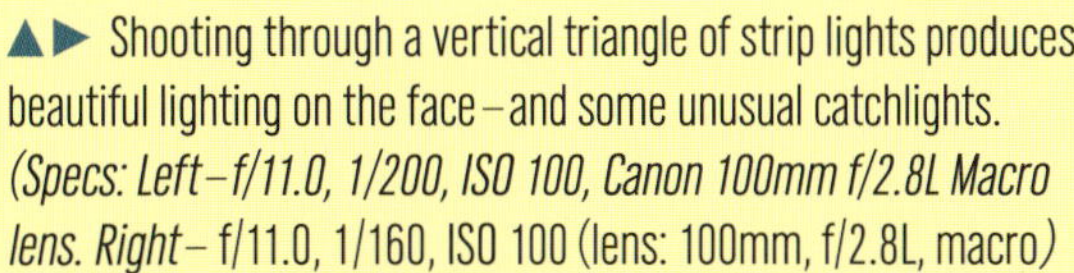
▲ ▶ Shooting through a vertical triangle of strip lights produces beautiful lighting on the face—and some unusual catchlights. *(Specs: Left—f/11.0, 1/200, ISO 100, Canon 100mm f/2.8L Macro lens. Right—* f/11.0, 1/160, ISO 100 (lens: 100mm, f/2.8L, macro*)*

Creating Catchlights

When shooting, we are sometimes just thinking about making the light look nice. Where the catchlights fall is often of no concern—but in advertising photography, and particularly in beauty images, your client may want something specific. Of course, you can manipulate the catchlights and where they fall using Photoshop (or you can even remove them), but here are some fun ways to *create* really unique catchlights while also making amazing light.

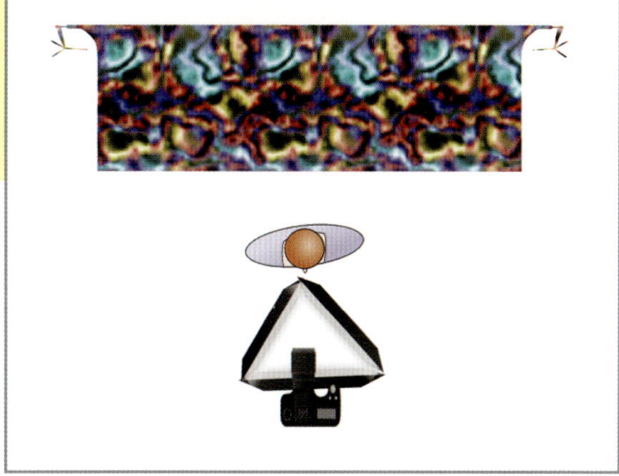

Shapes

The images above show a triangular catchlight with beautiful, even, window-like lighting on the face. The triangle looks rather unnatural in comparison to a round catchlight—but if this

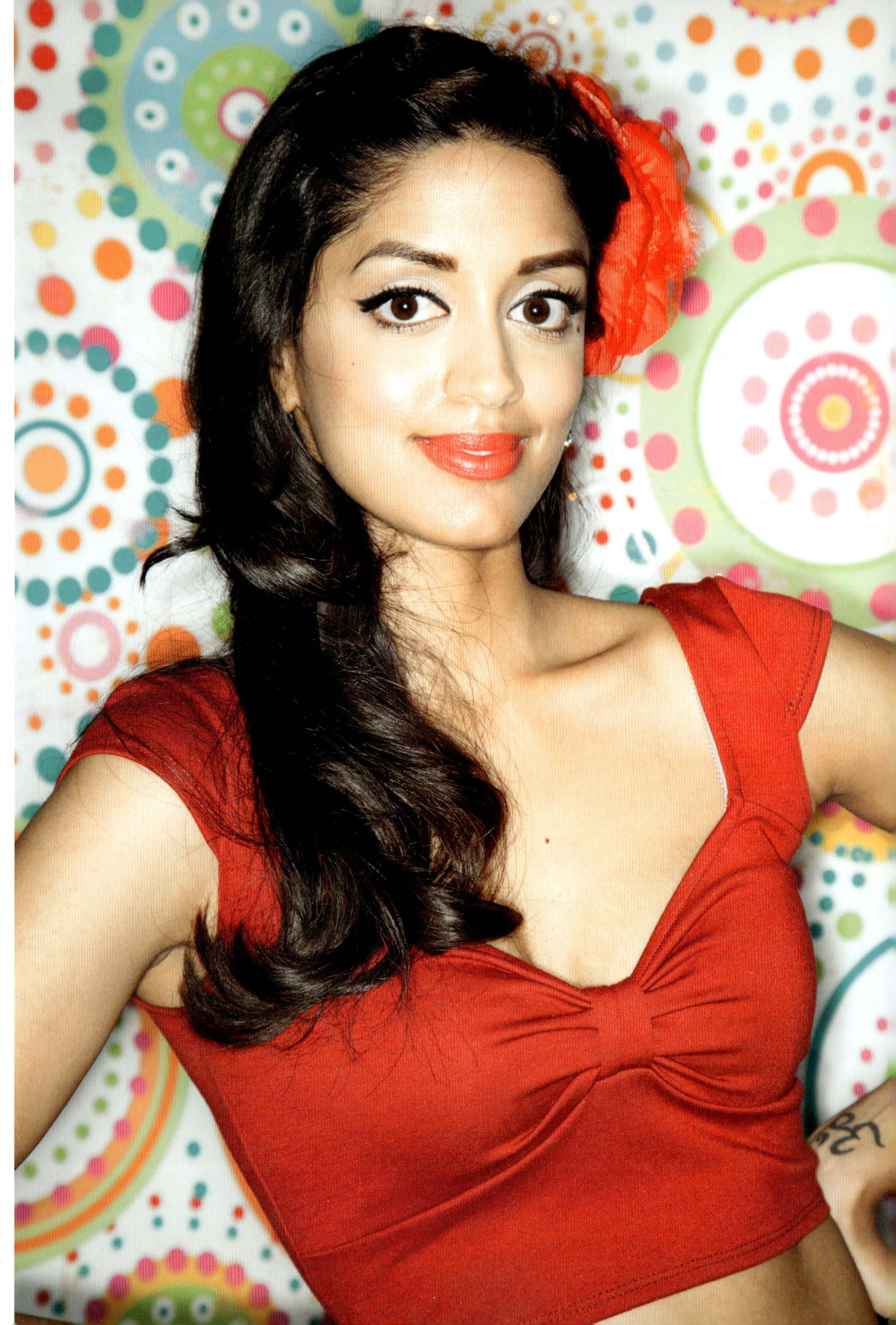

is an intentional effect, the lighting setup is fantastic. To create it, I arrange three strip lights in an upright triangle a few feet from the model. Each light faces flat toward the model. I then shoot through the center of the lights, much like shooting through the circle of a ring light. The quality of lighting this produces is very diffused and even, like window light.

Ring Lights

Ring lights are commonly used in fashion photography for directional light that hits your subject evenly and in a circular pattern. The basic design, whether a strobe model or a smaller speedlight-based one, is a circular light source with an opening in the middle. The lens is centered in that opening, so it is surrounded by the light. The closer your subject is to the background, the more you will see a subtle, characteristic shadow surrounding the model. Like the light source itself, the catchlight from a ring light is round and very distinctive. For the images to the right and on the facing page, I lit the model with the Ray Flash by ExpoImaging, a ring-light modifier that attaches to a speedlight.

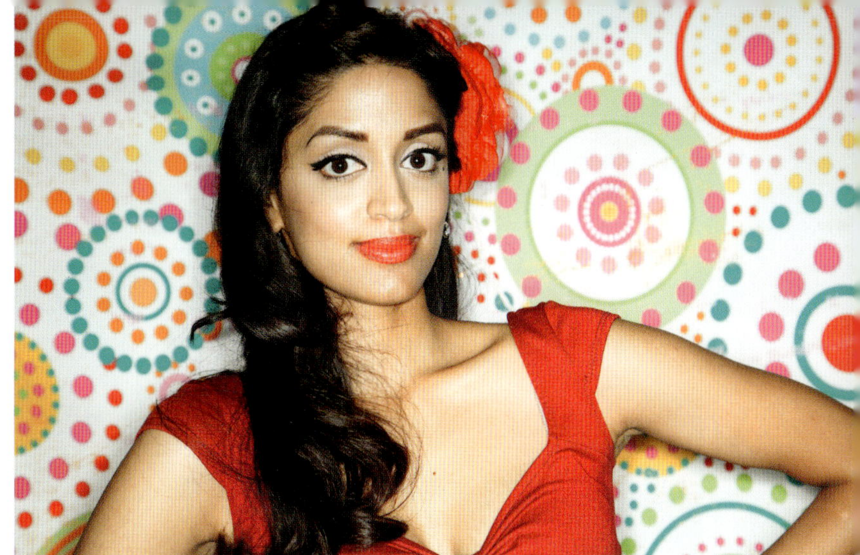

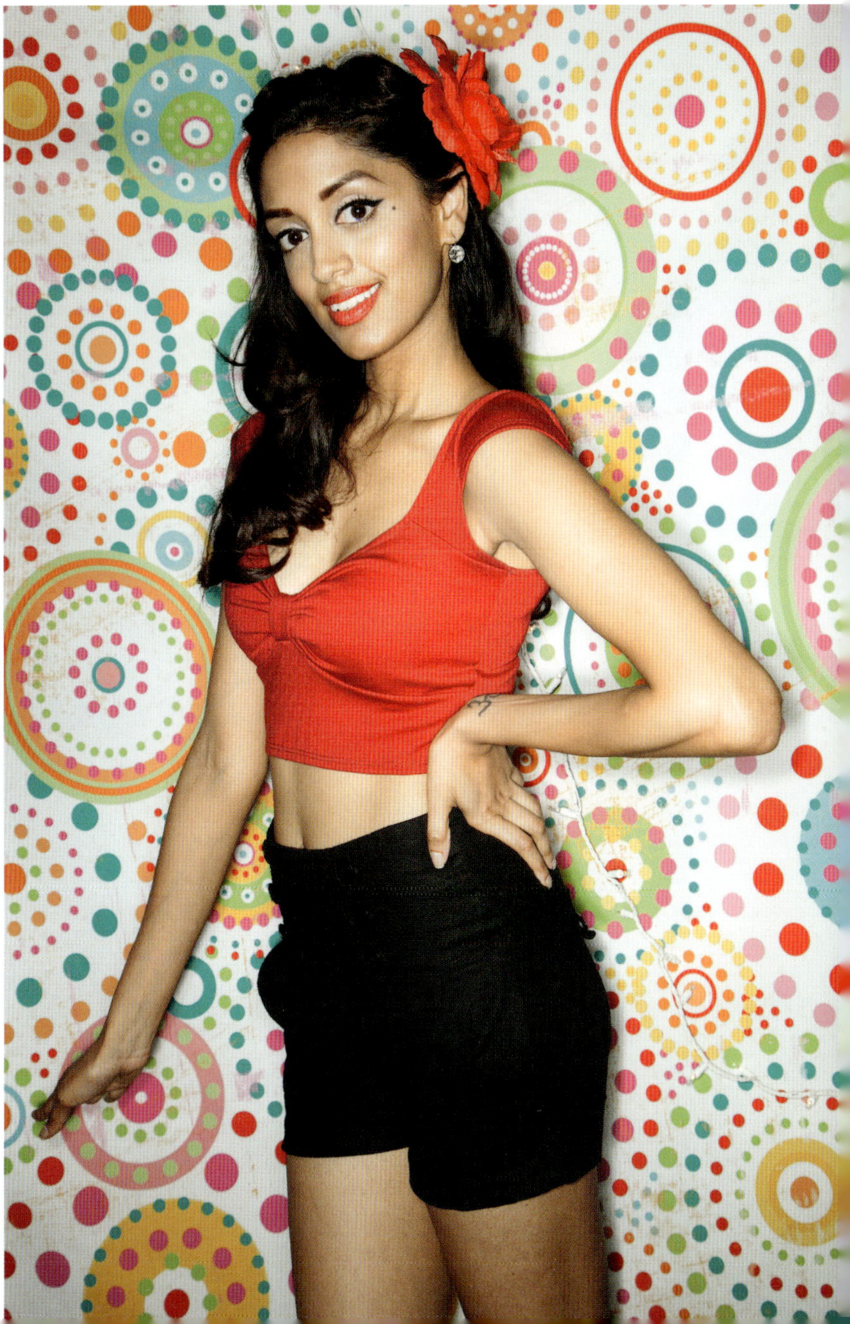

◄ ► *Facing page and right:* Lighting with the Ray Flash ring light. *(Specs: f/7.1, 1/160, ISO 200)*

The image below is a good example of being close to the subject with the light and using a longer lens. Here, the strobe ring light was close and directional, so the lighting dropped off around the edges of the model's face. The 100mm lens at f/5.6 created great compression and a shallow depth of field. This is a good example of an image where beauty meets fashion.

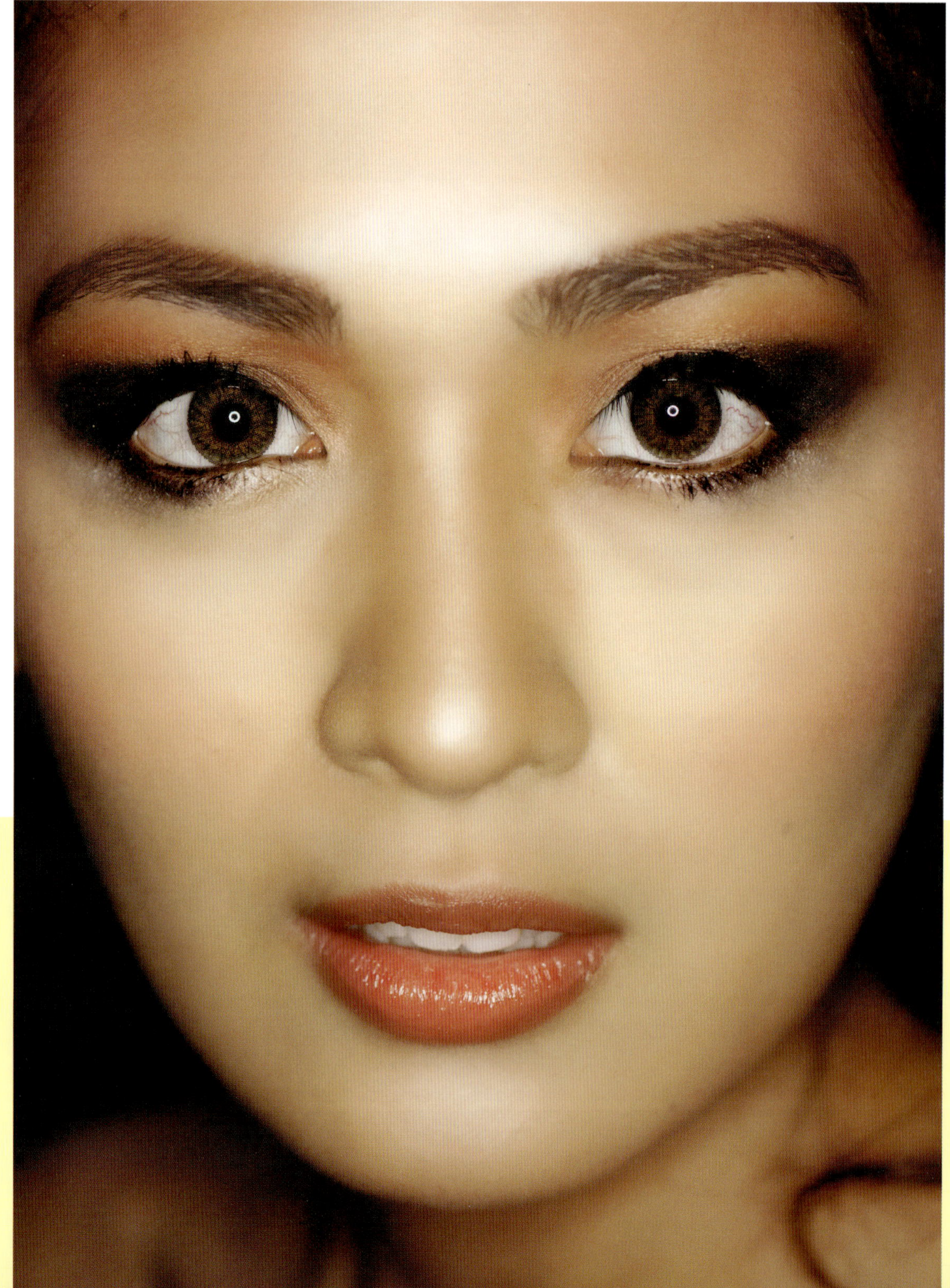

Putting It All Together

Styling

I contacted a couple of cosmetology students to help me out with this shoot. In exchange for their time, they received high-resolution images for their portfolios. When doing test shoots, this is a great way to collaborate. Makeup and hair are very important—especially in beauty photography. Without good styling, you really have nothing.

Models

In addition, I cast two aspiring models from an online classified advertisement. I did an audition a few days before the shoot to make sure the models actually looked like their photos and that they seemed responsible enough to show up.

Keep in mind that photography is not just about *you* taking a good photo or lighting the subject well, it's a collaboration—and having an appropriate model is half the battle. If you are shooting as a test for your portfolio and your model does not look appropriate, your images will not sell your work. What do I mean by "appropriate"? I mean the model needs to fit your genre. If you are shooting beauty, your model should be beautiful and

have a symmetrical face. Height is probably not a factor for beauty headshots, but if you are doing a high-fashion magazine shoot and photographing your models from head to toe, then using a tall, thin, well-proportioned model is very important. If you choose a short, petite, athletically built model for a high-fashion shoot, your images probably will not work as well.

Formalize Your Agreement and Follow Through

When setting up a trade with models and makeup artists, it's a good idea to have a contract and model release for everyone involved. Your paperwork should specify that you will give them a couple of retouched images of their choice in exchange for their time.

It's also a good idea to give your collaborators a timeline so they know when to expect the finished product. If you tell them you will have photos to them in two weeks, they will be patient and excited. If you don't tell them anything, they will be calling you impatiently wondering where the images are. Being upfront and clear will help keep everyone happy.

After the shoot, be sure to follow through. If you don't, you won't have a lot of repeat help—and you'll miss out on one of the best aspects of good collaboration: it can lead to actual jobs or referrals. (For more on casting and production, refer back to chapter 2.)

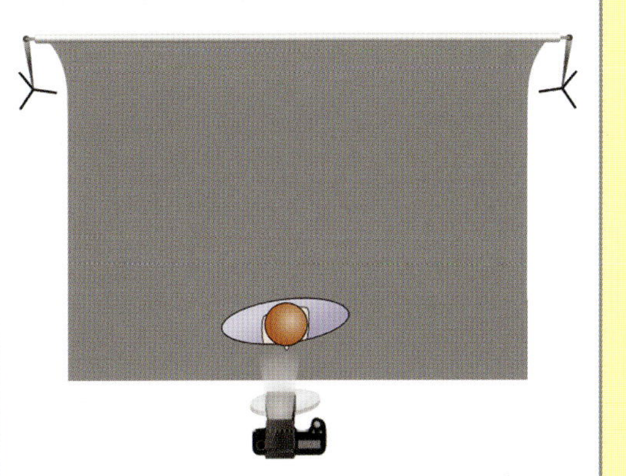

◀▼ Facing page and below: Lighting with the strobe ring light. (*Specs: f/5.6, 1/125, ISO 1250, 100mm f/2.8L Macro lens*)

4. High-Key Lighting

High-key lighting is often used in fashion magazines, catalogs, and magazine covers, among other things. You will often see this on magazine covers because the even lighting makes it easier to overlay text and titles—especially when there's a white background.

A Four-Light Setup
Equipment
For high-key lighting, strobes with modifiers are your best bet, but you can absolutely do this with speedlights and umbrellas, softboxes, or other modifiers designed to work with flash.

For the setup I'll be describing in this section, you'll need four light sources. If you don't have that many strobes, you can rent a couple of lights or combine two strobes with two speedlights. As long as you can get them all to sync to the camera, you can make this

> **Unless it's a super high-end commercial shoot, your client is likely to be on a budget and appreciative of your effort to make the lighting happen without extra fees for rentals.**

work. And don't feel that there is anything unprofessional about combining light sources like this. Unless it's a super high-end commercial shoot (and there are very few of those out there), your client is likely to be on a budget and appreciative of your effort to make the lighting happen without extra fees for rentals.

And, yes, you *should* be charging extra for rentals. In most commercial shoots, you will bid your shooting fee and include a separate fee for rentals, which includes the use of your personal gear. So if your client is on a budget, you can offer to wave the personal-gear rental fees and they will feel like they are getting a deal. And, really, they *are* getting a deal—because the wear and tear on your personal gear costs you money. In the digital photography world, our equipment (cameras especially) does not last forever and requires expensive maintenance, frequent replacement, and regular upgrades.

Two Softboxes, Two Umbrellas
The easiest way to do a high-key lighting setup and achieve a pure white background without shadows is to use a four-light setup: two lights in front of your subject and two lights behind the subject to illuminate the background.

In the setup shot on the right, showing a student photographer working on a high-key set, you see four lights where the blue arrows are located. Note that the two backlights have flags in front of them to avoid light spilling directly back into the lens and creating a haze on the image. This also prevents unwanted spill on the model from behind. Spill is not always a problem; it will depend on the modifiers you use and how much distance the shooting space enables you to put between the lights. In this setup, the front-light modifiers were softboxes and the backlight modifiers were umbrellas. If the backlight modifiers had been softboxes, there probably would not have been much spill and, thus, no need for the flags. The images created with this setup are shown below and on the next page.

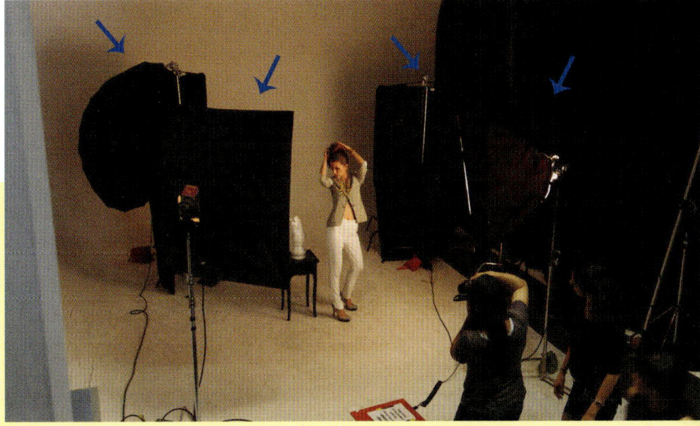

▶ Student photographer Mimi Mui photographing a model with a four-light, high-key setup using black flags to control spill. *Image by Preston Perkins.*

▼ Here are two of the images Mimi created using this setup. *Images by Mimi Mui. (Specs: f/8.0, 1/125, ISO 100)*

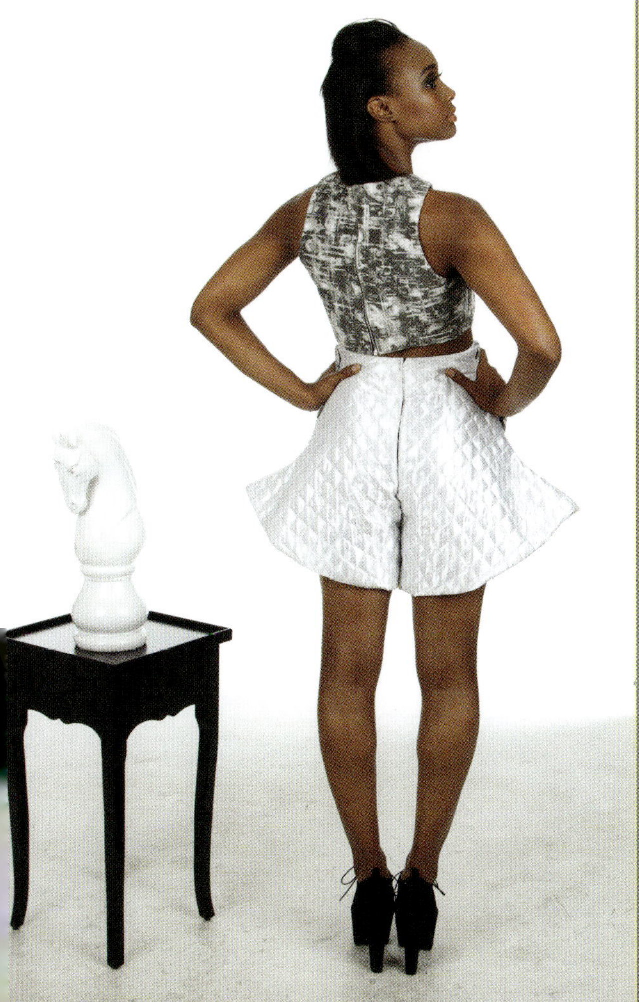

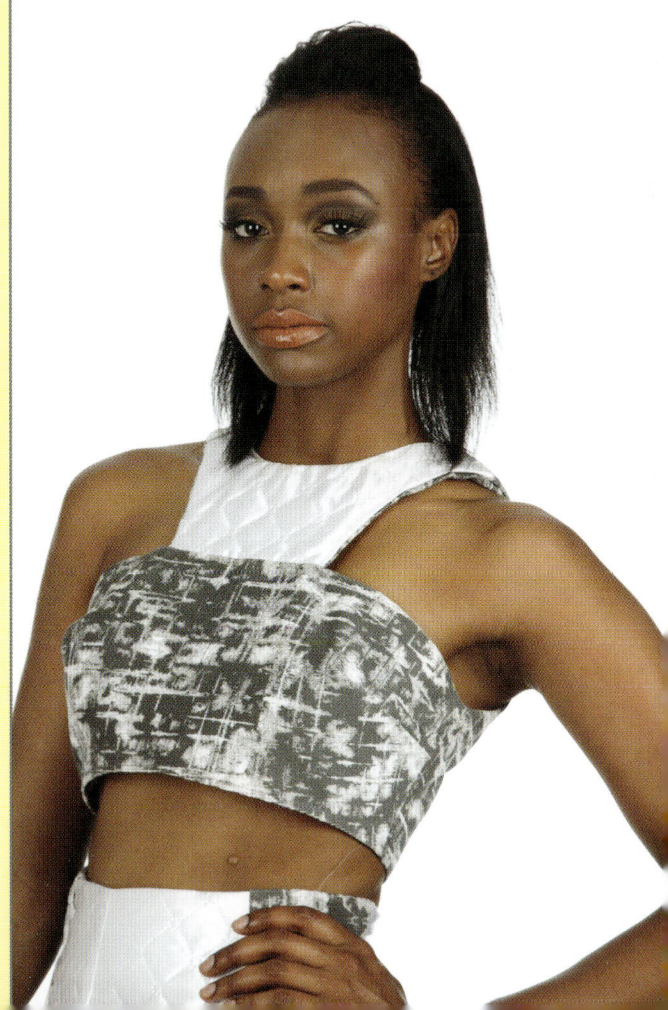

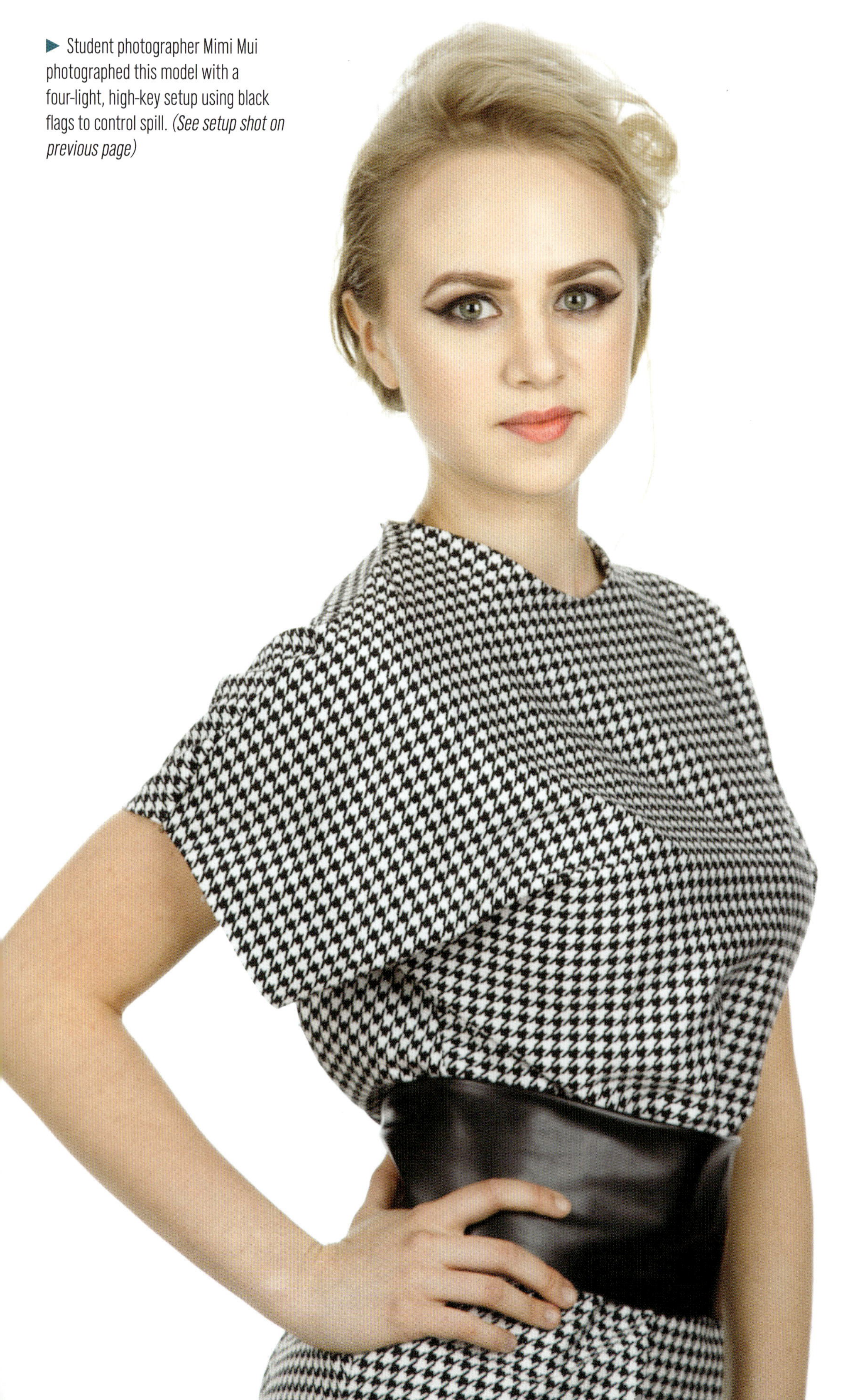

▶ Student photographer Mimi Mui photographed this model with a four-light, high-key setup using black flags to control spill. *(See setup shot on previous page)*

Four Umbrellas: Two Shoot-Through, Two Reflective

For the next example, I used four strobes with umbrellas. The two umbrellas for the front, positioned to either side of the subject, were lined with silver. The lights were bounced into the umbrellas to reflect back onto the subject. The two lights on the background were translucent shoot-through umbrellas; they were pointed directly at the white backdrop and positioned to either side of it. These translucent umbrellas created more directional light and there was a lot less light loss than with bounce umbrellas used in front of the subject. This gave me 1 or 2 stops more light on the background, so it washed out the white and eliminated any shadows thrown from the front lights. Having the background exposed correctly and very white is helpful when working in Photoshop to cut out a model's form from the background.

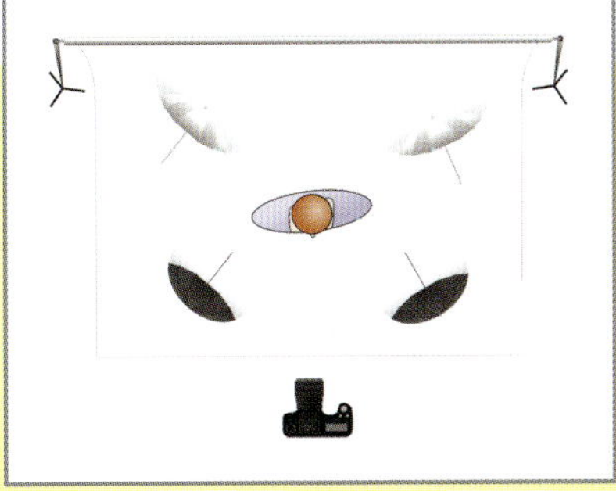

▶ The model was photographed with a four-light setup. I used two silver reflective umbrellas from the front and two shoot-through umbrellas at the back. This made it easy to cut the model out of the background in Photoshop.

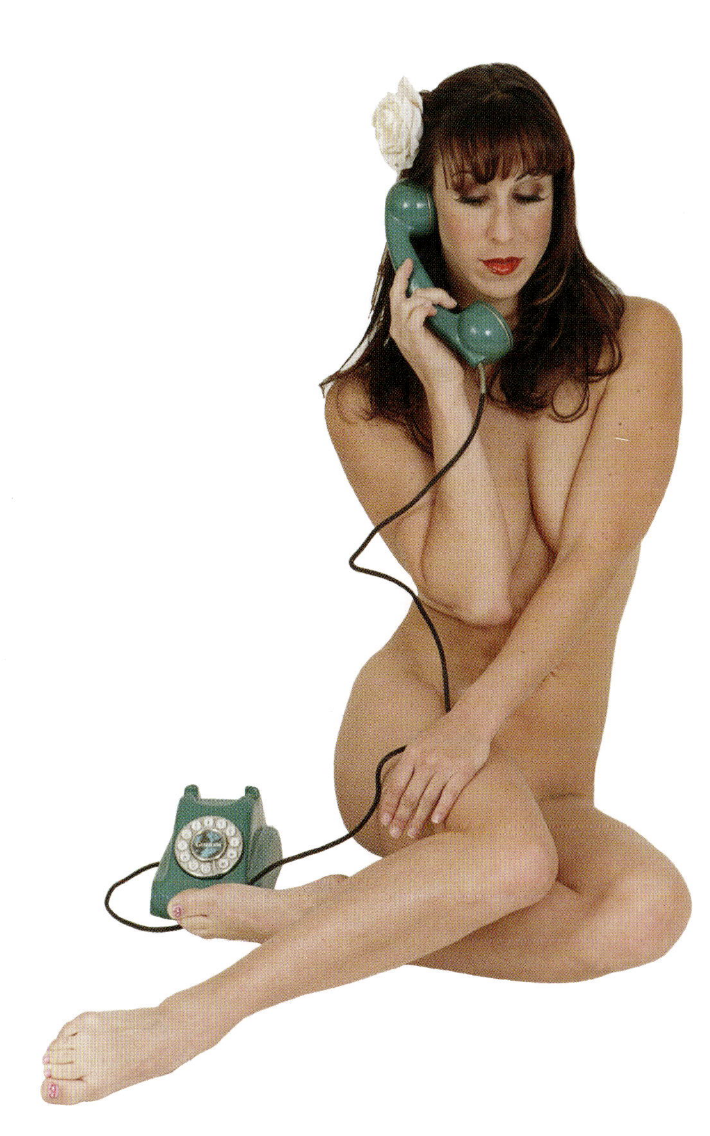

Controlling the Light

The farther away you have your subject and front lights from the background, the less you have to worry about the shadow of your subject being cast on it. However, moving those front lights away also means the overall background will go darker because the front lights can't reach it. This is why we add the backlights, so we can evenly light the background and keep it white.

If you are in a smaller space, however, you may have to worry about the backlight spilling forward onto your subject or even creating lens flare (a hazy look) in your images. Backlighting your subject is not a problem if it's not overexposing parts of the model where you want to see detail—and if the lights are far enough back, that spill won't happen. But if you are stuck in a small shooting area and have

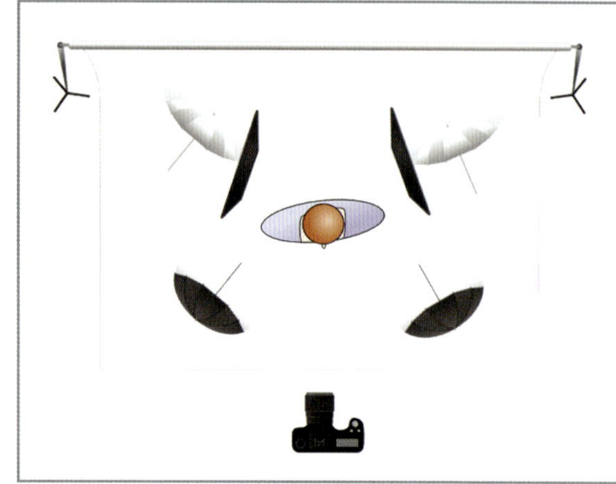

▲ Adding black flags or black panels in front of the back lights to avoid spill in the four-light high-key setup.

nowhere to go, placing a flag in front of the backlights will also eliminate that spill. Earlier in the chapter, we touched on an example of this. Now, let's look at another one in the image sequence below and on the facing page.

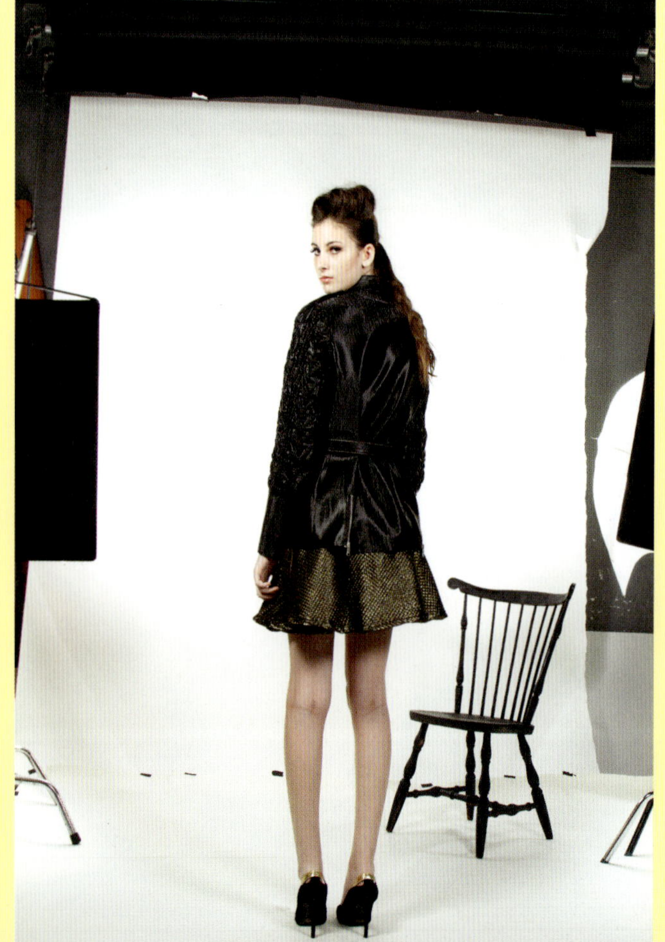

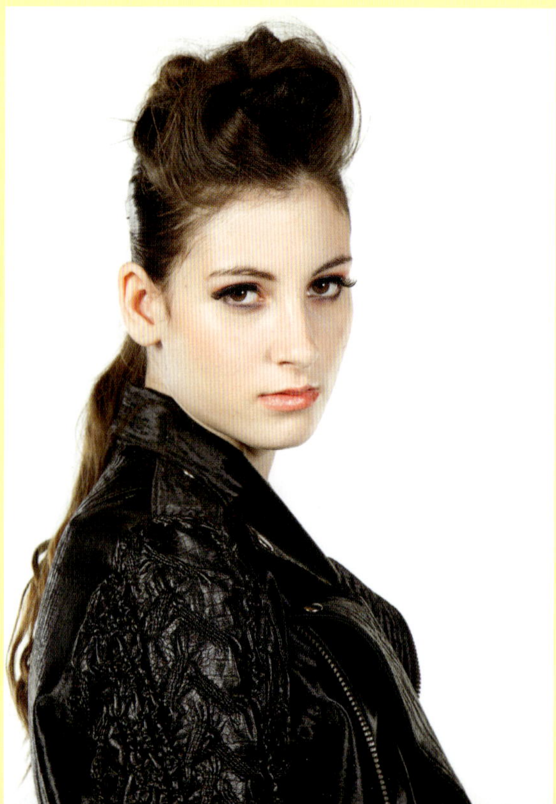

▼ ► This page and facing page: Black flags were used in this small studio space (left image). The resulting images in closeup views (below and facing page). *Images by Christoper Martin.*

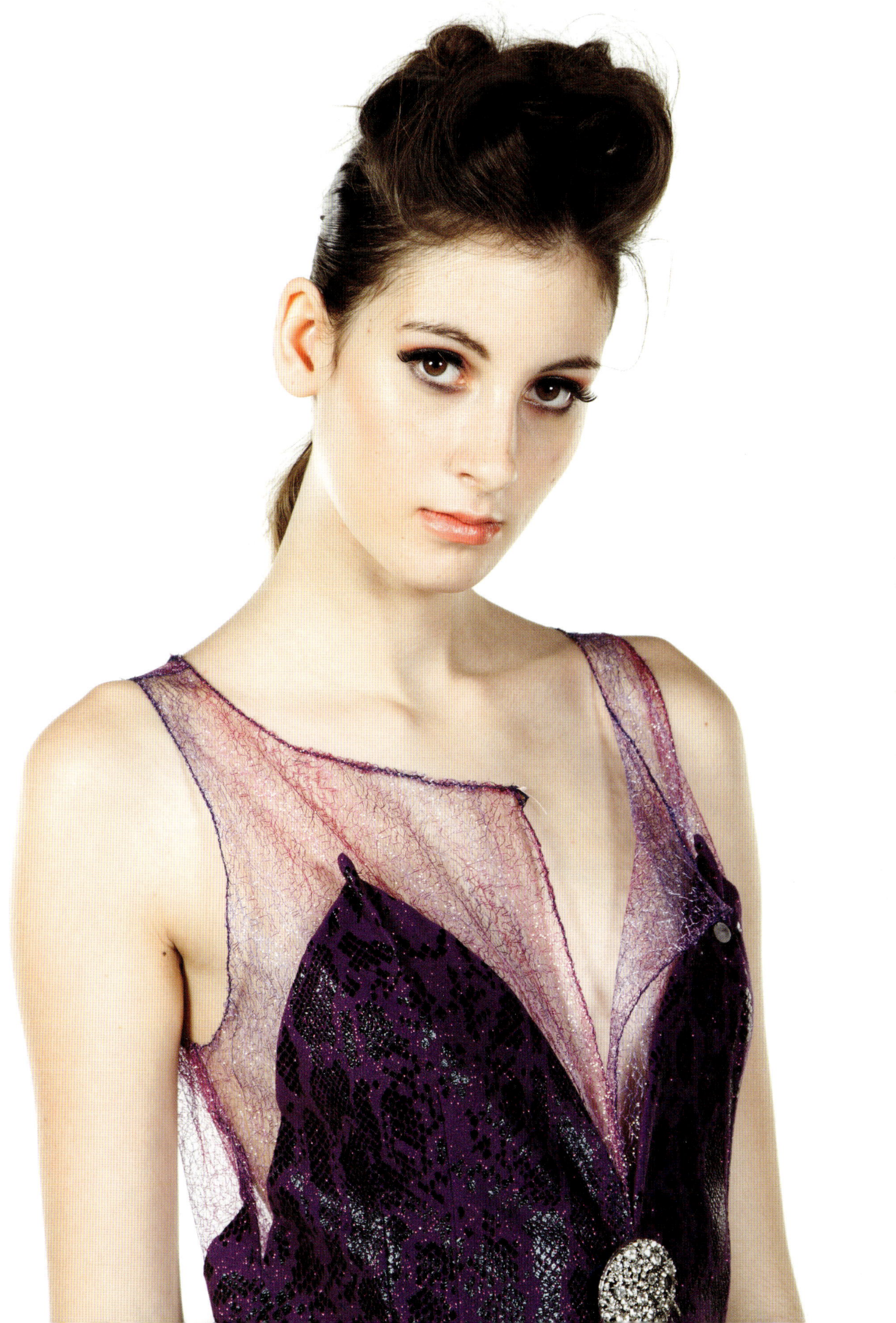

Working with Client Concepts

Magazine Cover Shoot

Often, clients will be very specific about what they want the final images to look like, and it's your job to work with them to create the product they are asking for. Pay attention to what the client is asking for in terms of lighting, model type, and theme. Get past what *you* might like and try to tell the story *they* want told. Create a feeling that is close to any samples the client has given you. An example of this appears below (left). Notice that the text on the magazine reads "Having Fun with Technology" and that the image, all on its own, demonstrates a "fun" emotion in the model—*and* it fits the text.

Shooting Tethered

A very handy way to make sure your client is getting what they want is to shoot tethered. This means you are transmitting your photos directly to a computer monitor as you shoot. On that monitor, the client can watch the progress of the session and give immediate feedback so you know you're headed in the right direction.

There are many ways to handle the technology involved with shooting tethered. You can shoot with a Bluetooth device or you can use a USB-to-mini-PC cable to connect your camera and computer. (*Note:* Even if you go the Bluetooth route, I recommend having a USB cable available as backup—just in case of technical problems.) In terms of software, Canon cameras come with a program called Canon Capture that allows you to shoot tethered. Aperture and Adobe Lightroom also allow for tethered shooting.

For the purpose of this example, I will use Lightroom to show how I shoot tethered for magazine covers using the Overlay option. I start by asking the client to give me a .PNG image file of the magazine cover with a translucent background layer (below, right). This will have the text and title that the photo will go behind. Using the Overlay option, I can place my photos *behind* this graphic as I shoot live, allowing the client to preview the image with the text in place over it and evaluate what works best in terms of cropping and position. It's just a preview, but it's a useful way for you and your client to be more in tune visually.

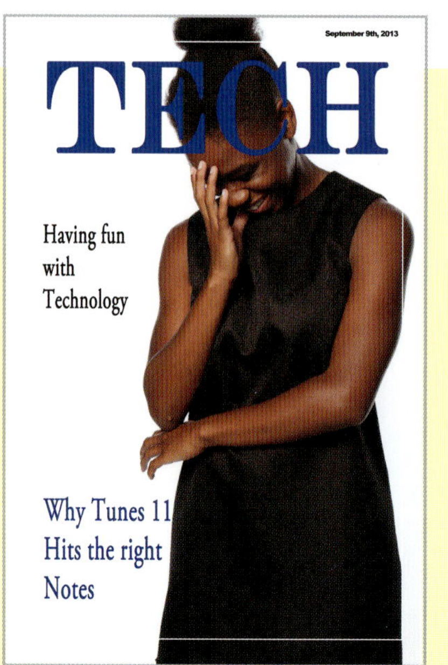

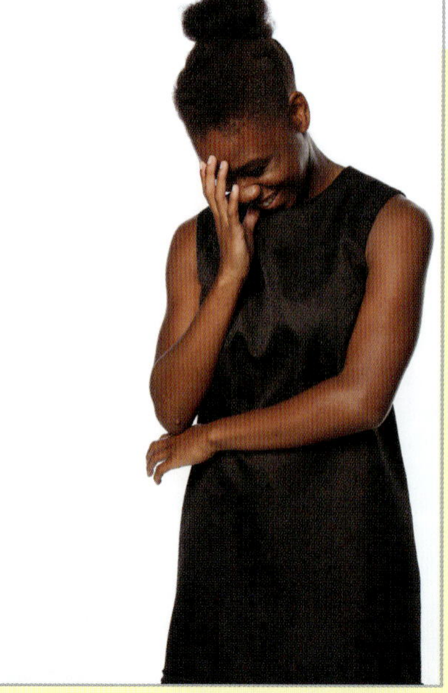

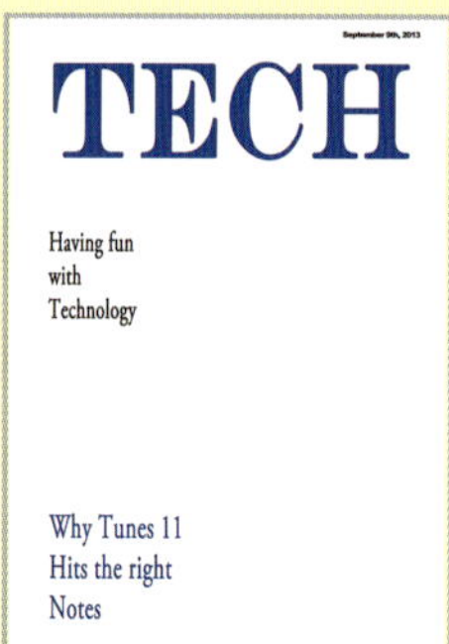

◀ The image and the text work together graphically and logically. The image alone shows emotion and a blank space for the text. *Image by Edurne Salas.*

◀ A PNG magazine-cover template from client.

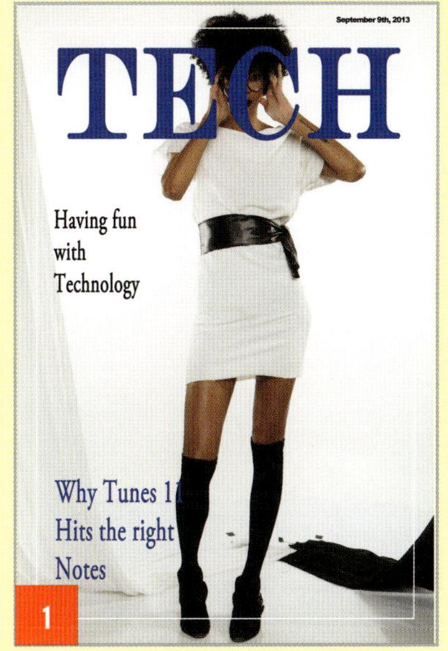
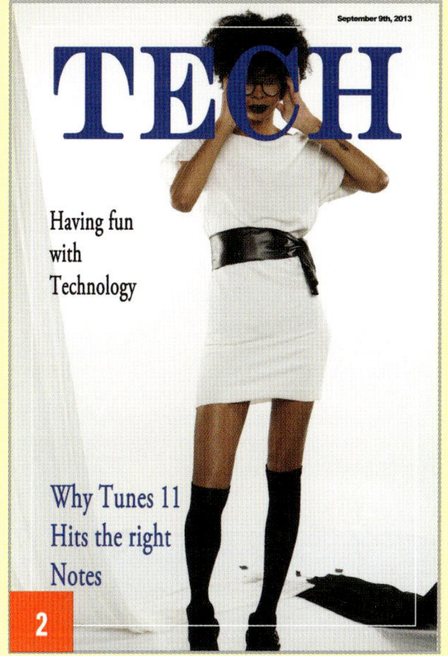
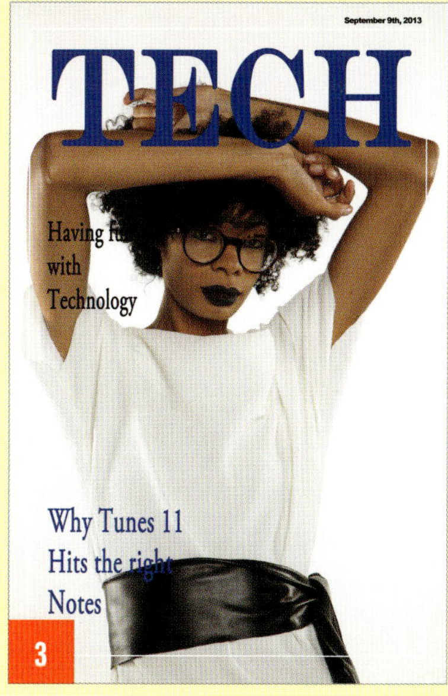
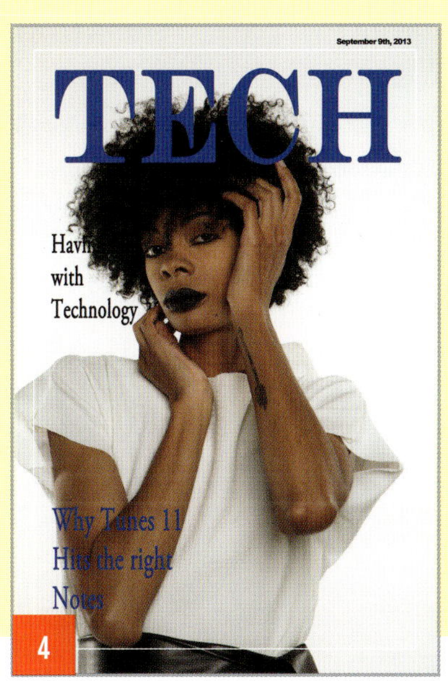
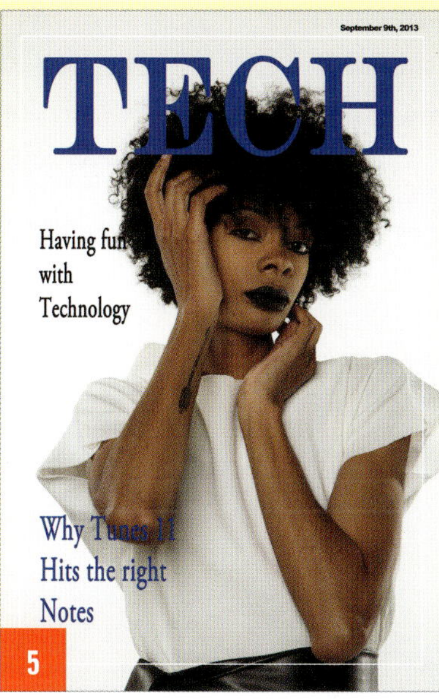

◀▲ **1.** Here, the text covers the model's face. **2.** Moving the image around in the template to place the model's face within the "C" may be better. In some cases, the client might choose to put the model's head in front of the text, blocking part of it – but that would be done in postproduction. **3.** Changing the model's pose and leaving some room above the head may work with the title text. **4.** This pose may work great, along with the extra headroom above for the title text to lay. **5.** Flipping the image (or posing the model the opposite way) leaves some blank space for the text and this may work better. *Images by Trang Nghiem.*

(*Note:* You would not export this template with the photo to create the actual magazine cover. In most cases, the final process of creating the magazine cover with the text and photo together is not the photographer's job.)

In the sequence of images above, you can see how the cropping and posing come into play when working with the .PNG template of the magazine cover. Having the template in place, while the images are being photographed, enables the photographer to make quick adjustments to cropping and posing and optimize the image to suit the layout. It can also avoid a re-shoot if it turns out that the images aren't workable with the text design.

High-Key with Props

Can you still achieve a high-key image when you add props into the images or set elements in front of the background? Yes, but when we talk about high-key, we usually want a blown-out white background and even lighting on the subject without much in the way of shadows. In the first image below, you can see that adding a small prop does not change any of the lighting elements. When the image is shot up close, as in the second photo below, there is no loss of light.

Obscured White Backgrounds

For the images on the facing page, the photographer had a little fun with the setup by adding some sheer material to the background on the high-key set. These images show

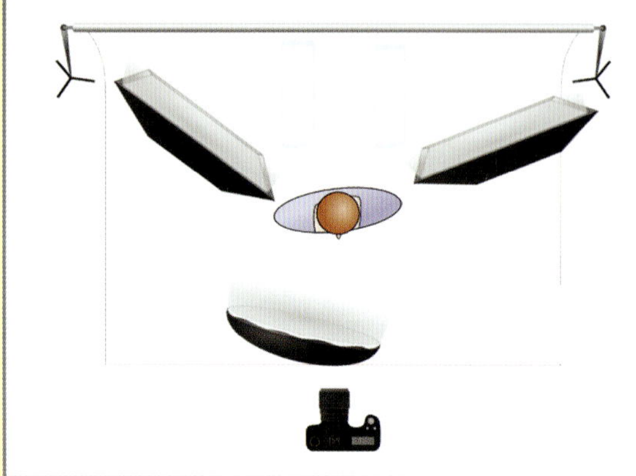

▲▶ Above and facing page: A high-key image in a small space using three lights and obscuring the background with fabric. *Image by Gabriella Muttone.*

how you can pretty much achieve a high-key lighting effect with only three lights in a small space. The front light was a large Mola beauty dish with a diffuser. The background was lit with two medium softboxes. To make this a true high-key image, we would probably have added some fill under the subject to get rid of most of the shadow under the chin. A white bounce card would probably suffice if you only had three lights to work with.

▼ A high-key image with a prop added (left). A close-up (right) shows that the lighting is not affected by adding the prop. *Images by Madeleine Dalla Torre Castillo. (Specs: f/16.0, 1/125, ISO 100)*

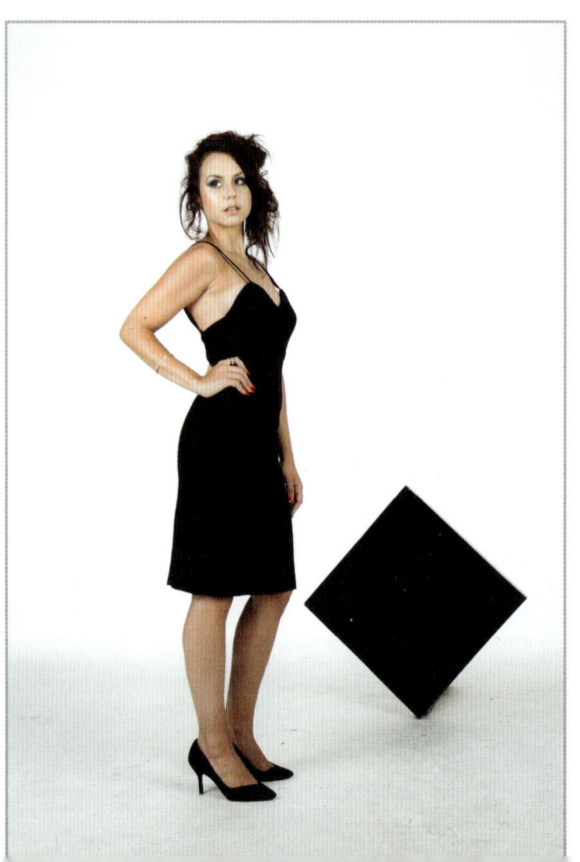

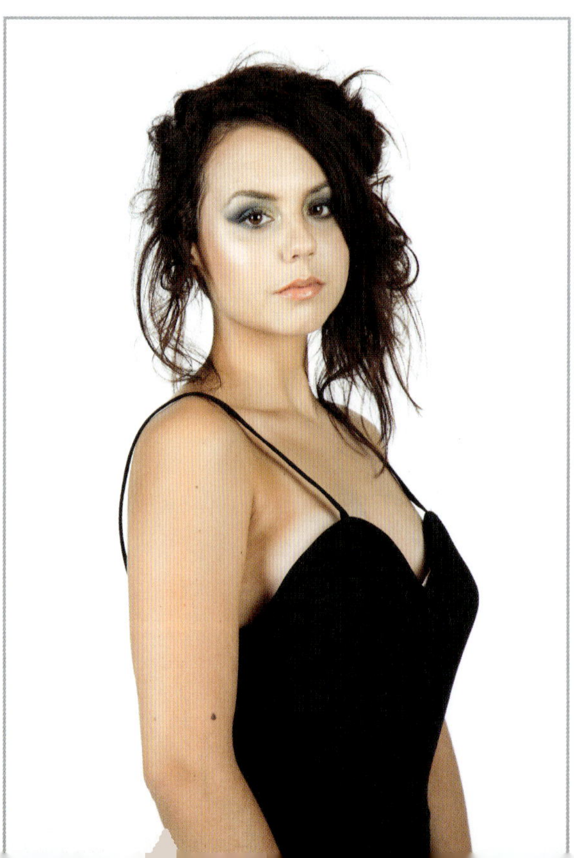

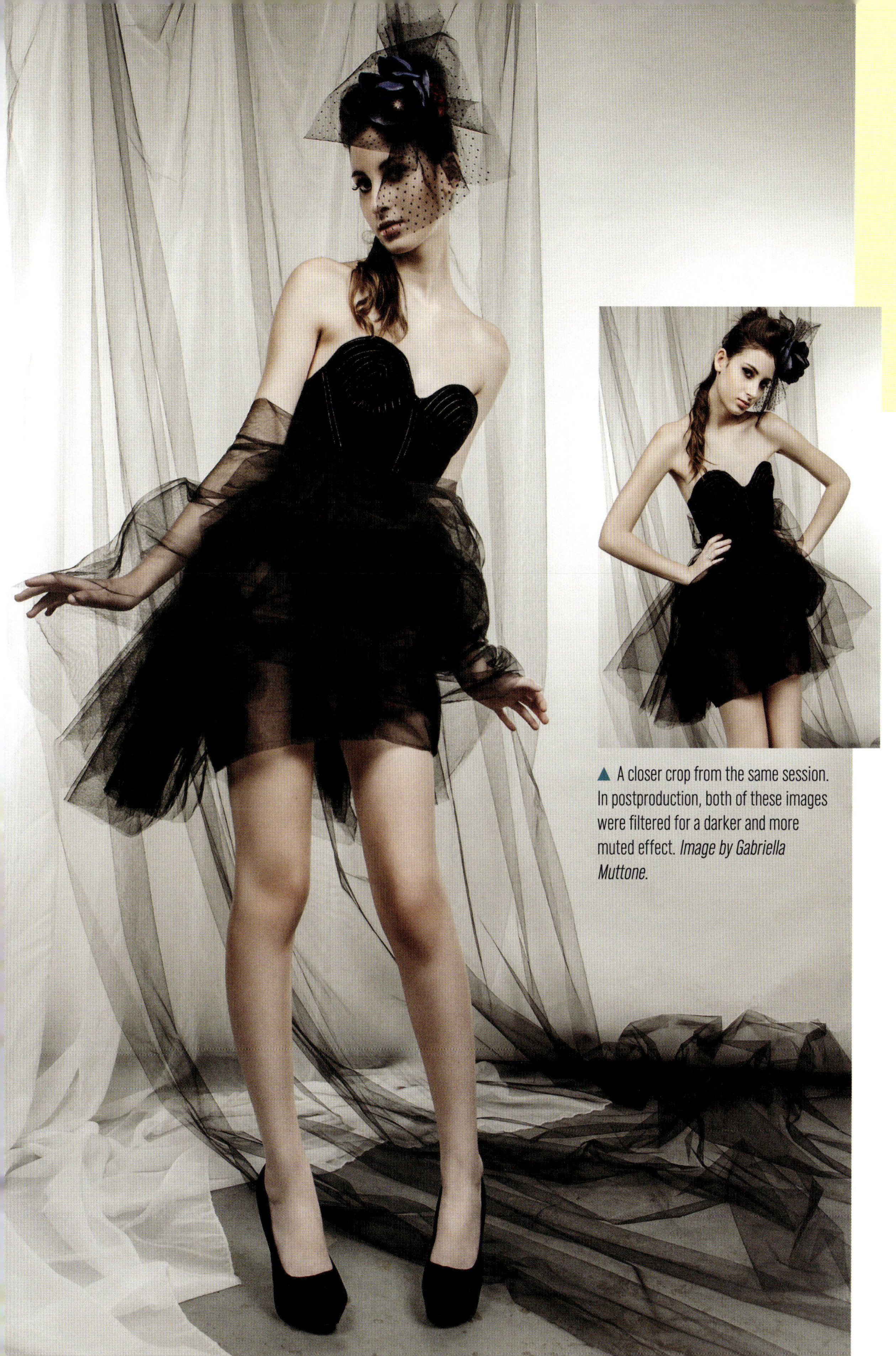

▲ A closer crop from the same session. In postproduction, both of these images were filtered for a darker and more muted effect. *Image by Gabriella Muttone.*

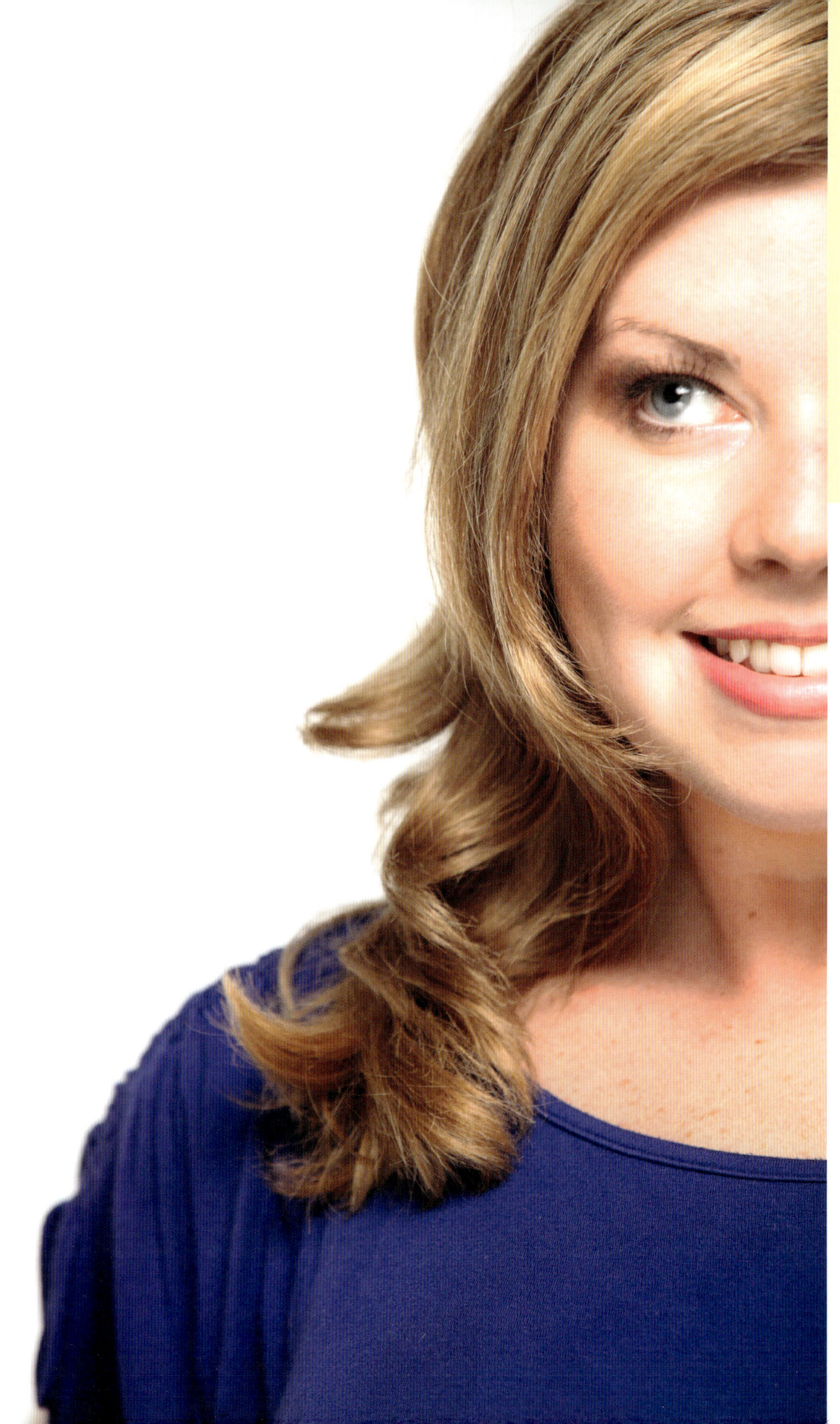

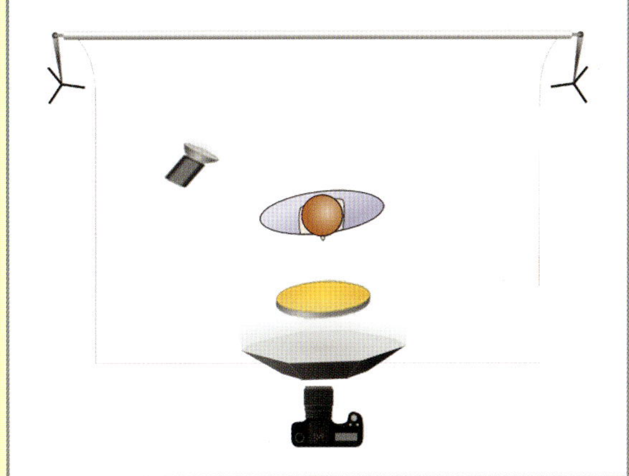

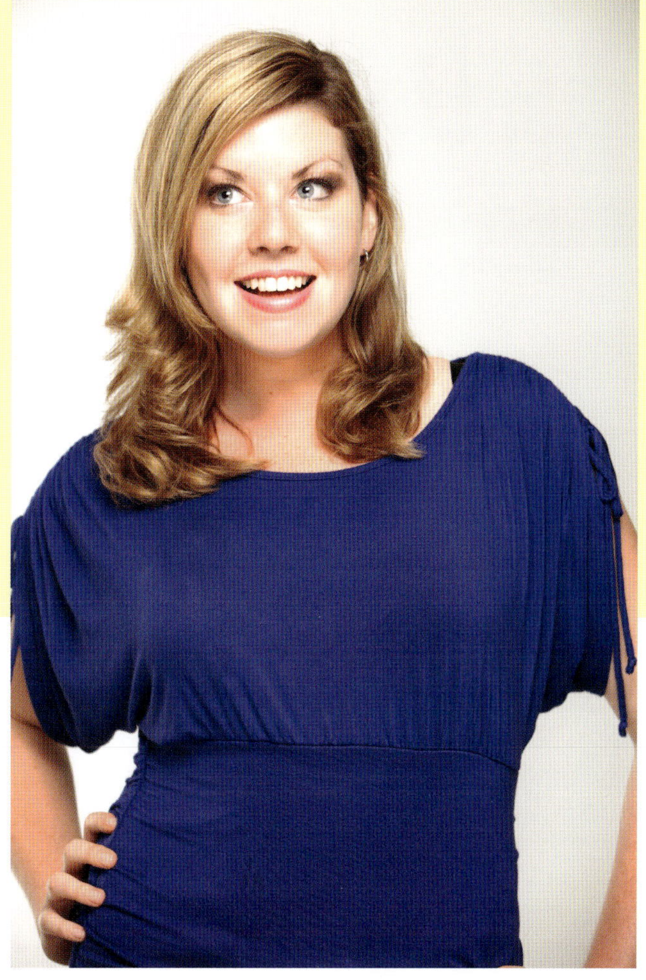

Two-Light High-Key Headshots

High-key lighting is used for many different kinds of photography. For these headshots, I used a clamshell setup (see chapter 3) plus a light on the background. The main light was above the actor and feathered down toward her face. From below, a gold reflector was used to bounce light back onto her face and fill in most of the shadows. A second light behind the model illuminated the background. The studio area I was shooting in was all white, which helped bounce light all over and eliminate more of the shadows. In the second image (this page), notice that the background is going a little gray on the right-hand side. This is where we lost the full high-key effect. To really make that background white and high-key, I would either have needed a second light on the opposite side of the background, or I could have turned up the backlight to blow the background out. The model was only a few feet from the background and it was a small space, however, so pumping the backlight up might have created a bounce-back spill situation leading to image-degrading lens flare.

Learning to do high-key correctly is a good idea, because there are so many different kinds of jobs that can call for this style of lighting design. Remember that it's okay to blow out the background to make it go white, but you should not overexpose your subject's skin or create hot-spots.

5. Lighting Groups

Key Techniques ▶ Using large light sources; Multiple light setups; Shooting with gels
Application ▶ Production stills; Cast photos

In this chapter, we will cover lighting groups as it applies to film, television, and music production stills. We will also cover techniques for keeping the lighting consistent for individual character photos and the group cast photos. These techniques can also be applied to industrial or local advertising shoots. For example, you may be hired to shoot group and individual photos at a local car dealership for a regional commercial and advertising campaign. Or perhaps you'll be hired to shoot band photos for CD covers and promotions.

Lighting Design

If you are working on a large, big-budget production, you may be creating photos that the art director has designed. In that case, they will often give you a lighting diagram that eliminates a lot of the guesswork. At first, however, you will probably do most of your work on lower-budget productions where you will either have to design a lighting setup yourself or come in and shoot with an existing lighting setup during filming.

Large Sources

When lighting multiple people, having a large light source or multiple light sources is the key. Large light sources can be easier to manage, but the resulting images may not be as dynamic or dramatic as those shot with multiple-light setups. Let's start by looking at some quick setups with larger light sources.

Modifiers

Placing two large softboxes in front of your subjects, to either side of the group, is a good, easy option for lighting groups. You can use one *very big* softbox, centered above the group, emulating a large window light source—but most of us don't have access to such large modifiers or even the space to use them when shooting.

There is a lot of debate about square/rectangular softboxes and octaboxes (round softboxes). The only real difference is the shape of the catchlights in the subjects' eyes—either round or square. Round modifiers can spread the light a little more evenly around the subject, but there really isn't a huge difference unless you are only using one light. If you are using two lights placed evenly on either side of your group, square boxes and round boxes will yield very similar results.

If you like round catchlights, you can also consider using umbrellas, which may be more

readily available and economical than large octaboxes. Compared to a softbox, the umbrella
will have more spill at the sides—light that
would be contained by a softbox. This means
that umbrella light will be less directional.

A Two-Umbrella Setup

Most people have two strobes in their lighting
kit, so let's start by using two lights with umbrellas. You can really do *most* groups with just
two lights, but it's best to keep your subjects
close together (in terms of depth, front to
back). Otherwise, there will be light falloff and
the people in the back will not be lit as well as
those in the front.

The images that open this chapter are from
a session I shot with a band. I used a two-
light setup with umbrellas. I wanted there to
be a little bit of shadow, so I used one shoot-

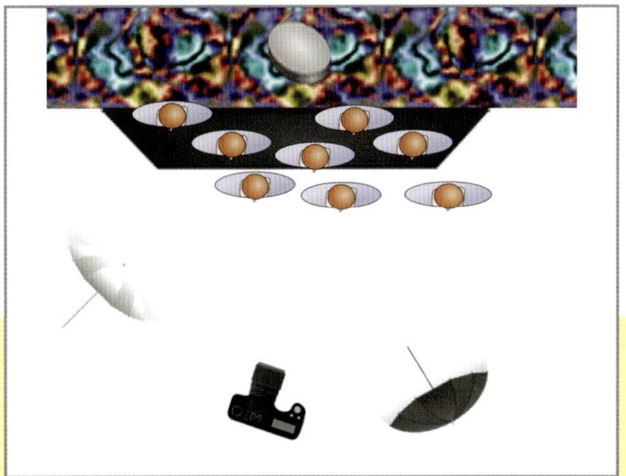

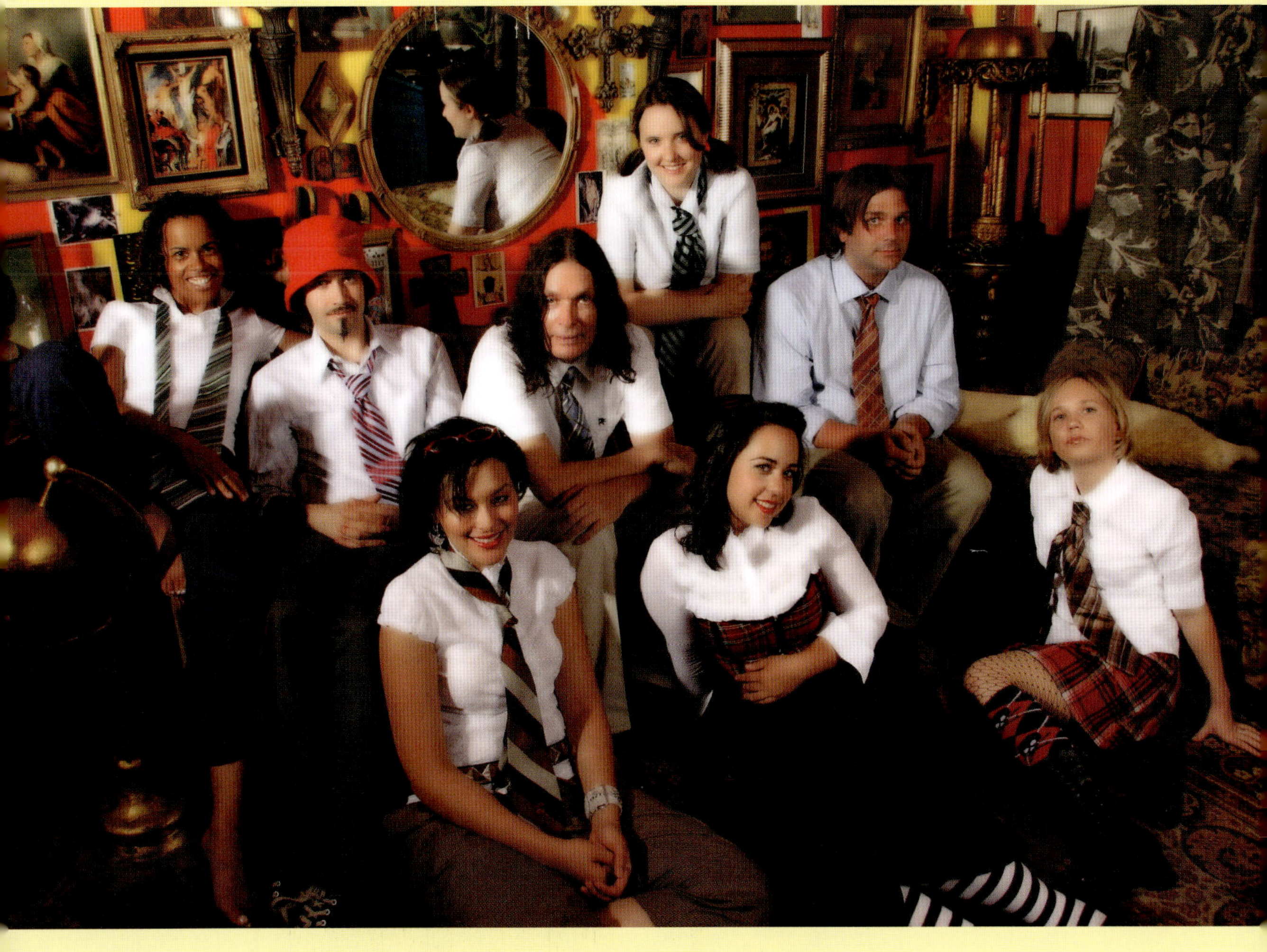

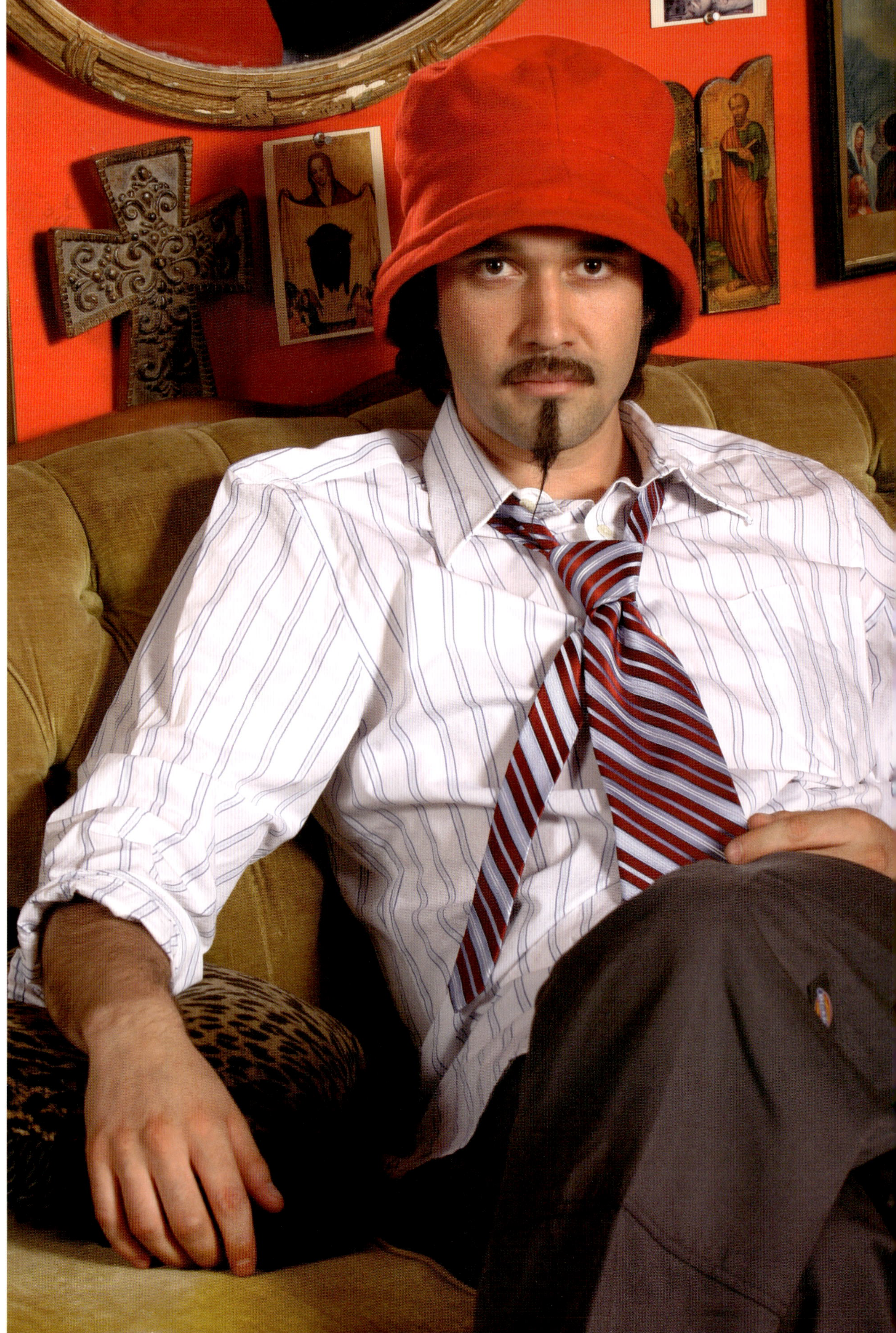

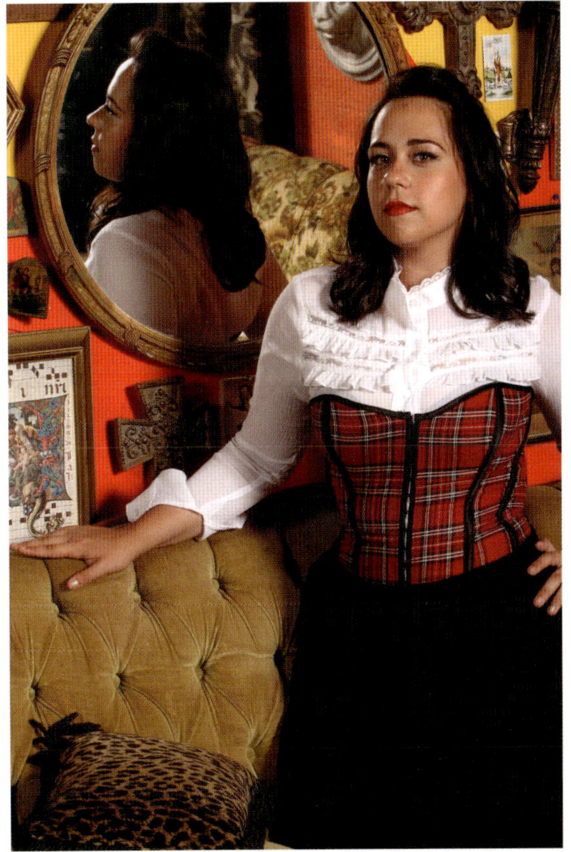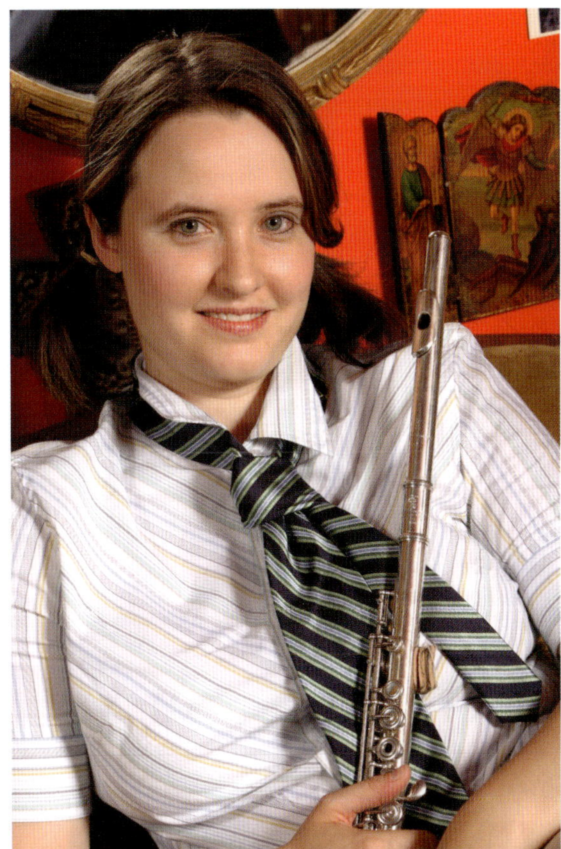

◀▲ Facing page and above: Individual photos of the band members were shot on the same set with the same lighting. *(Specs: f/11.0, 1/180, ISO 400, Canon 70-200mm f/2.8L at 17mm at 78mm [facing page], 70mm [above left], and 105mm [above right])*

through umbrella and one bounce umbrella. The shoot-through was placed to camera left and a bit off to the side of the subjects so that it fell evenly on the people in the back. The second light was to camera right and a little more centered and over my shoulder so it was directional and there was some falloff to the right side to create a little shadow and depth on everyone's face. This umbrella also helped light the people at the back-right of the frame, whom the shoot-through might not have lit as evenly.

In this rather small space, the subjects were right up against the background wall, making it easy to light the whole area. In a bigger space with the subjects farther away from the back wall, I might have needed more strobes to light the background, which is an essential

Take a Quick Inventory

The band photos were shot on a "found" set—the wall, couch, and every prop in it existed at the studio just as it is in the photo. There was no moving things around on the wall or anywhere else, so taking a quick inventory of potential issues before placing the lights and camera was important. You should especially take note of reflective surfaces. In this case, the scene included a wall mirror. By shooting from the side, we avoided catching my reflection or getting any light bouncing off the mirror itself.

element in this image. With eight people and an elaborate set to light, keeping them all close to each other in depth (front to back) and close to the background was a good way to make it work. Since this was a small space, having a wide-angle lens came in handy. I shot at 17mm with a 17–35mm lens.

I shot the individual photos of each band member (previous pages) on the same couch; I did not move the lights. Even if the band says they just want a group shot, I think it's a good idea to take a little extra time and do some individual headshots so they have them. These days, with websites and other online promotions, they may need these images for things like the "About" page, featuring bios of each member. I switched to a 70–200mm lens for a more compressed portrait-lens look.

A Simple Multiple-Light Setup

Now, let's look at a setup where more lights were used. These are promotional images for a television pilot about vampires that was produced by my company, PBJ Candids Productions. Most of the pilot takes place in a bar set, as seen in the photo on the facing page, so doing the cast photos on this same set was the best way to tell the story. We wanted a dramatic look to the photos, something similar to the lighting for the filming.

Planning and Production

For this shoot, we did not have the luxury of time. This was an ultra-low-budget television pilot and the actors and crew were either volunteering their time or working for very little money, so it was not possible to devote a separate day to shooting stills. Instead, the producers chose to have us come in during prep on a filming day.

While the first set of actors were in makeup, we set up the lights and did some test shots. Before their makeup was finished, we then brought the entire cast on-set to do a final lighting test shot as a group. That took about five minutes. In larger productions, you would use stand-ins. It's important to have your lighting done *before* you bring your actors on-set, so you are not wasting production time.

As each actor came out of makeup and wardrobe, we then shot their individual cast character photos, including a headshot and a full-length image. This was a great use of time because each actor came out of makeup at a different time, so we were not taking up production time.

Once the actors were all fully in makeup and wardrobe, and all the individual images were done, we brought the entire cast in for the group shots. We did a few different arrangements, tweaked the shot, and finished in about twenty minutes. As soon as we finished, the production crew got to work setting up their first shot as we quickly moved our lights off the set.

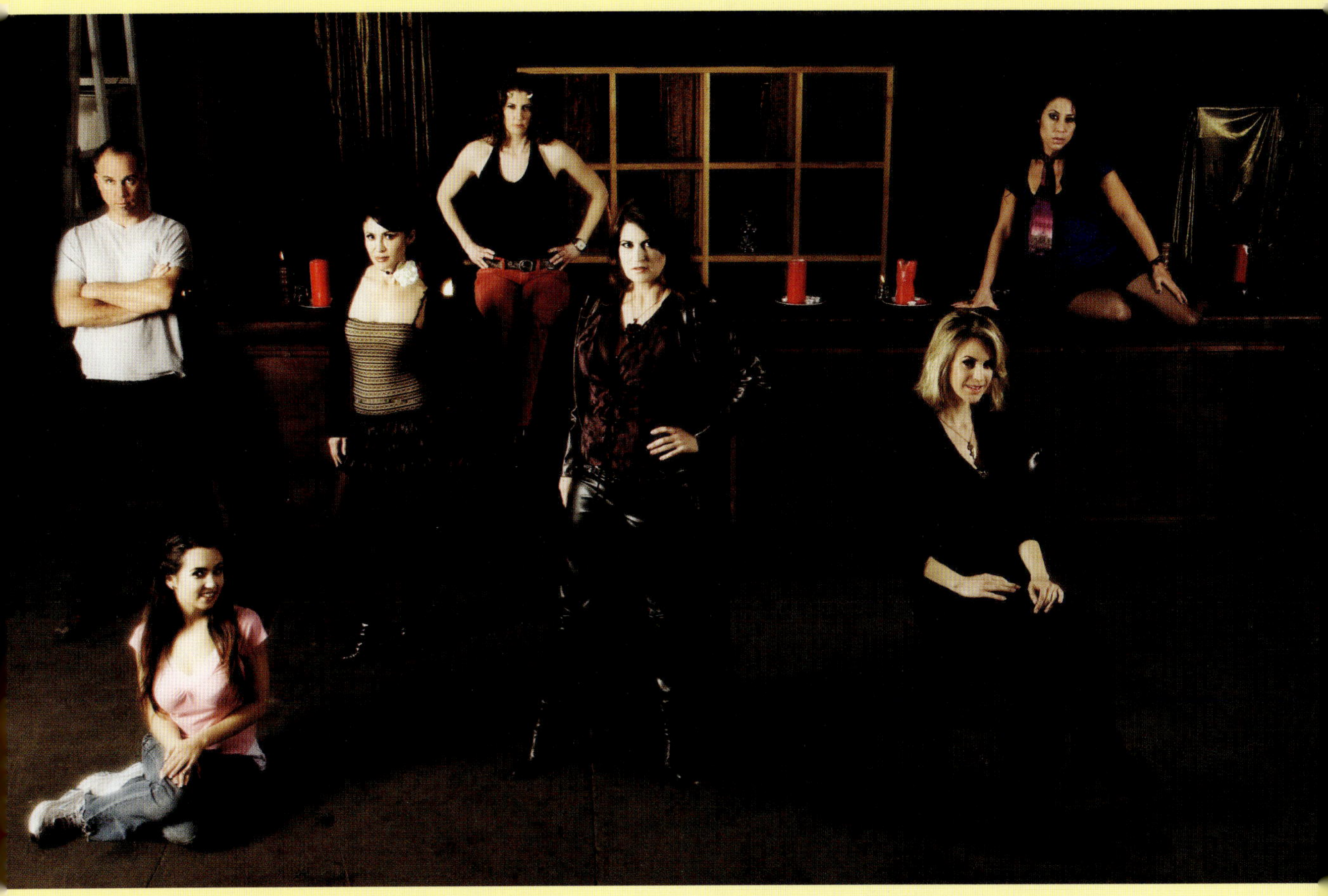

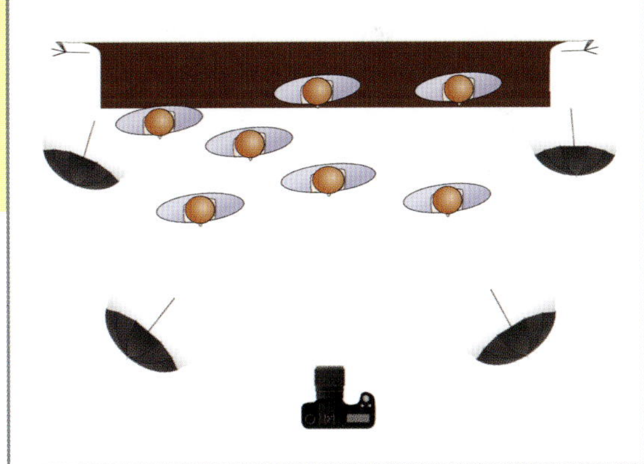

Group Portrait

We used four monolights with umbrellas with silver linings. If you look at the shadows cast on the floor by the actors, you can see there are multiple lights. The key light was to camera left and about 8 feet high. This was our hottest and most powerful light. The other front light, to camera right, filled in the shadows just a bit. It was powered down to preserve the shadows that the key light produced on the sides of the subjects' faces, giving us that more dramatic look. The two lights to the back of the set were set high about 8 feet above and directed downward, in toward the subjects and feathered back. These lights were

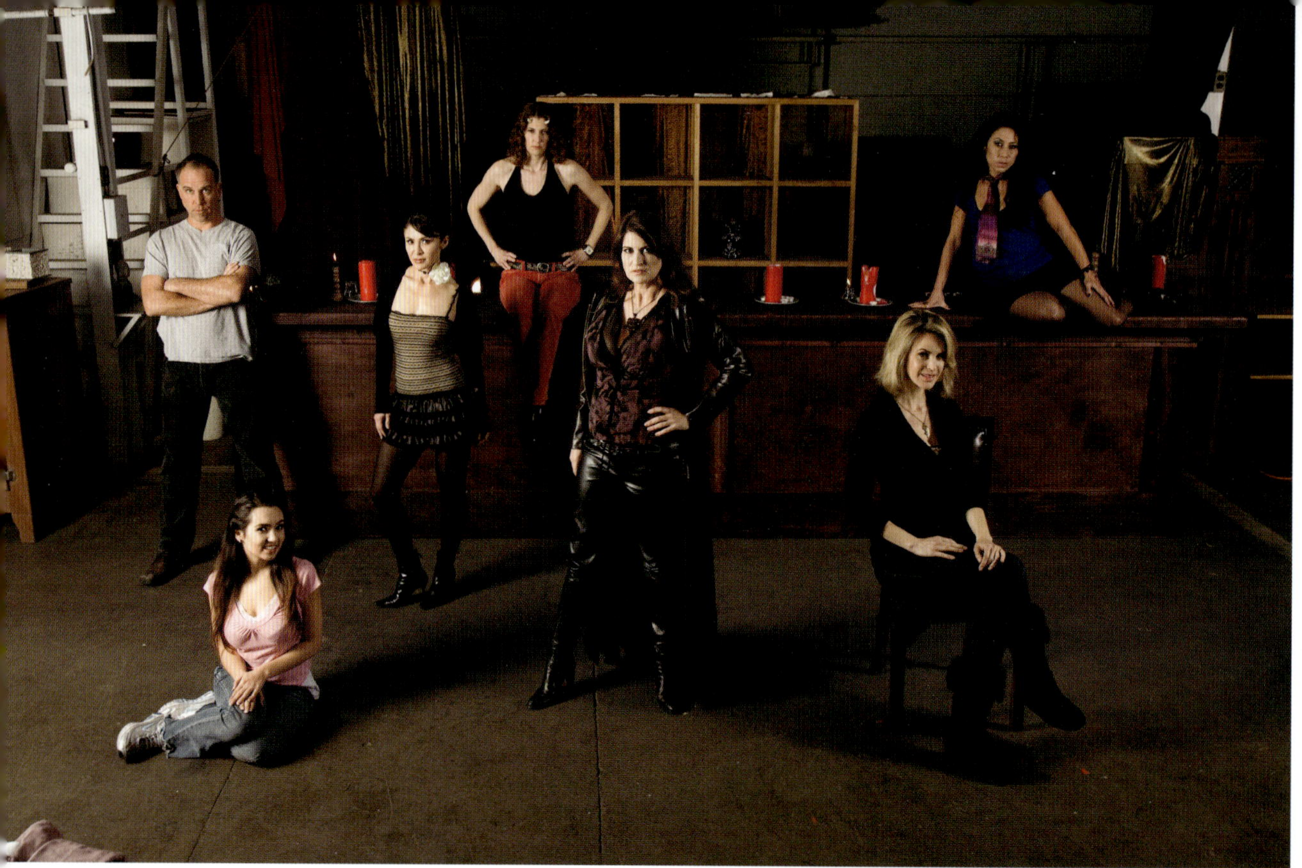

▲ Original photo before postproduction. *Image by Ted Pang. Lighting design by Jennifer Emery and Mario Jennings.*

also set a couple of stops lower than the key light. The camera-left backlight was quite close to the cast members so that we could light them evenly and balance the cast members in the foreground. The camera-right backlight was farther away and powered down to just fill a bit of the back cast. (*Note:* If you need less power from a light and you already have it powered down as low as possible, try pulling the light farther back from your subjects.)

Above, you can see the original image before postproduction. The set was built in a warehouse and the background shows some falloff from the backlights being feathered. In postproduction, we darkened the background and cleaned up the sides of the image. We also wanted it to be even more dramatic, so we brought down the levels on the entire image and gave it more contrast to accentuate the blacks. In the facing page image, you can see how it was used in a final poster. Again, we were shooting on a live set, so we had to just work with what was there and clean it up after the shoot—which can often be the case when shooting promotional stills for low-budget productions.

> 66 We had to just work with what was there and clean it up after the shoot – which can often be the case when shooting promotional stills for low-budget productions. 99

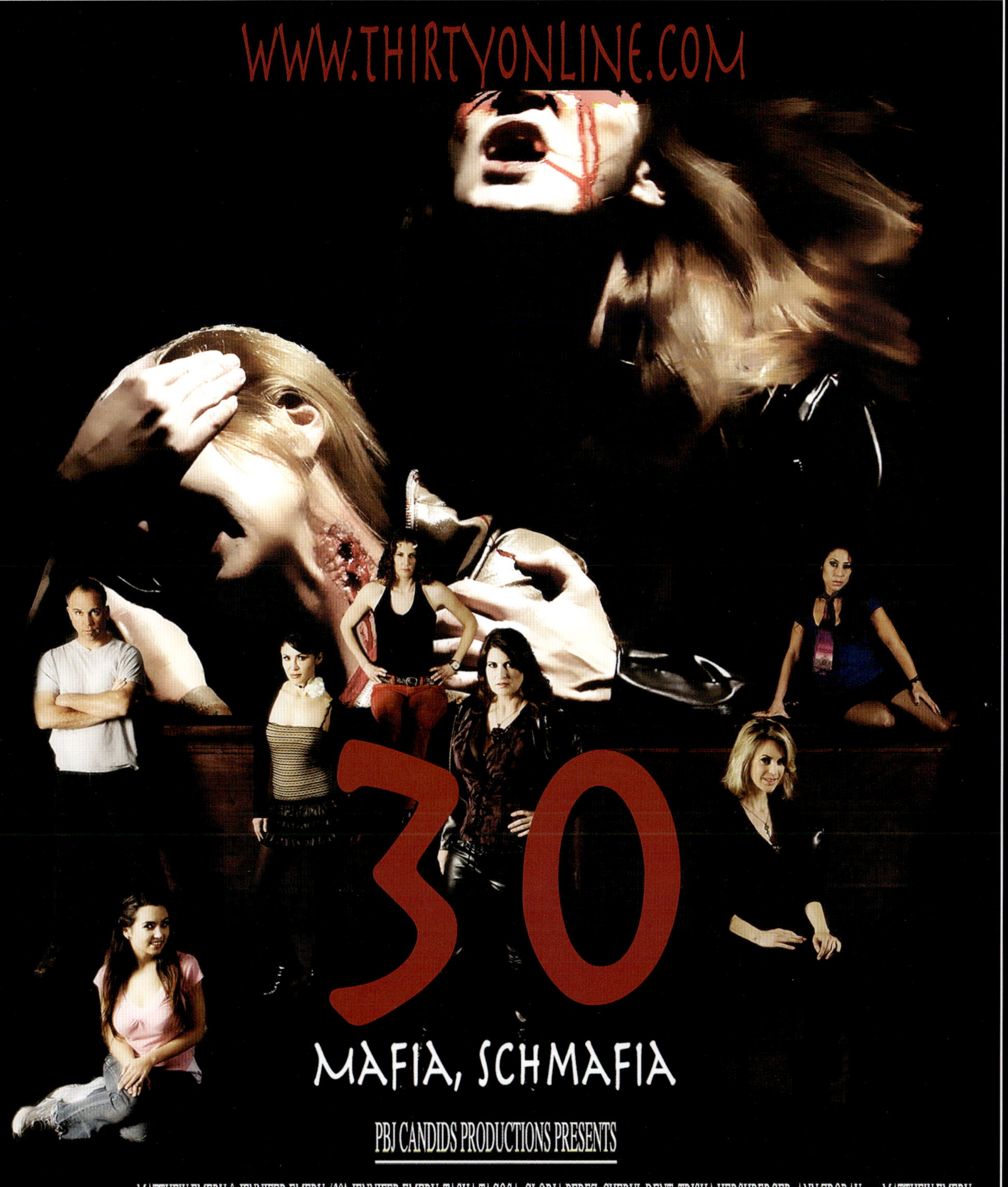

Final use as a poster and flyer. *Poster art by Jennifer Emery.*

Individual Portraits

An important note is that we did not change the light positions between the individual shots and the group shots. During the individual photos, we simply moved the camera and/or subject around the set and used a longer lens to create more compression and a more shallow depth of field. To give each image a bit of a different feel that suited the individual character, we placed the actors in different spots on the set so the lighting would hit them a bit differently. For some shots, the camera-right light was turned off (or was so far from the actor that it did not register), creating a Rembrandt lighting effect. However, the lighting is generally the same, so there is a consistent look to the individual images and they all make sense visually with the group shots. Not having to light each person individually also saved a lot of time, which was essential.

It's important to note that the images were taken *in character*. Often, you can just tell the actors to be in character for the still shoot—but it's nice if you know something about the characters and can tell the right story in the image. If the director or assistant director (AD) is on the set, they can help, but doing some homework beforehand to learn what needs to be conveyed is best. In this sequence, notice that all the headshots are shot in a similar way. They are all horizontal, in similar locations on the set, and with the similar lighting. The full-length shots, then, give the viewer a little more information about the character by adding a pose that conveys the overall personality of that particular character.

I shot all of the images with a 100mm f/2.8 lens and moved closer or farther away from the subjects for headshots and full-length views. I chose this lens because it is crazy sharp and has great compression and bokeh results. All of the images were then taken into Photoshop and developed with the same action so they match. And, of course, skin retouching and smoothing were applied.

The images shown on the next few pages were the final picks, selected for use on the website and in the video trailer. I have included all the cast photos so you can see how they work harmoniously with the group image at the start of this section.

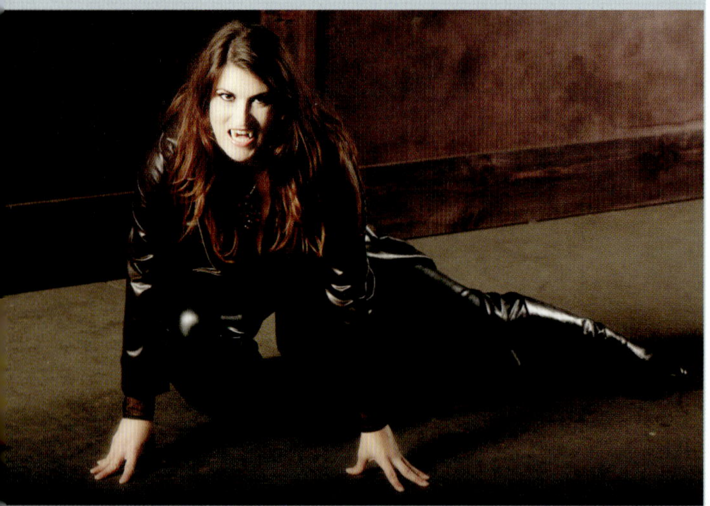

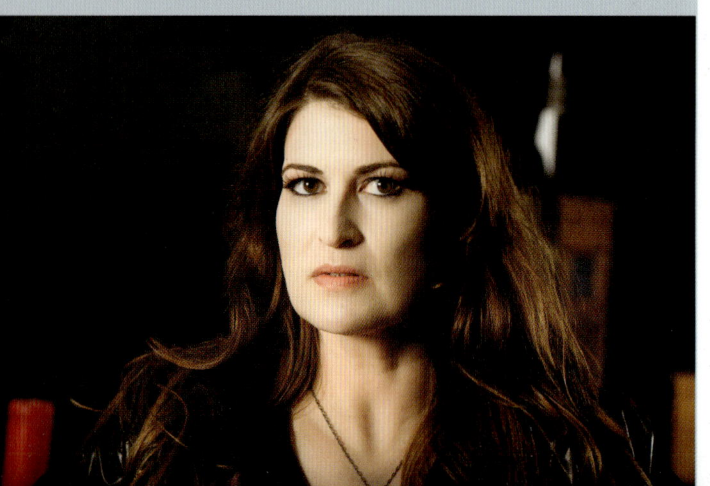

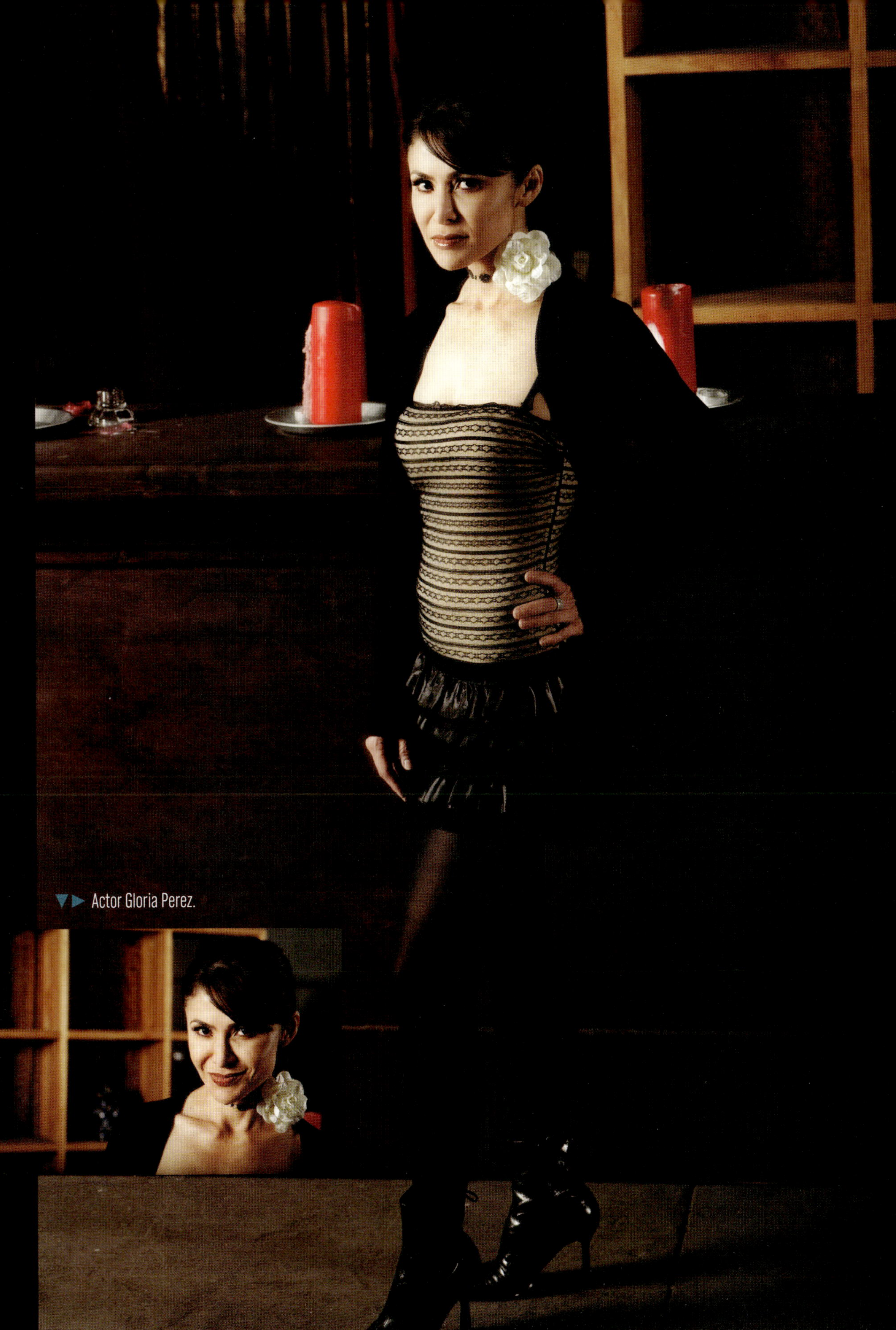

Actor Gloria Perez.

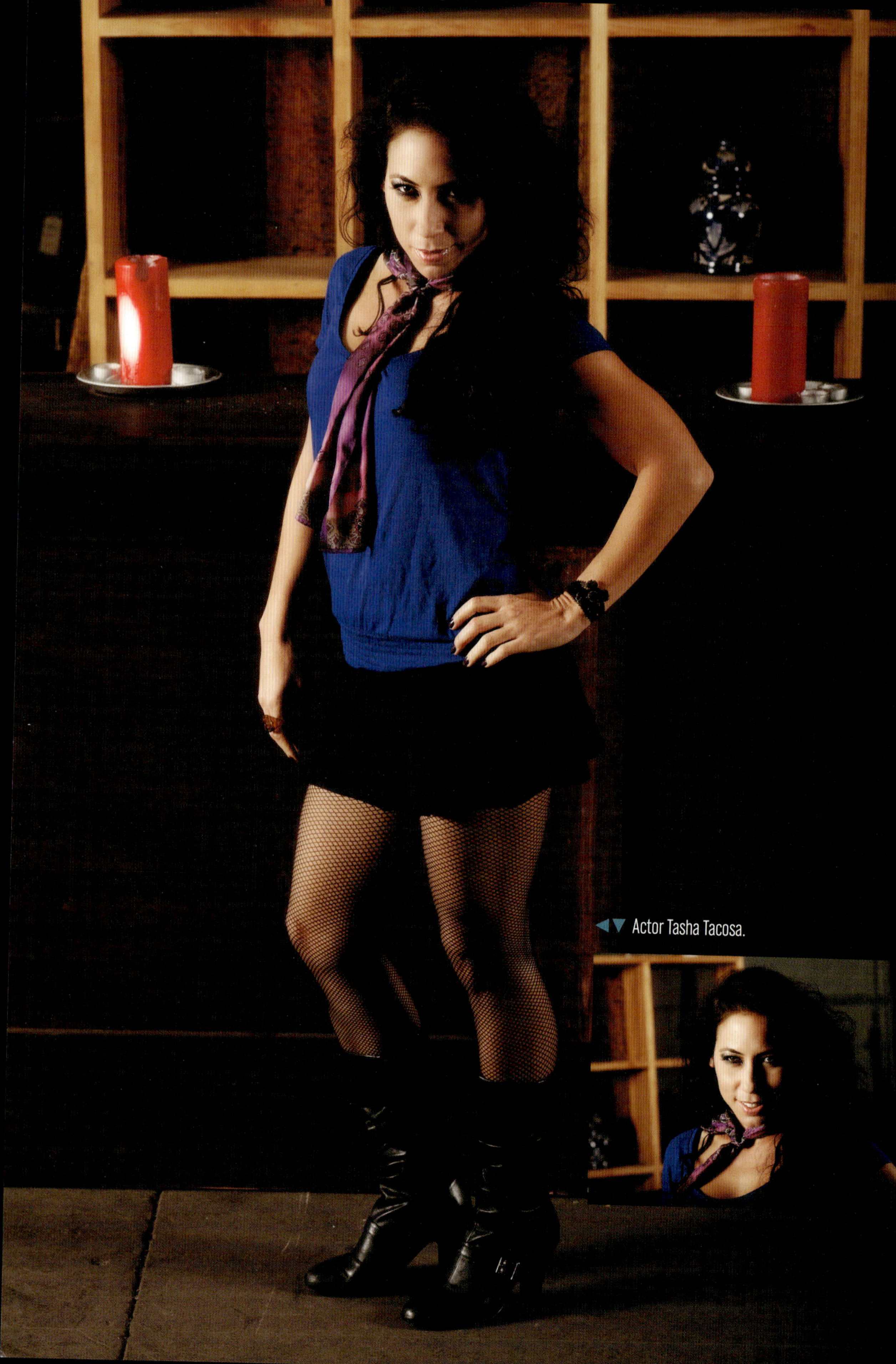

Actor Tasha Tacosa.

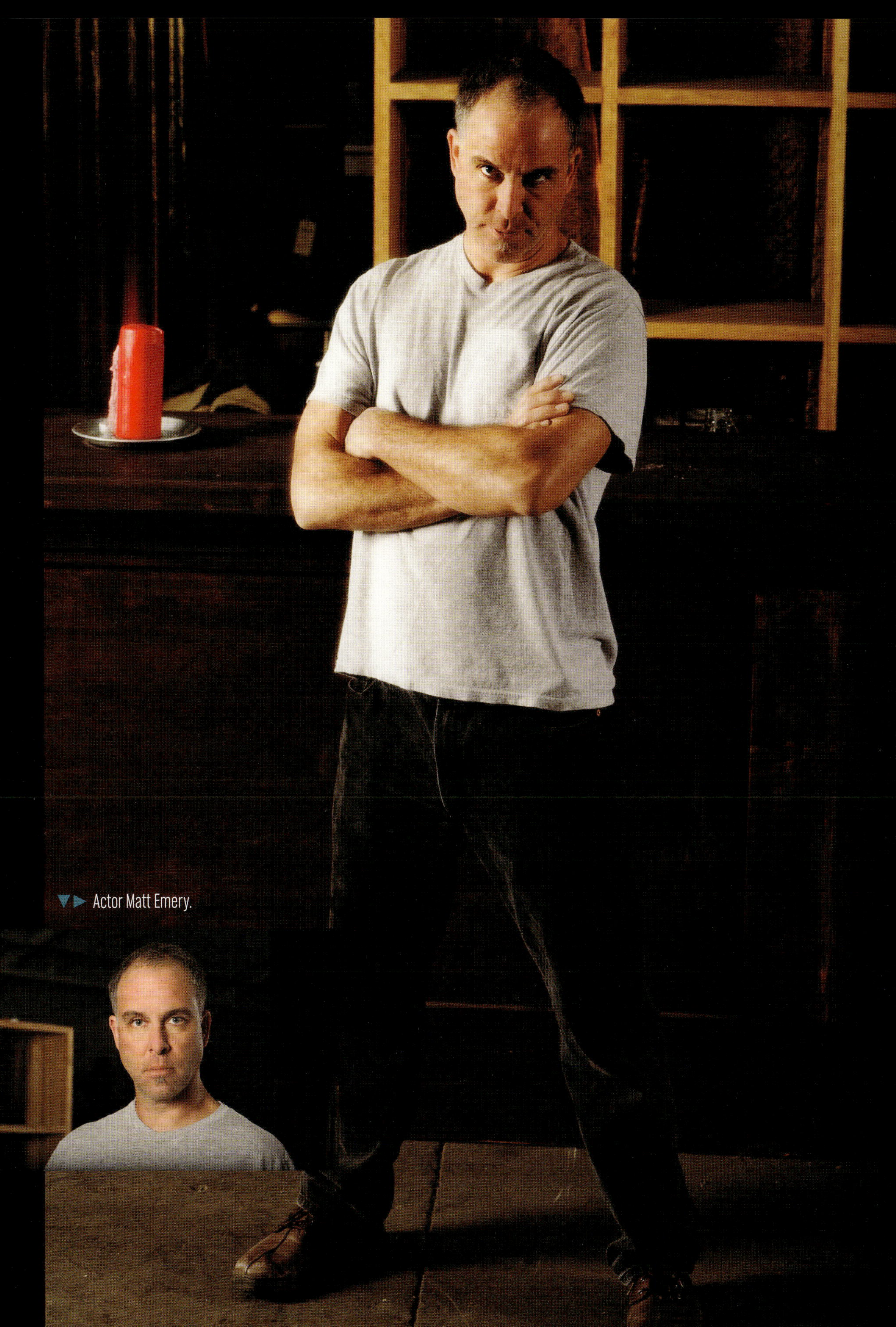

Actor Matt Emery.

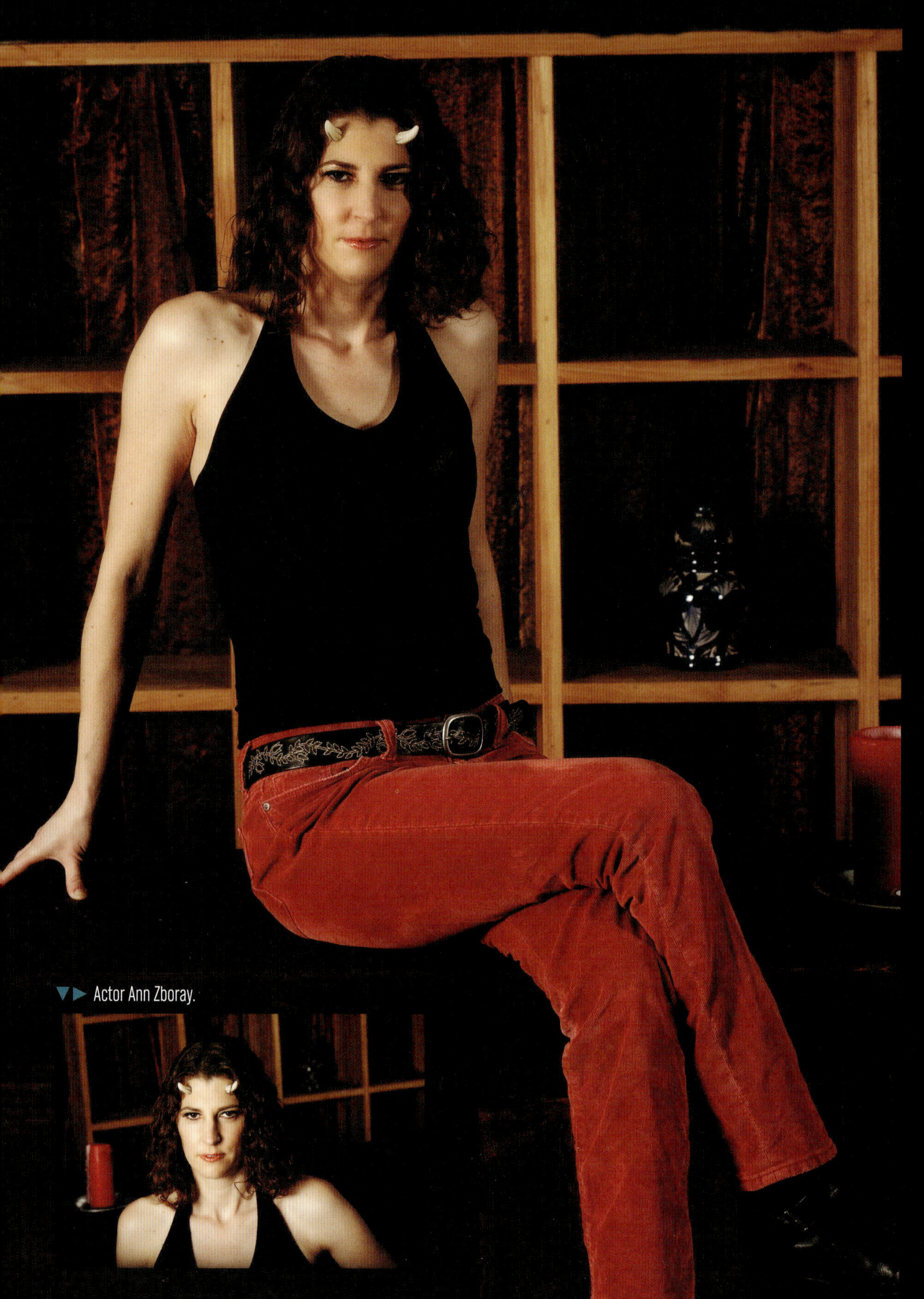

▼▶ Actor Ann Zboray.

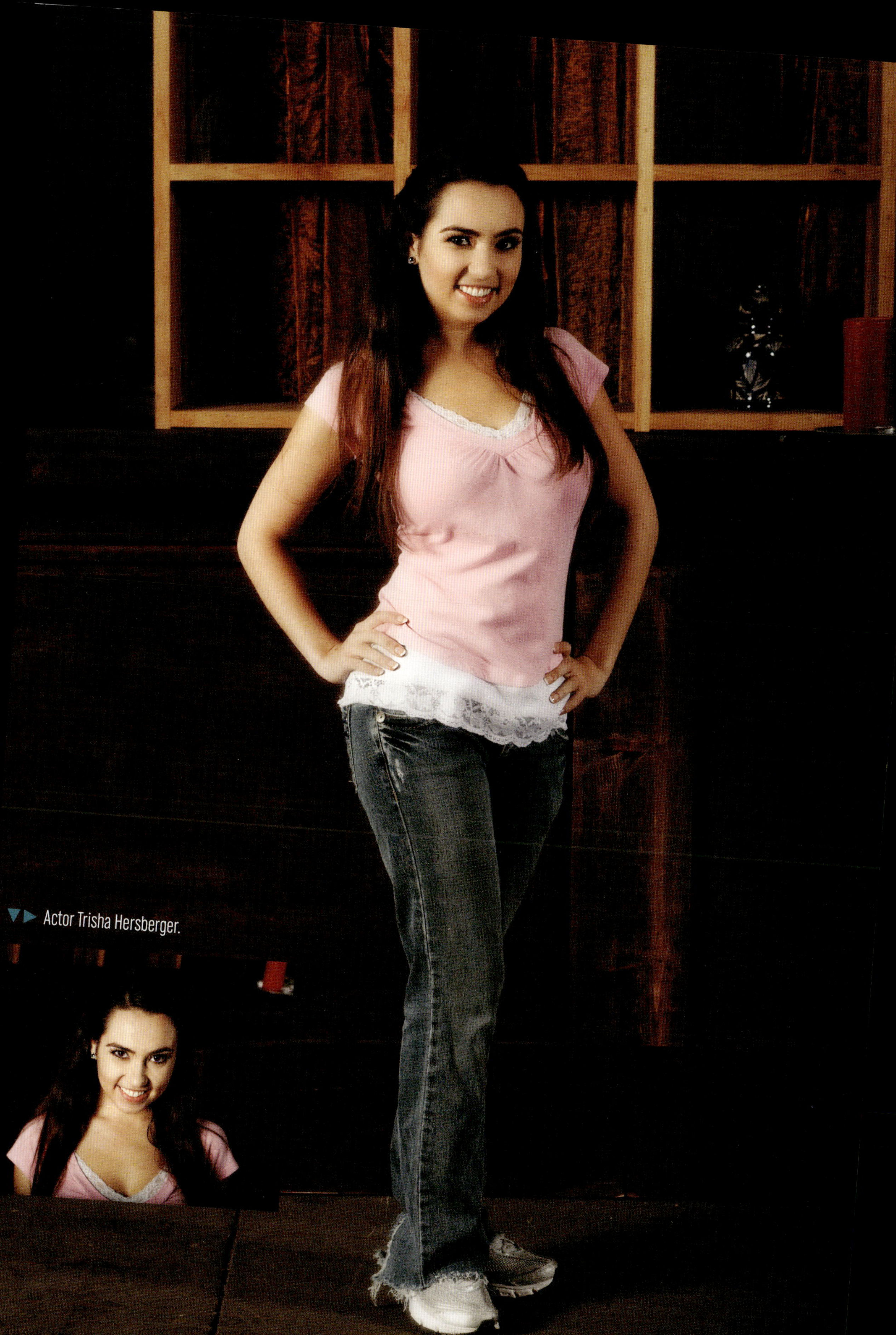

Actor Trisha Hersberger.

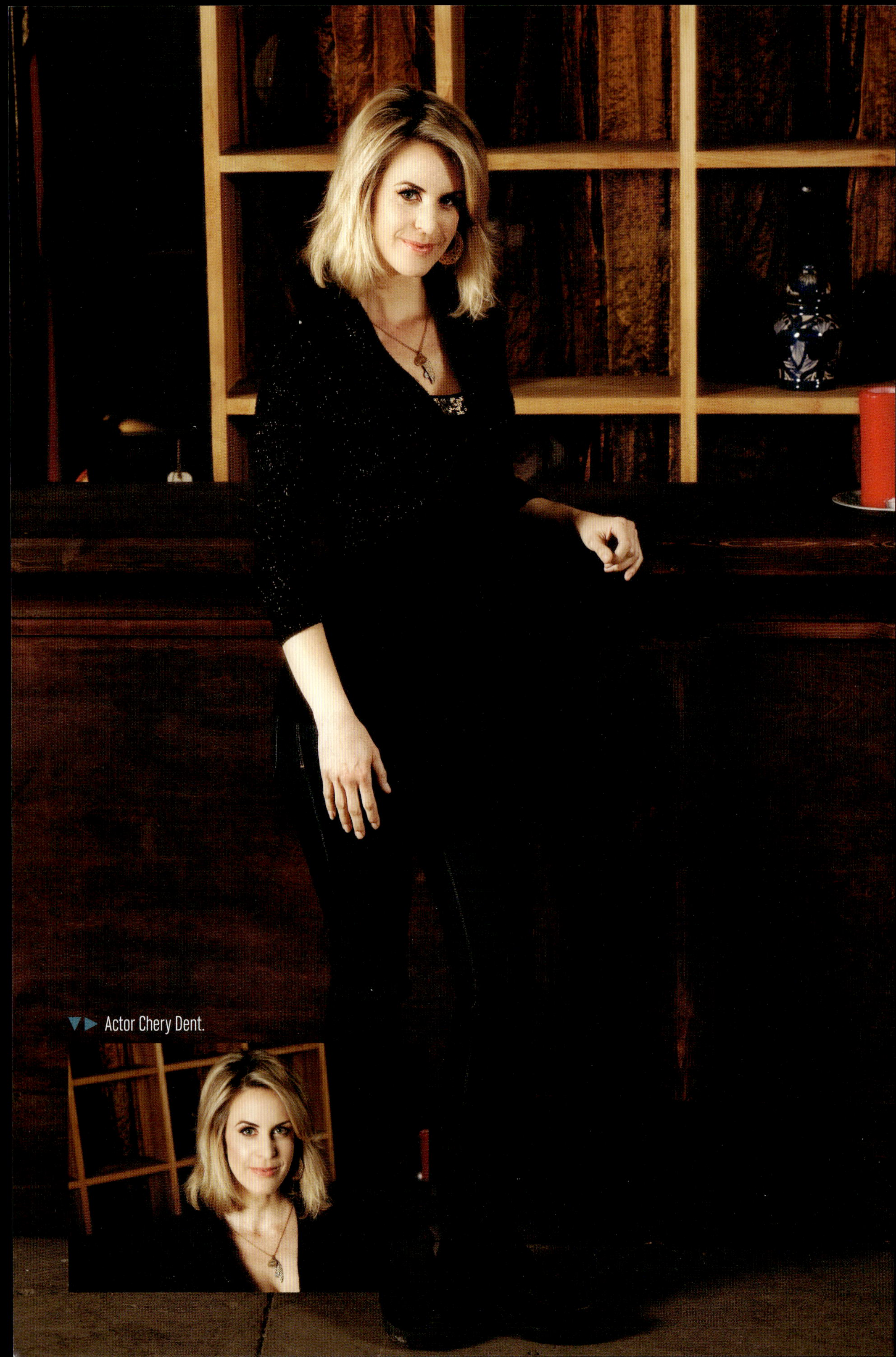

Actor Chery Dent.

Drama with Multiple Lights and Gels

Next, let's talk about a more dramatic multiple-light design created during a test shoot. It's a good idea to practice specifically for the kinds of photography you want to get jobs shooting. So, if you want to shoot television and film stills, then go out and shoot some images that look like that. In this case, I used an online casting service to find actors who wanted to work in exchange for portfolio images. My concept was to shoot cast photos for an imaginary television detective series. I liked this idea because I knew it would be easy for each actor to provide their own wardrobe—since most people own a suit-like outfit. I had my "cast" arrive one hour early and made sure they were done shooting within four hours total. (More on production and casting in chapter 2.)

Group Cast Photo

The next group shot we're going to look at (next page) seems like complicated lighting, but with a little planning you can have this set up in about thirty minutes—especially if you come prepared with a lighting diagram to hand to the crew. In this case, my test shoot was conducted during a class I taught, so the "crew" consisted of photography students. What can you do for crew on a test shoot? Try getting a couple other photographers together, renting or borrowing your lighting equipment, and running the shoot together.

We started with the key light, a large Octabank, in front of the subjects and to camera left. This was slightly feathered down toward the subjects. We placed the key light as far

back as we could get it in the space to avoid spill on the background—which was a gray roll-up door about 8 to 10 feet behind the actors. We set lights with grids and gels (one blue, one orange) to either side of the cast. A light directed at the background was fitted with a red gel to give the gray door a little something extra. The cast to camera right was still a little dark, so we added a small strip light on that side just to fill in a little.

> 66 What can you do for crew on a test shoot? Try getting a couple other photographers together, renting or borrowing your lighting equipment, and running the shoot together. 99

The two "headlights" you see flashing toward the camera are strobe heads with 40 degree grids. To get different effects from these lights, I just shifted the camera a bit from side to side. Sometimes I got a flare effect; other times, when the light was hidden behind the actors, I just got some rim light. Mostly, I was going for that "headlights" effect—as though we were seeing the headlights of a police car behind the detectives. It was just a little something to make the viewer feel more like it was the cast of a cop show.

When trying to get the output on your lights correct in a complex lighting setup like this, you need to take a reading of each light individually and then see how they work together. I first tested my key light to get the

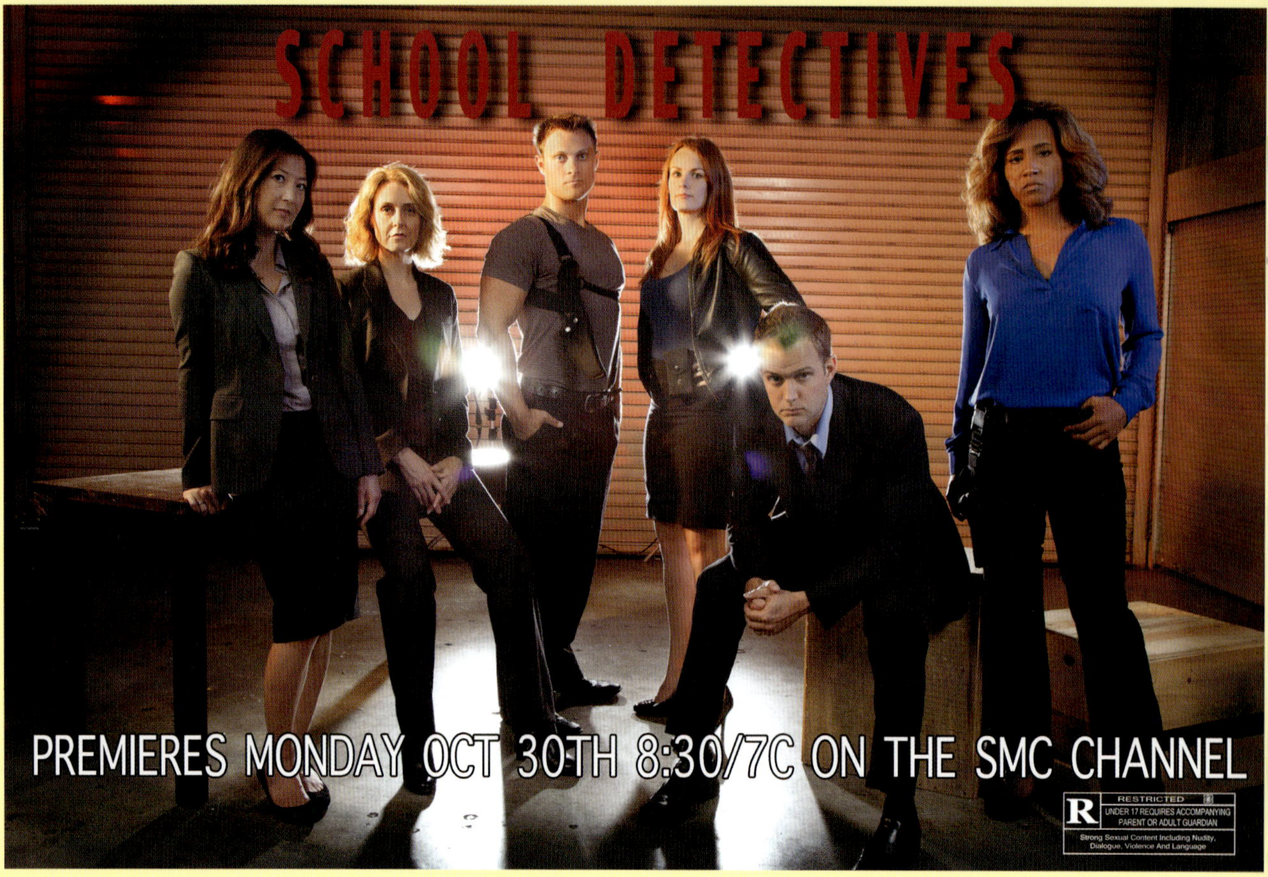

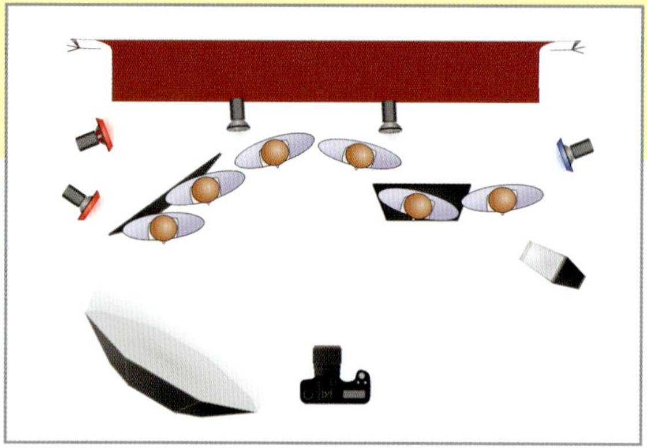

▲ Multiple strobes were used at varying powers, with the Octabank as the key light, on this test shoot for an imaginary television detective series. *(Specs: f/8.0, 1/200, ISO 160)*

overall light how I wanted it. Then, I worked on the red background light to make sure I could get it to show and not be washed out by the big Octabank. Once those two were working together, it just took a little tweaking to get all the rest of the lights properly balanced.

Individual Cast Photos

Let's look at some of the individual cast images (pages 67 and 68). I shot some with flare and some with more of a rim-light effect—but the overall lighting was not changed from the group shot, so the images all look like they belong together. Again, I just moved myself and the camera from side to side, either allowing the backlights to shine through or not. Depending on how the light hit my subject, I opened up or closed down my shutter, rather than changing the light output to work with each skin tone (page 69).

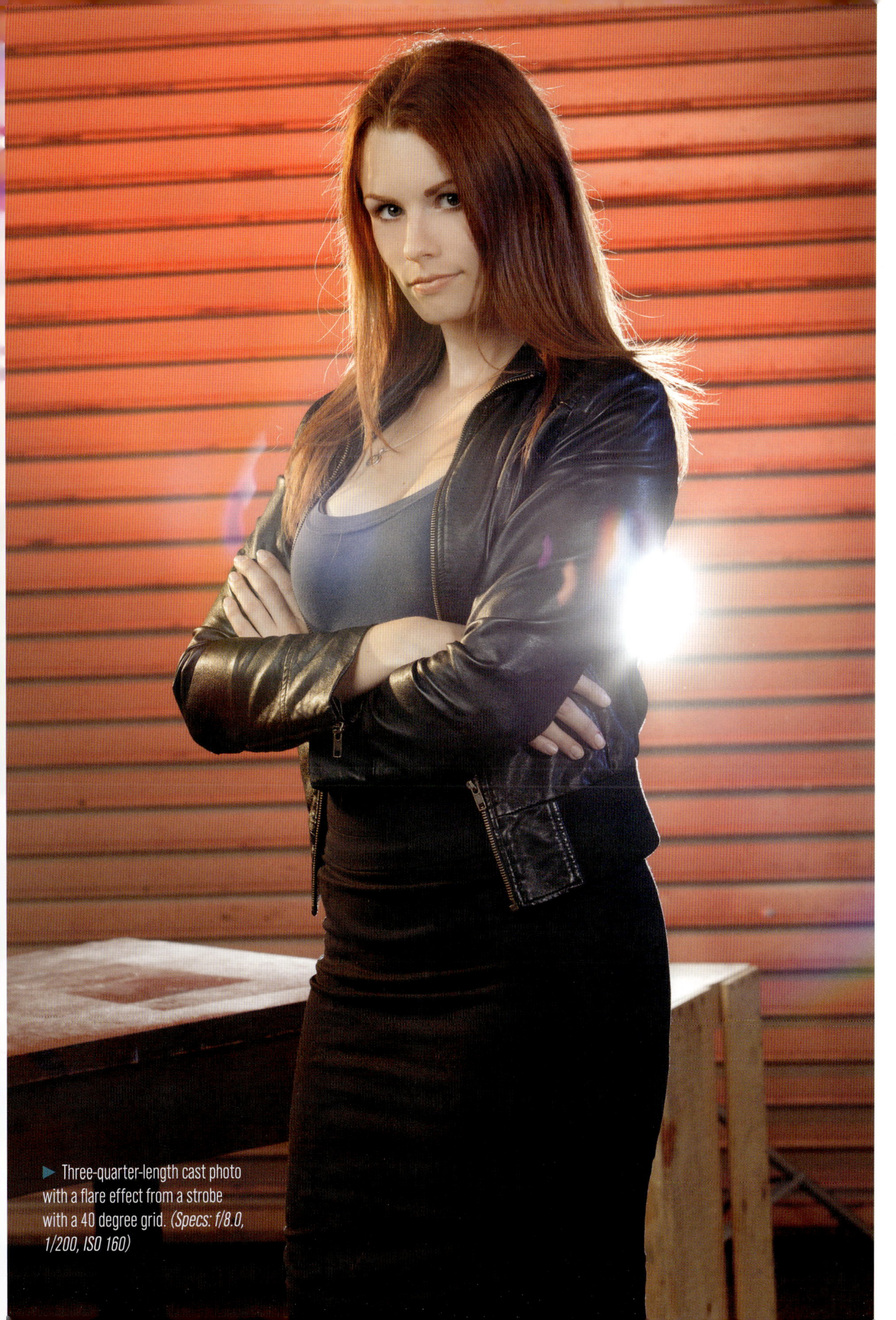

▶ Three-quarter-length cast photo with a flare effect from a strobe with a 40 degree grid. *(Specs: f/8.0, 1/200, ISO 160)*

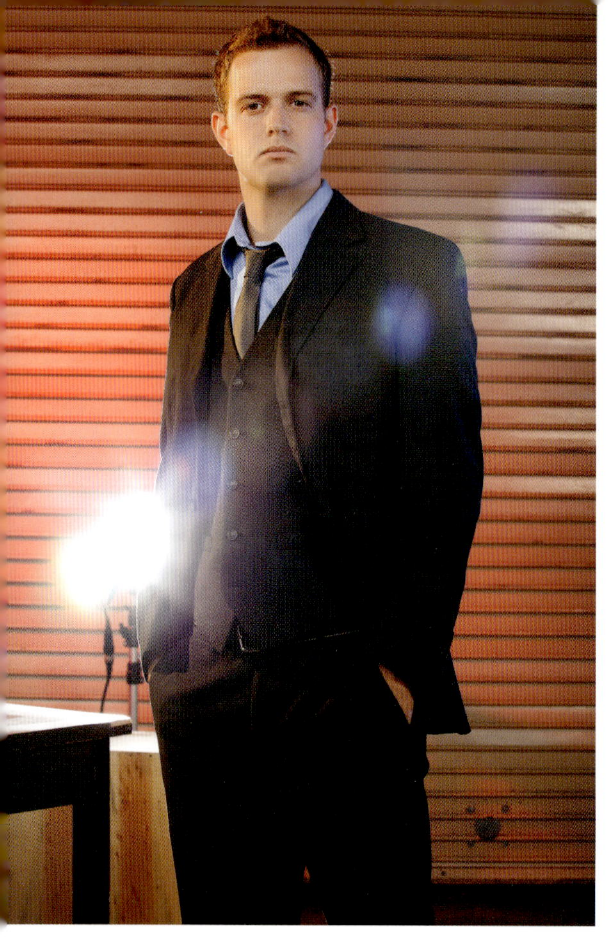

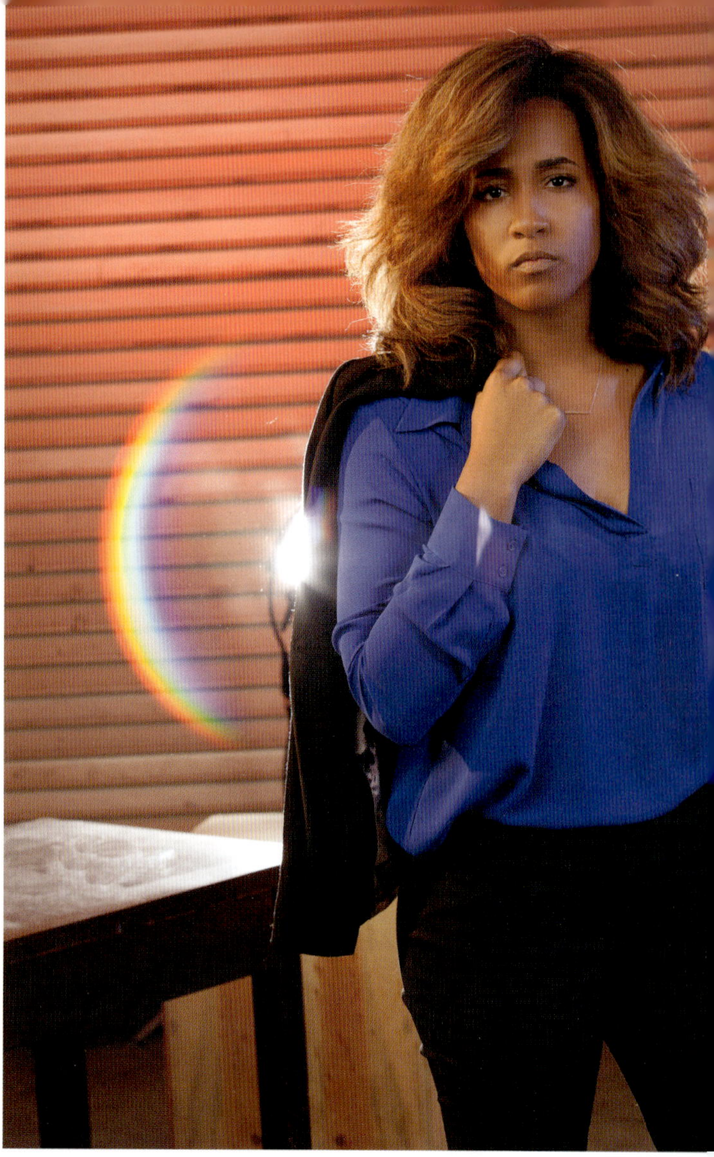

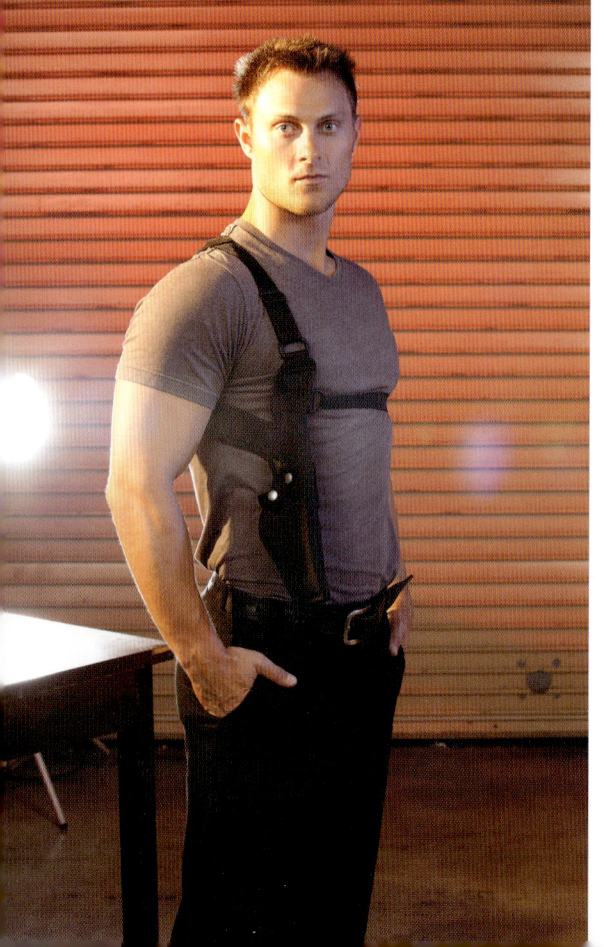

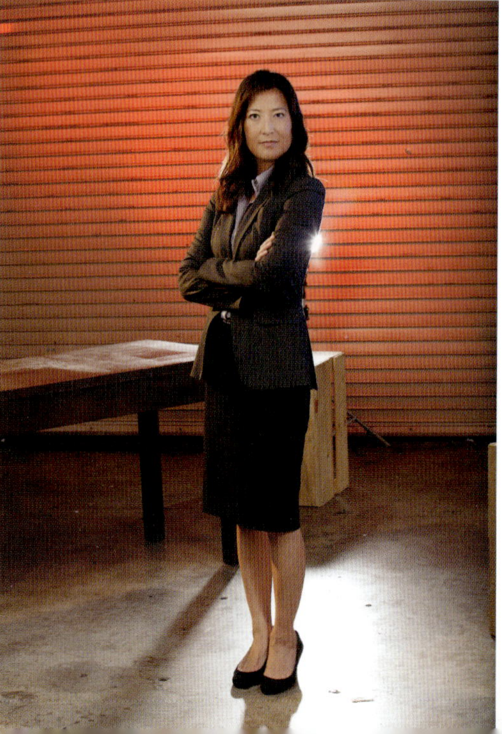

◀ ▲ Full- and three-quarter-length cast photos with a flare effect from a strobe with a 40 degree grid. (*Specs: f/8.0, 1/200, ISO 160*)

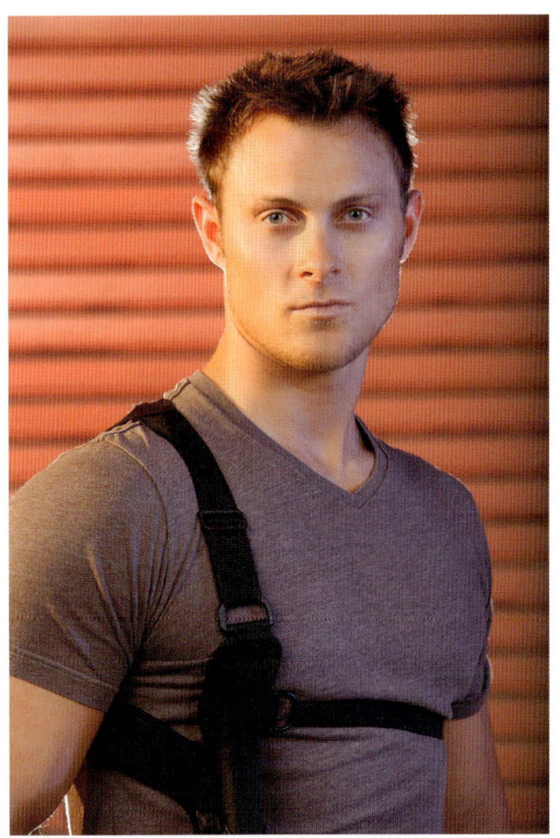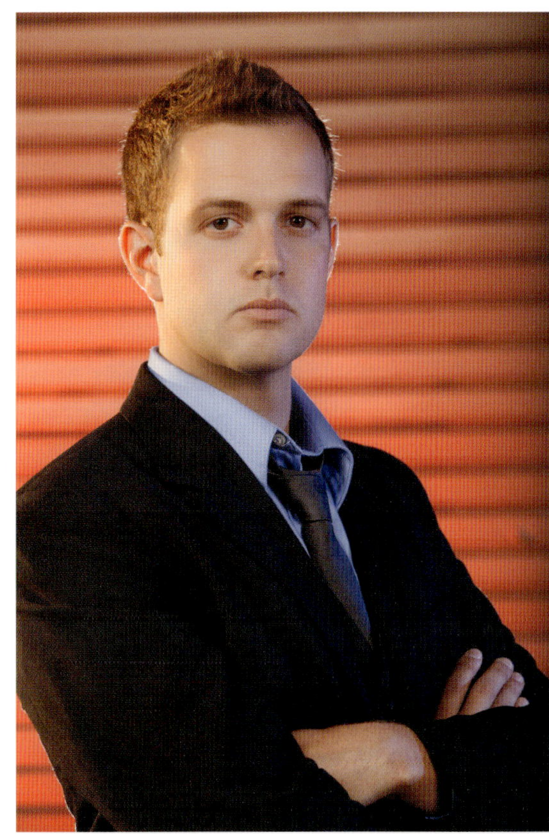

▲ Adjusting the shutter for a lighter skin tone, rather than changing the lighting output. (Specs: f/8.0, 1/200, ISO 160)

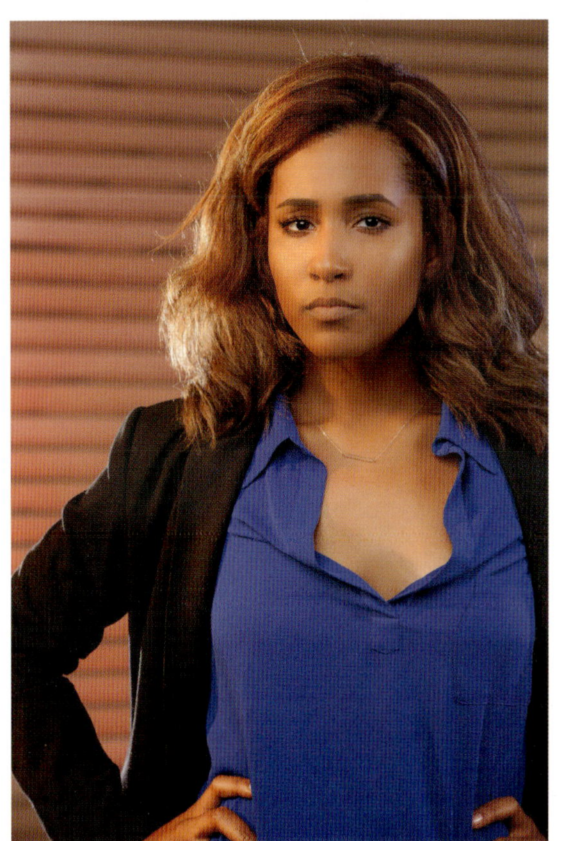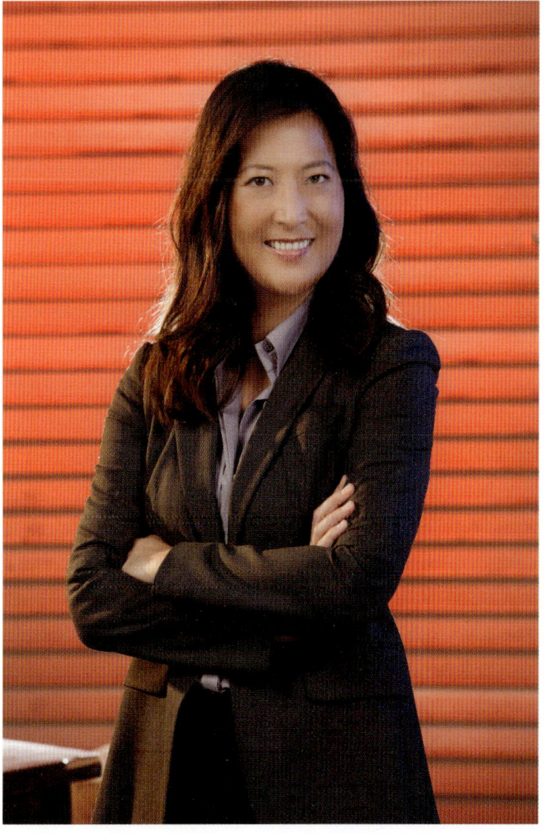

▲ Adjusting the shutter for a darker skin tone, rather than changing lighting output. (Specs: f/8.0, 1/160, ISO 160)

Movie Poster with a Three-Light Design

Let's look at one more test shoot for a movie poster. Again, I cast this with actors who were willing to shoot for trade. I wanted to do a space-type movie poster, similar to *Star Trek*, so in my ad I asked for people who had access to an appropriate costume or uniform. Some respondents had actual *Star Trek* costumes from Halloween; others came up with shirts that looked right on the money. We all brought a few props to use, and I built some set pieces to give the images a little something more than just a plain background.

Group Cast Portraits

The key light was an Octabank, centered and straight overhead. I added a large strip light on either side of the set. These had blue gels on them to produce the space-like look I was after. One strip light was directed straight in from the side of the cast from the left; the other was more to the front and farther away on camera right. I shot these all with a 70–200mm lens at around f/6.3 because I wanted good depth of field and for the background set pieces to blur out some. The silver triangles

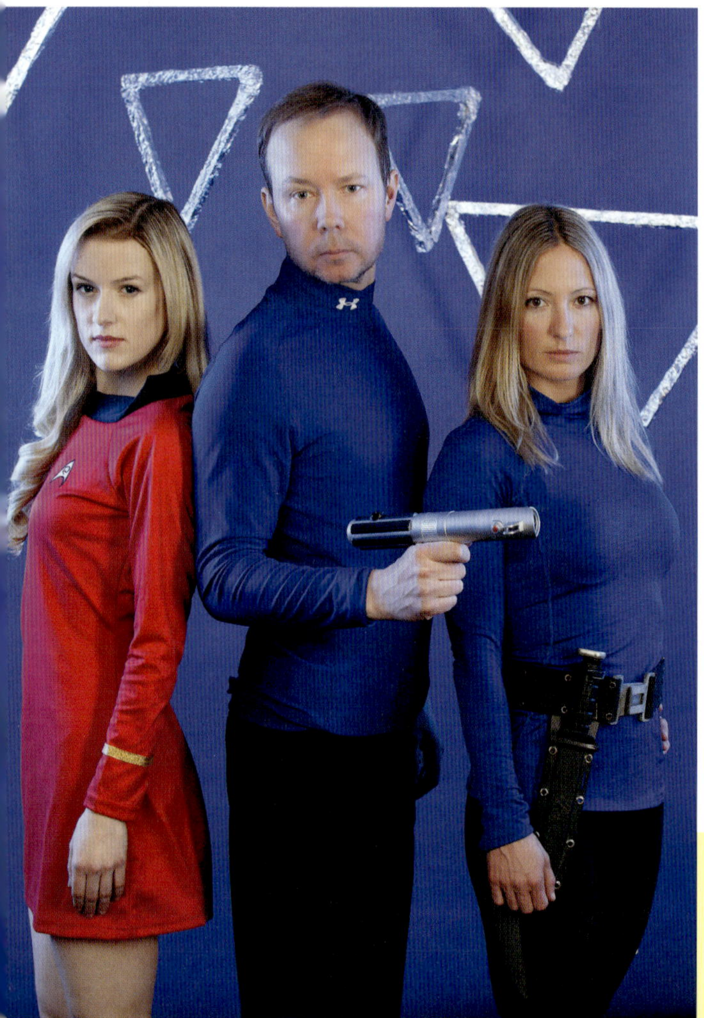

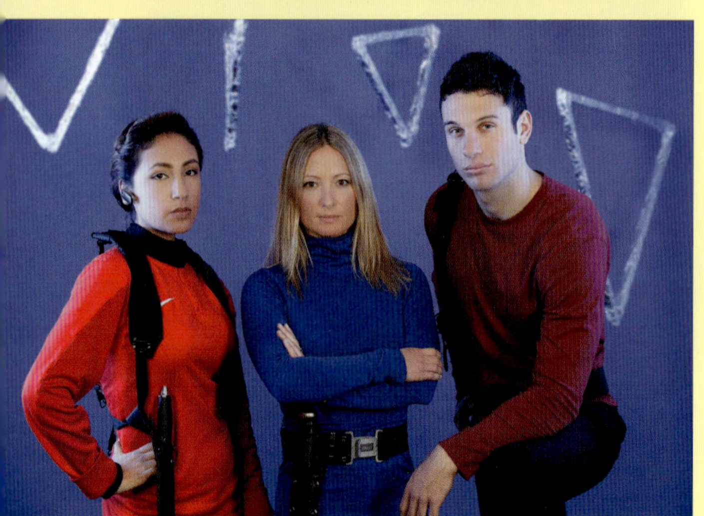

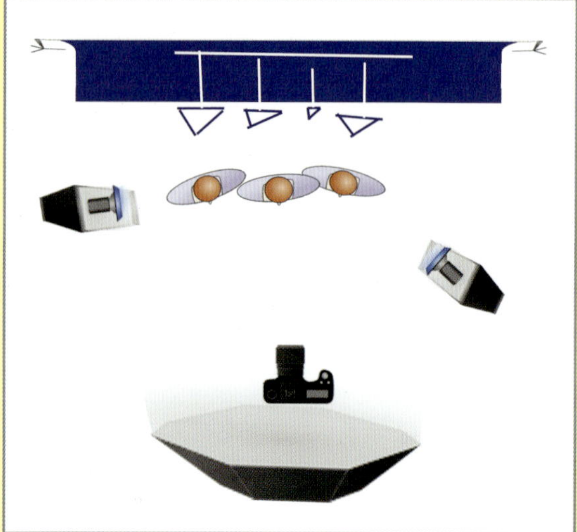

◀▶ Left and faging page: Pictures from a three-light setup with blue gels. These were shot with a 70–200mm lens at f/6.3 to blur the background elements while still achieving a good depth of field.

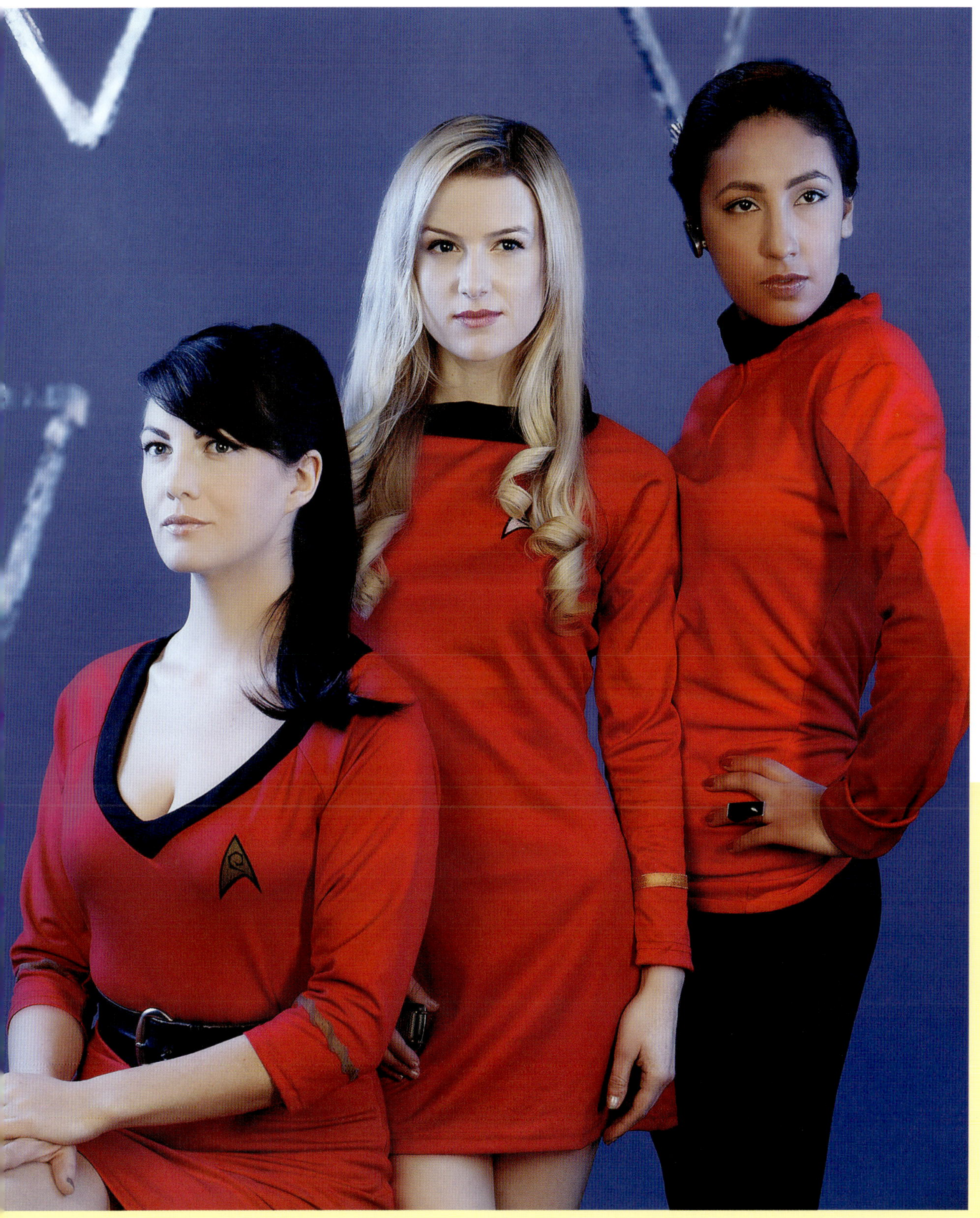

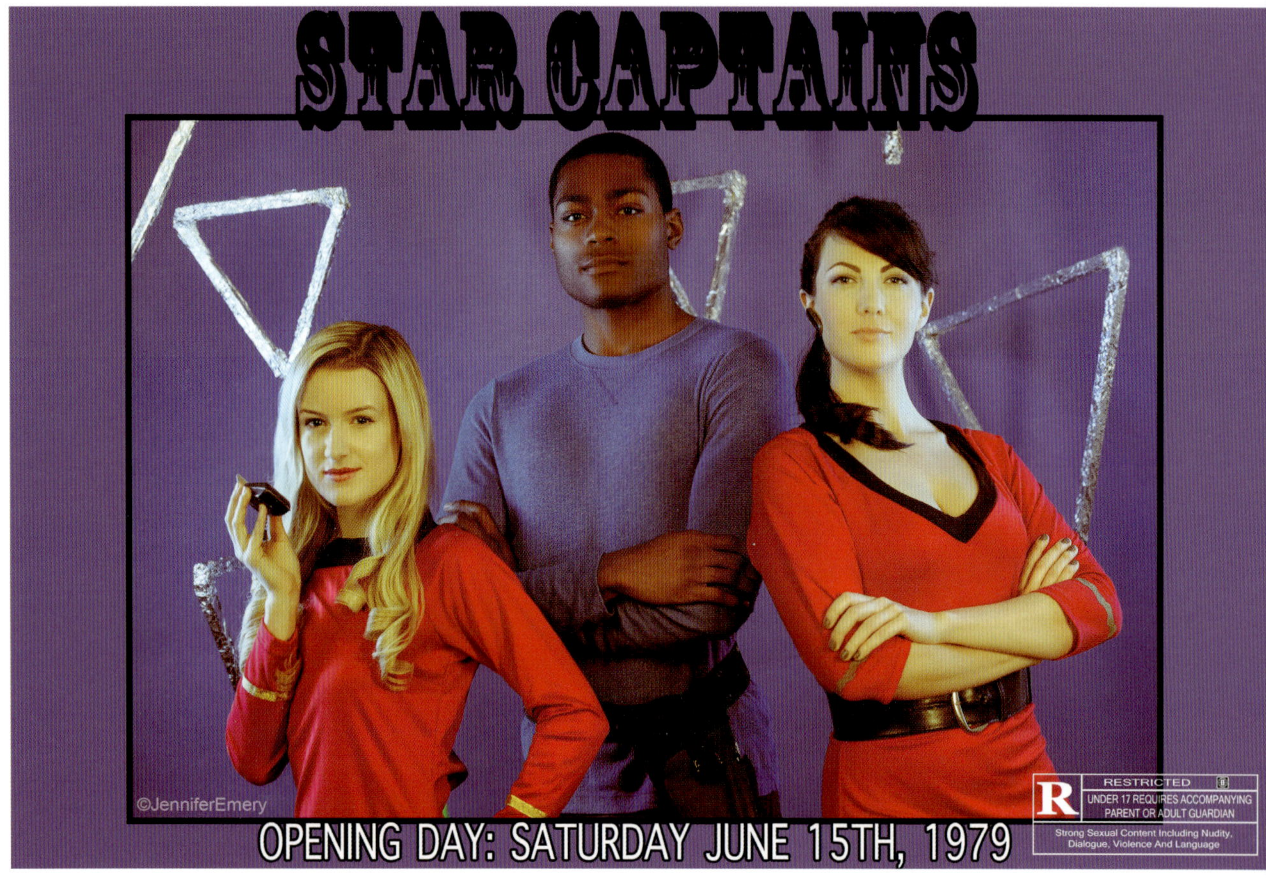

▲ A favorite image from the shoot was used to create a movie poster with a retro feel. *Poster art by Jennifer Emery.*

in the background were suspended from clear fishing line that I took out in postproduction. Notice that we tried quite a few different poses and arrangements with the actors.

The image above was my favorite from the session. I gave it an old movie poster look in Photoshop—like it was from a 1970s film.

Individual Cast Portraits

I also created individual cast portraits. Again, doing both closeup headshots and more full-length looks for each actor is a good idea (pages 73 through 75). After the shoot, I played around with adding some special effects in postproduction. There is a lot you can do in Photoshop to give your images some flair, but it's best to get *most* of it to come out of the camera how you want it.

▶ Facing page: Individual portraits of the cast. *(Specs: f/6.3, 1/100, ISO 320)*

▶ Facing page, bottom right: In postproduction, I experimented with adding a smoky look around the actor's lower legs.

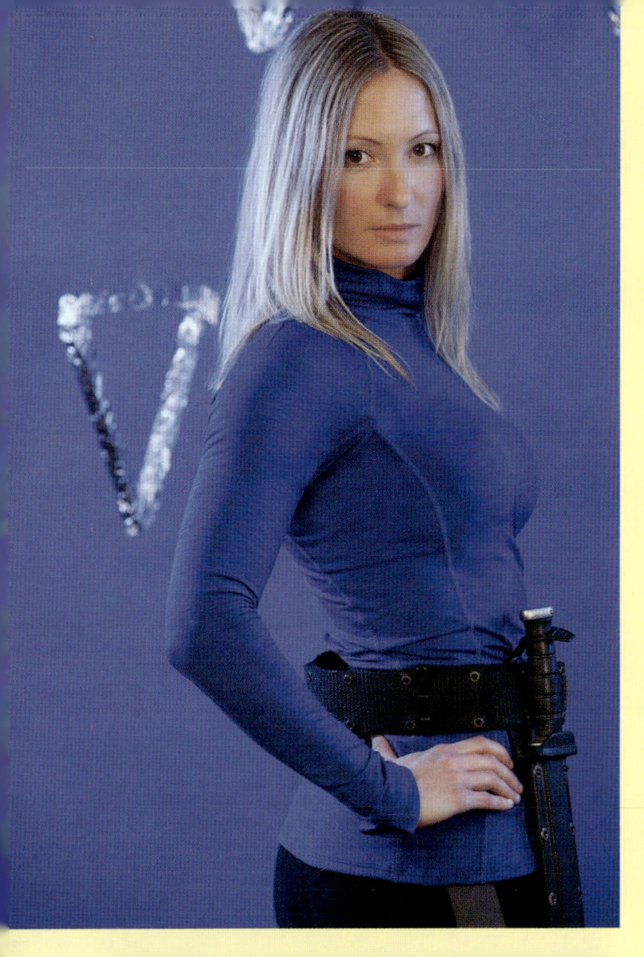
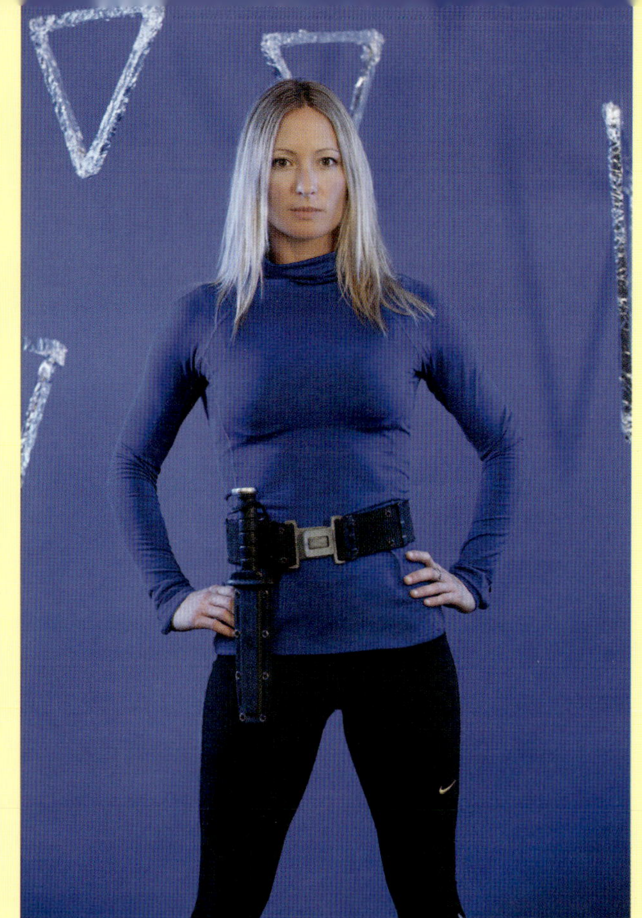
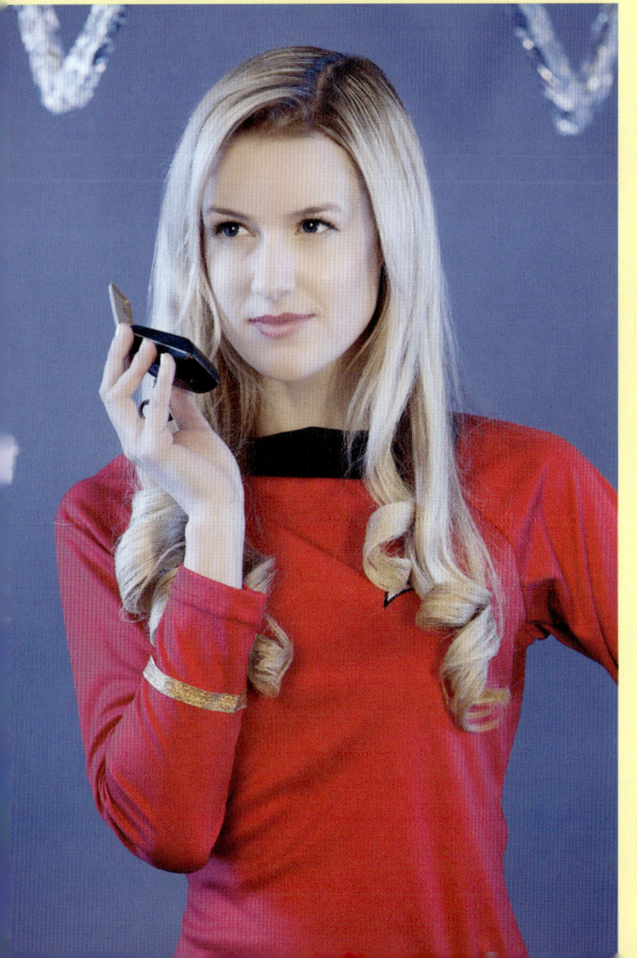
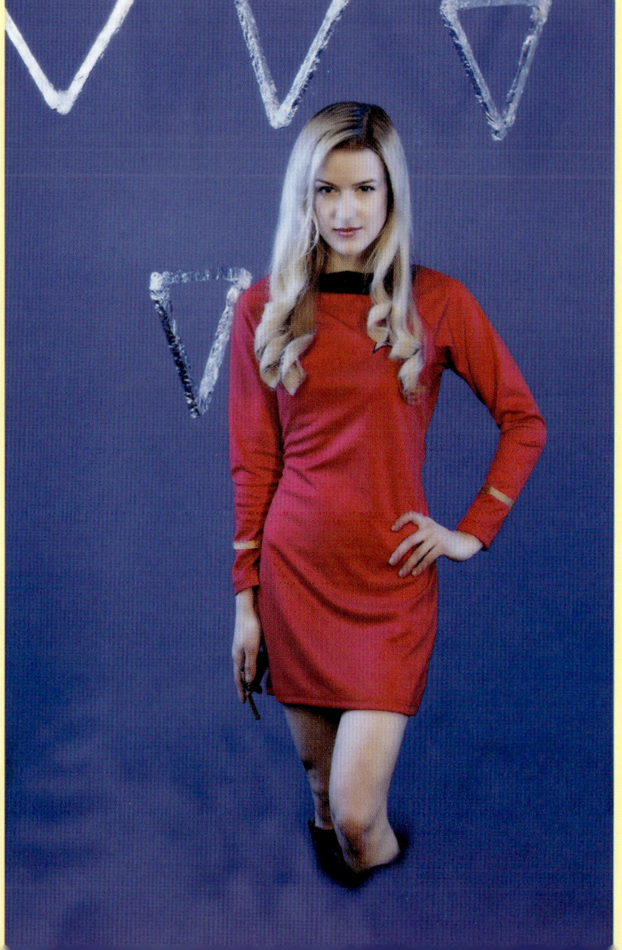

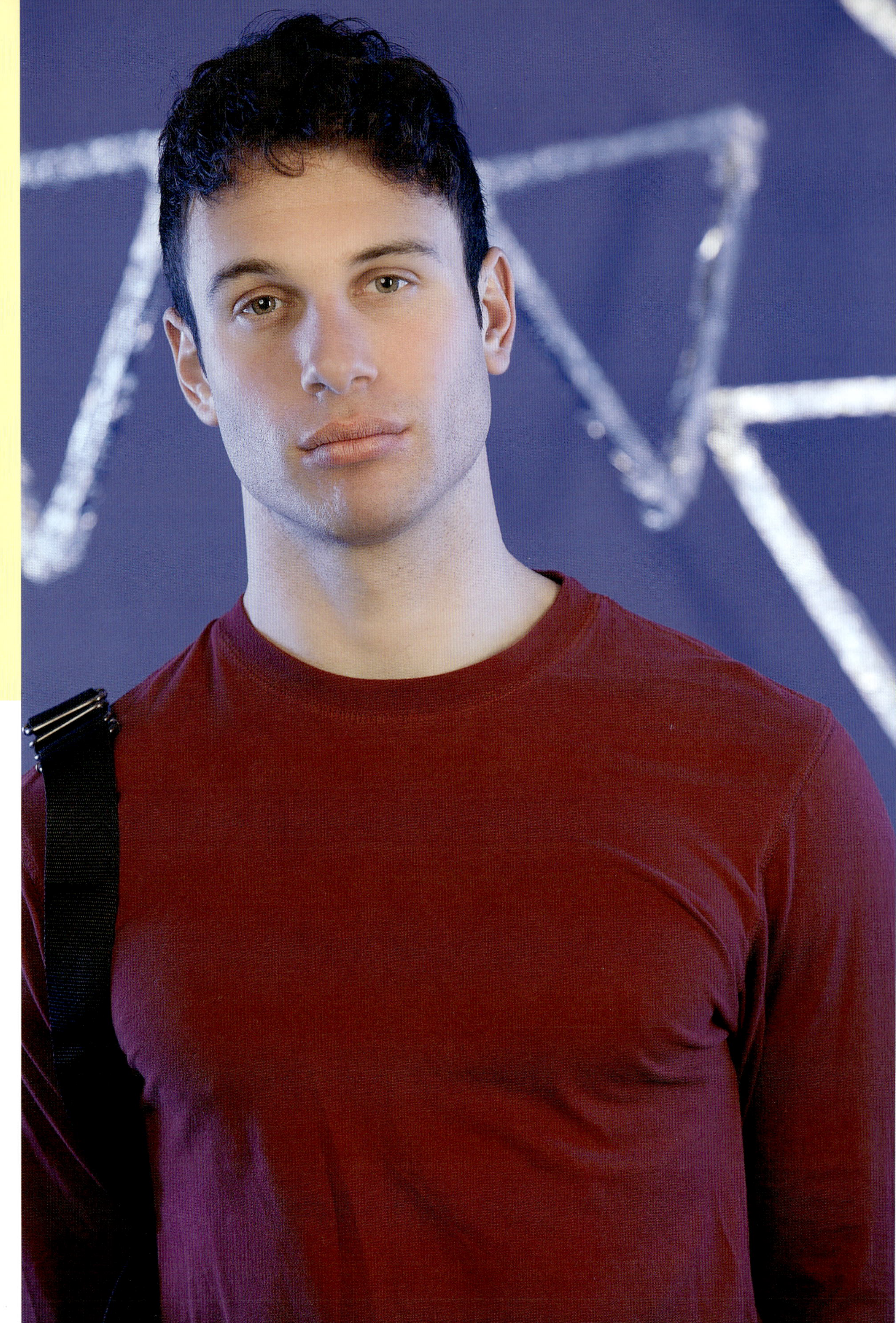

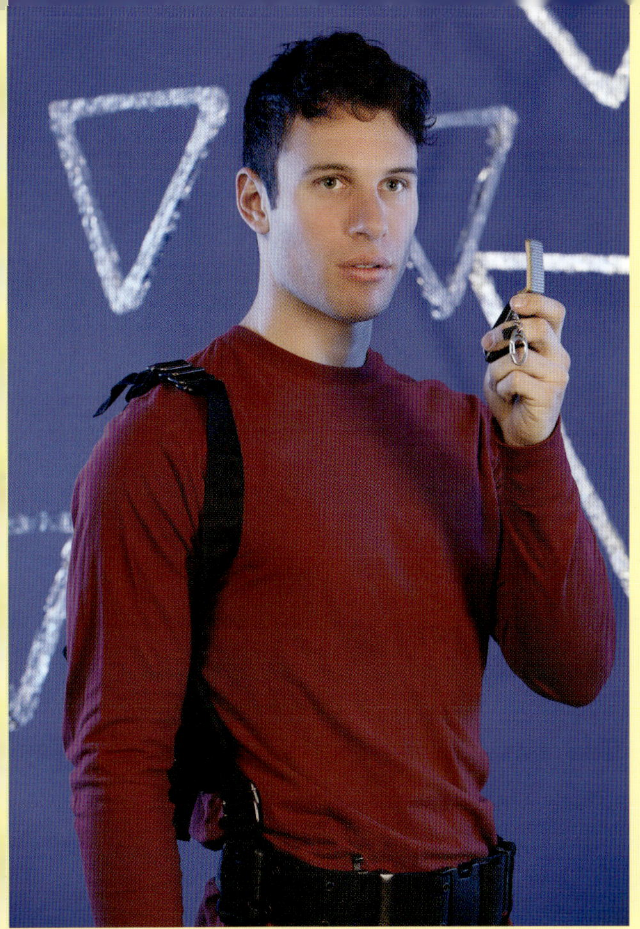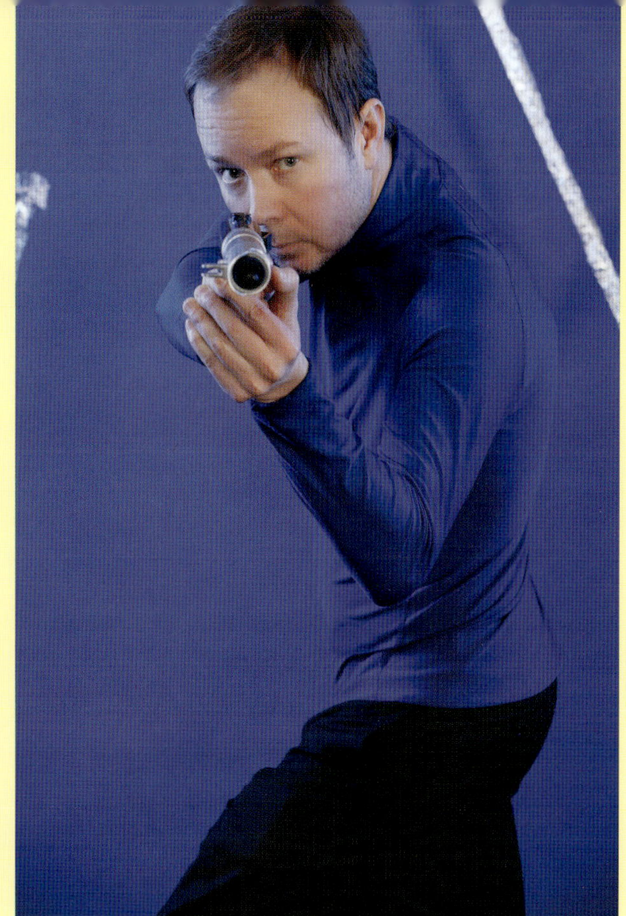

◄▲ Above and facing page: Individual portraits of the cast. (*Specs: f/6.3, 1/100, ISO 320*)

Even Lighting Is Critical

When photographing groups—whether it's for business portraits or cast photos—the main thing to think about is lighting all your subjects *evenly*. If there is much depth from front to back between your subjects, then you may need lights positioned toward the back and more lights positioned closer to the front, as in the four-light setup presented earlier in the chapter. If you have all your subjects rather close together in depth, maybe in a straight line, then the two-light setup will probably do. But does your background also need to be lit? Sometimes it does and sometimes it does not (because you want it to be obscured). These are all variables to keep in mind when choosing lighting designs for groups.

You may have noticed that the group portraits in this chapter include individuals with different skin tones. This is something you have to pay attention to. If you are exposing for your lighter-skinned subjects, you may not be exposing the darker-skinned subjects correctly (and vice versa). In most cases, you can make it work just by placing your exposure somewhere in the middle, but in some cases you may not have enough light on one subject, or you may have too much on another.

You may say that you often see very high-end magazine covers and commercial images where the photographers did not do a great job lighting the people with darker skin tones alongside those with lighter skin tones—and I would agree. I bet you can do better if you are really thinking about it, though.

Below is an image we looked at earlier in this chapter. Let's check it out again with the issue of skin-tone variations in mind. We are not trying to make anyone's skin tone look lighter or darker, we just want even lighting on everyone and for them to look like themselves. Here, the three actors in the middle back are lit a bit hotter because the side light is hitting them more directly and they are lighter in skin tone. The male actor, sitting to the front right, is a bit more in shadow but still looks in range—as does the female actor at front left leaning on the desk. The actress in the blue on the right has the darkest skin tone and is farthest away from the key light and that hotter left sidelight. Pumping up the key light was not the best option, because I did not want to fill *all* my shadows. Instead, I added a front-right strip light to put a little more light on her and the seated male.

Sometimes, you don't know who you will be photographing or what environment you will need to light, so you just have to do the best you can in each circumstance. But paying attention to how each individual in the group is lit is important. Being prepared is also important, which is why I always bring a tripod or extra light stand to use with my speed-lights/flashes—even if I have been told that a two-light strobe setup will do. If you have some extra light sources and radio slaves, you will always be ready to improvise and tackle unforeseen problems.

▼ Notice that the varying skin tones of the actors are evenly and realistically captured.

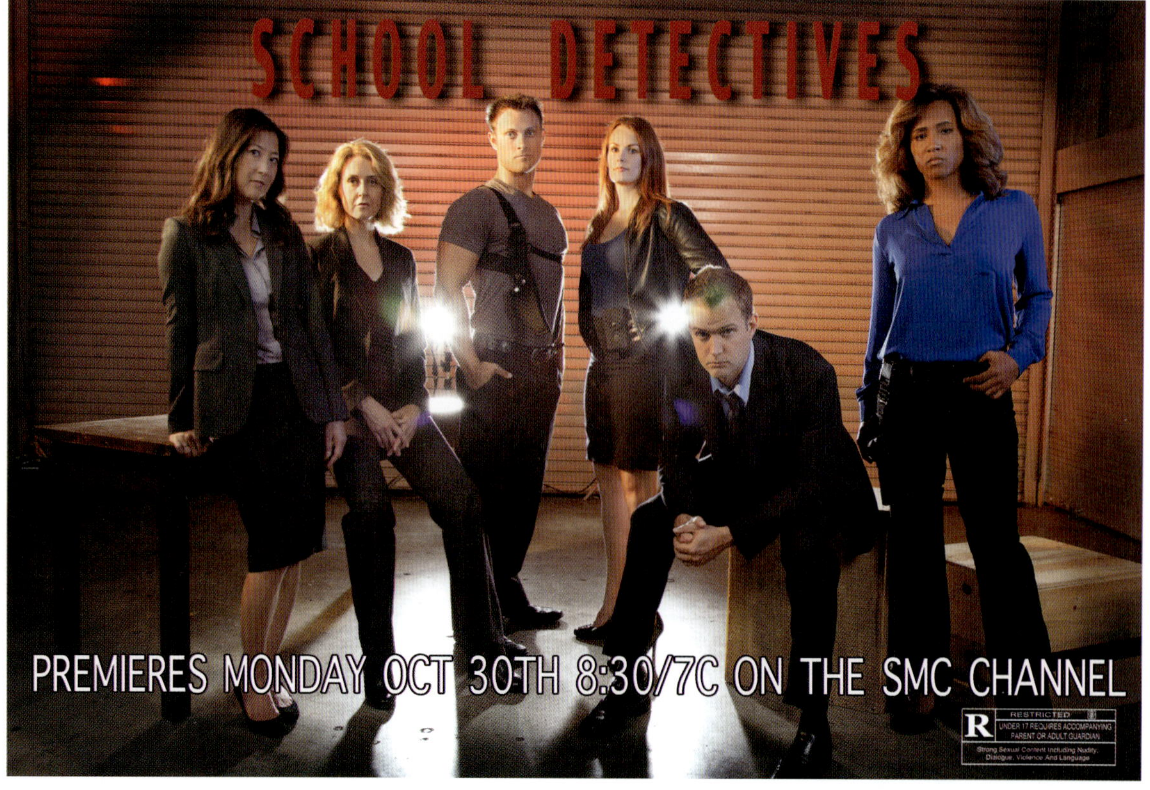

6. Body Contouring

Key Techniques ▶ Creating light and shadow to flatter the body; Posing the body
Application ▶ Sports profiles; Lingerie and bathing suit images; Nudes

Body contouring is essential for making people look good. This means using light and shadow to, in essence, sculpt the body. No one is perfect, but with good lighting you can make people look pretty close. Posing the body is also very important for flattering the subject. In this chapter, we will examine some useful lighting strategies and talk about how the model's position relative to the light can be used to refine the image for even more flattering effects.

Before we get started, let me just point out that we're not going to rely on the "fix everything later in Photoshop" approach. I know we all love the Liquify tool, but it's definitely best to get the shot right out of the camera and do only minor retouching after the fact. Photoshop may be a big part of our lives now, but it's not photography. Learning these sculpting techniques for lighting and posing will help you work with all kinds of clients—even fully clothed industrial and corporate clients. With a little practice and attention to detail, you can make anyone look good.

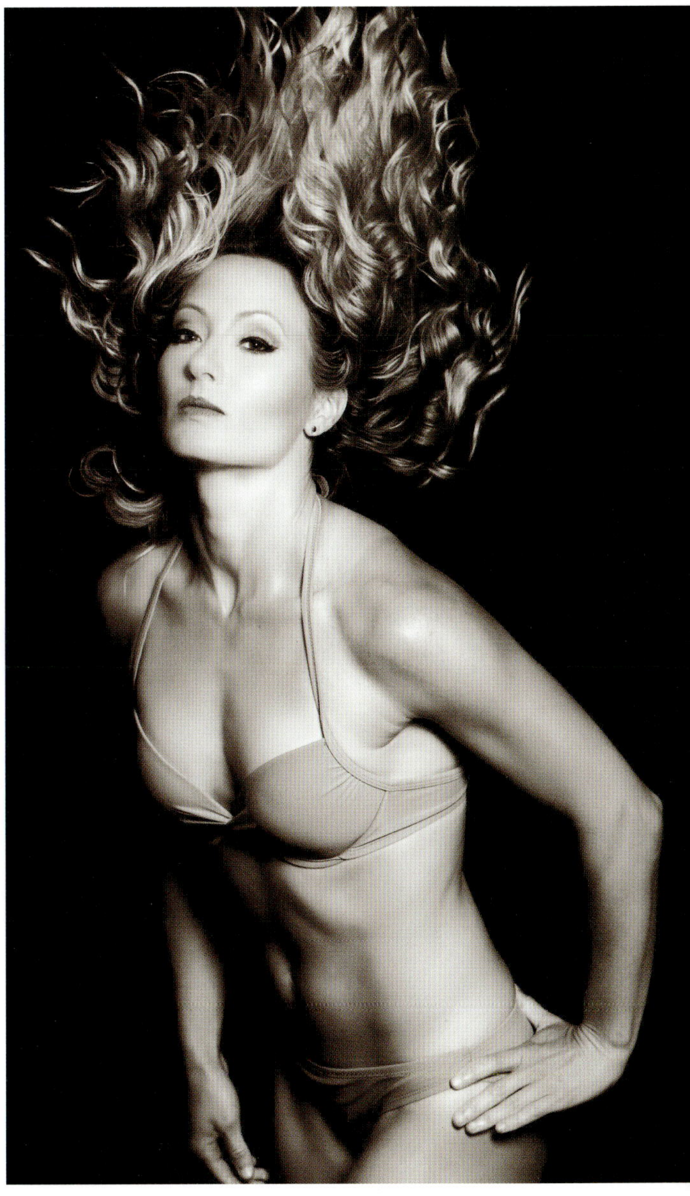

▶ Professional triathlete Kristen Hetzel from Team USA. *Hair and makeup by Deva Bales.*

If You Are Choosing the Models . . .

If you are casting models for a project, you will usually be looking for well-proportioned, long, lean figures, preferably with long torsos. To give you an idea, a Victoria's Secret casting call asks for models who are 5'9" and taller, with 34-25-34 (bust/waist/hips) measurements. I have even seen them ask for a particular torso

length measurement. Again, I'm not saying all your models need to be this ideal—but it may be close to what your client is looking for. (More on casting in chapter 2.)

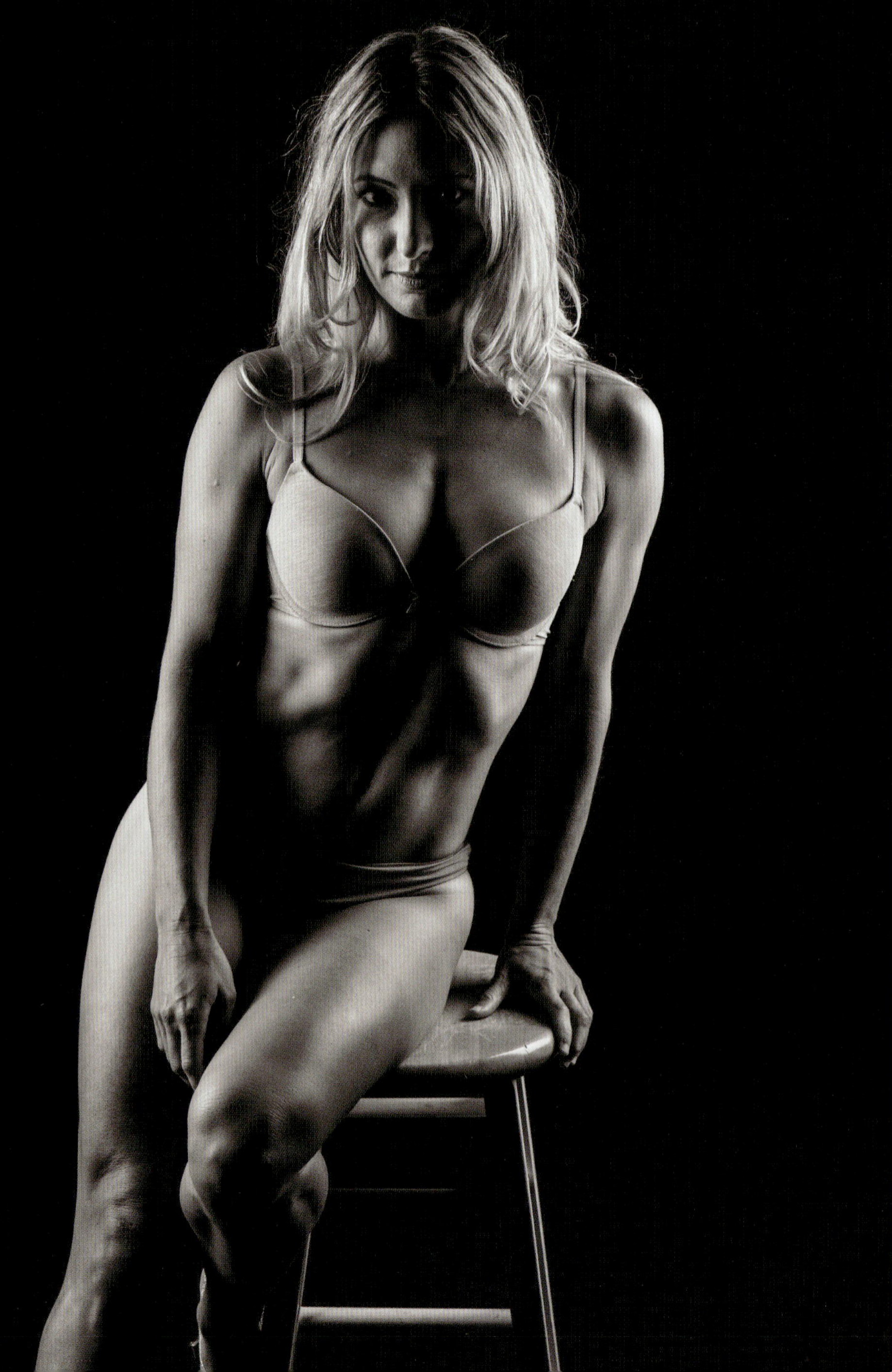

Posing Tips

Victoria's Secret catalogs are a good reference for posing and lighting ideas. If you are new to posing models for lingerie, bathing suit, or even direct-to-client boudoir sessions, using lingerie catalogs and bathing-suit magazines as references will be very helpful. Just showing the model the pose in the magazine can help get you where you want to go.

◀ I showed the model a photo of a similar pose and then simulated it myself on the stool to get the subject into this position.

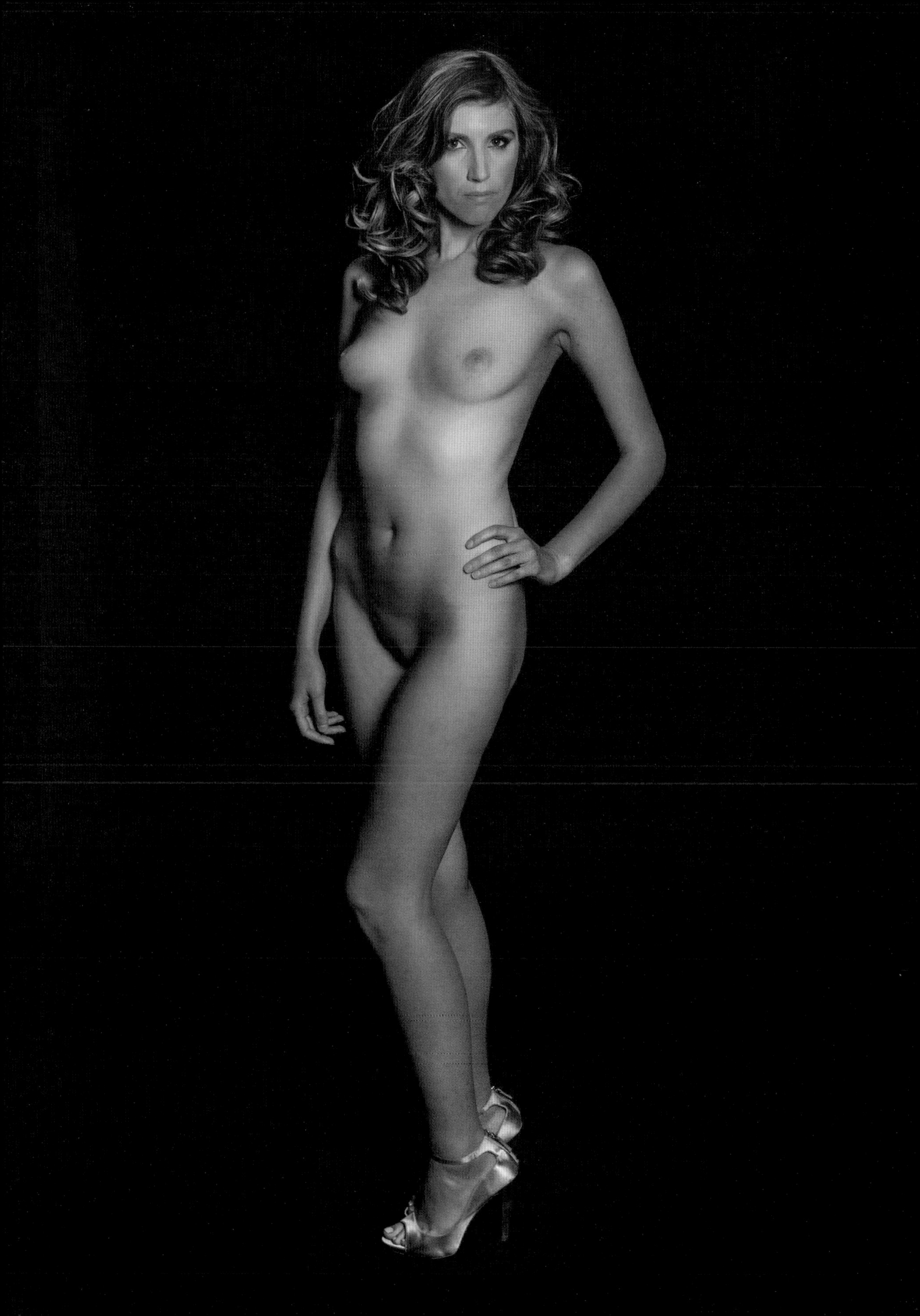

Promotional Portrait of an Athlete

Our first image sequence was created on a promotional shoot for a professional athlete. It is a good example of how body contouring with light would lend itself to a commercial shoot. These images could be used on a sports magazine cover or in an article.

Lighting

The images were created using a sideways clamshell lighting setup, similar to what was discussed in chapter 3 when we looked at beauty lighting. In this case, I used two large, vertical softboxes on either side of the model. Both lights were at the same power setting and the model was posed on a black seamless backdrop. There were no other light sources.

Because we were in a controlled space on a set with a black background, it was easy to control the contouring highlights and shadows. Note, for example, the shadow down the center of the model's body in the facing-page image; the two lights on the sides created a very flattering effect that thins the center of the body and accentuates her contours in all the right places.

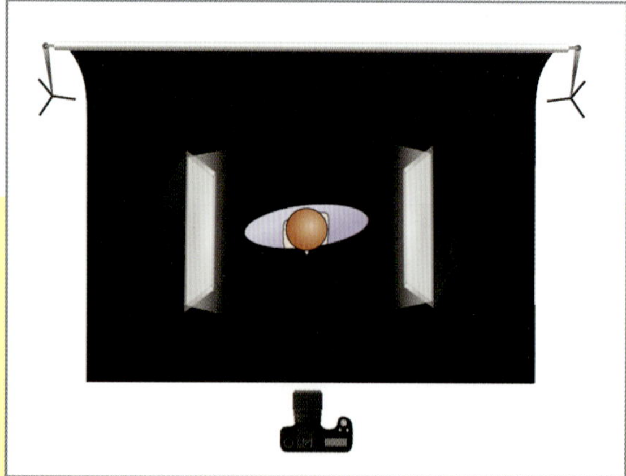

► Facing page: Note the shadow down the center of the model that accentuates the contours of her body. (Specs: f/8.0, 1/160, ISO 100, 50mm f/1.2L lens)

▼ Clamshell lighting with large, vertical softboxes. Both lights were at 500 watt output, giving f/8.0. *Image by Preston Perkins.*

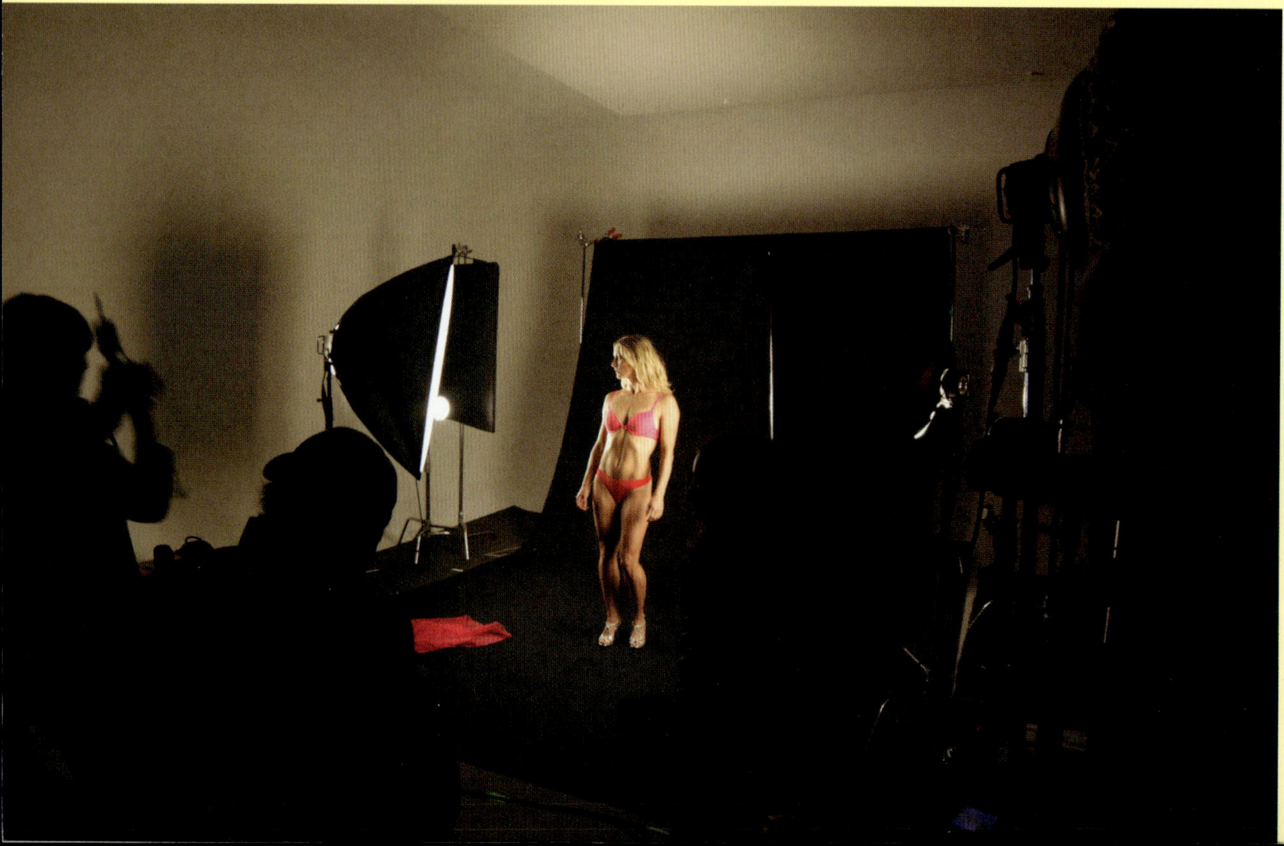

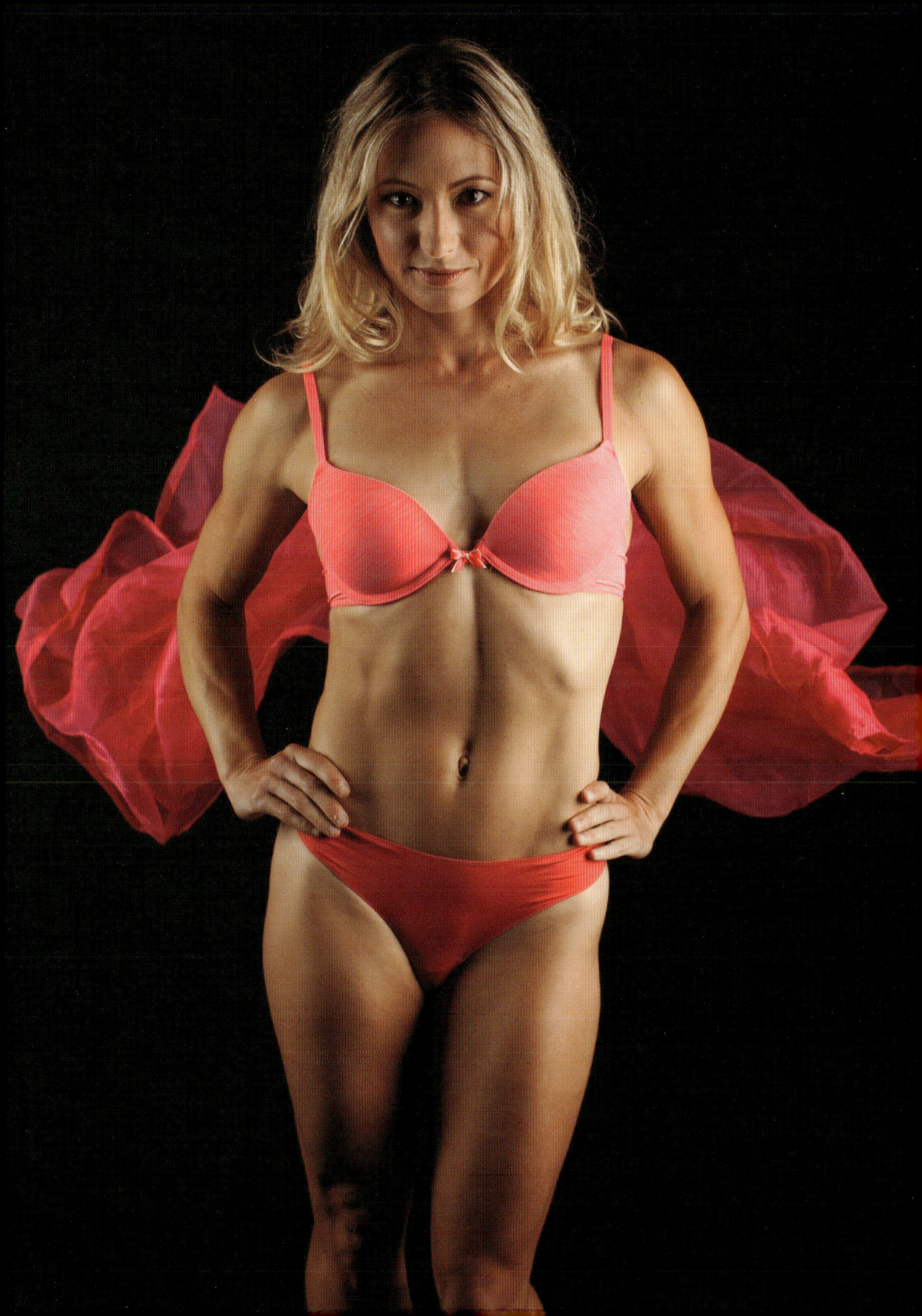

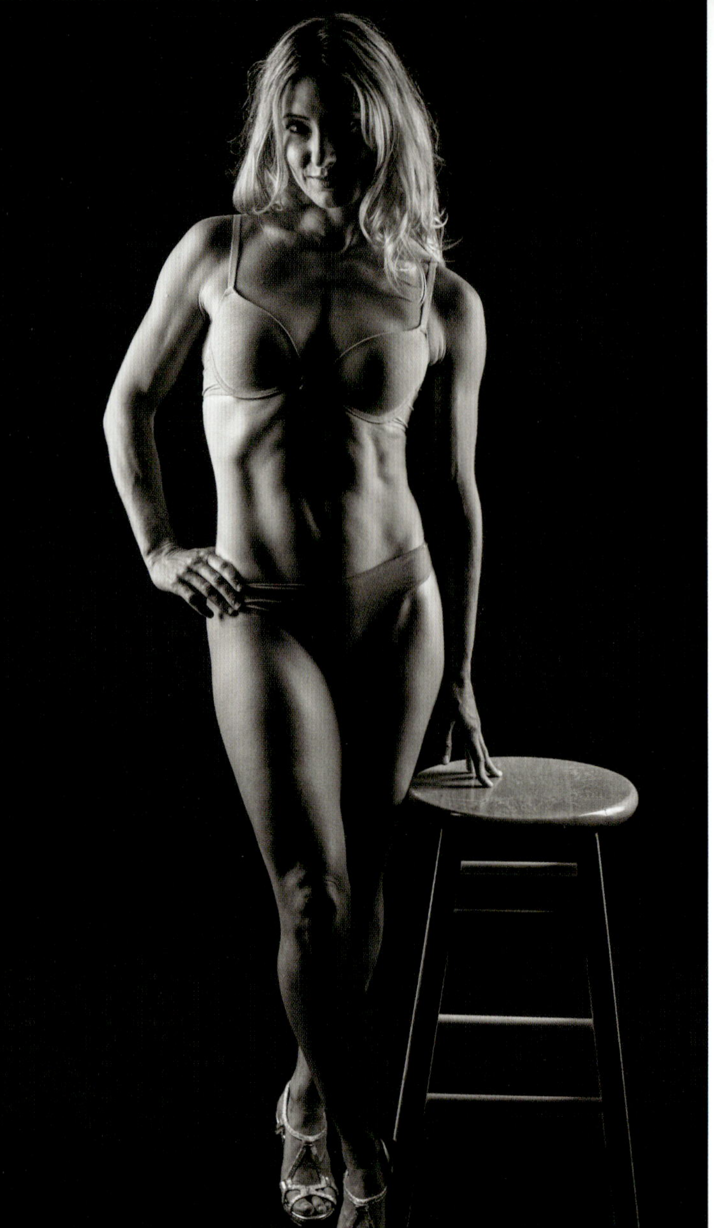

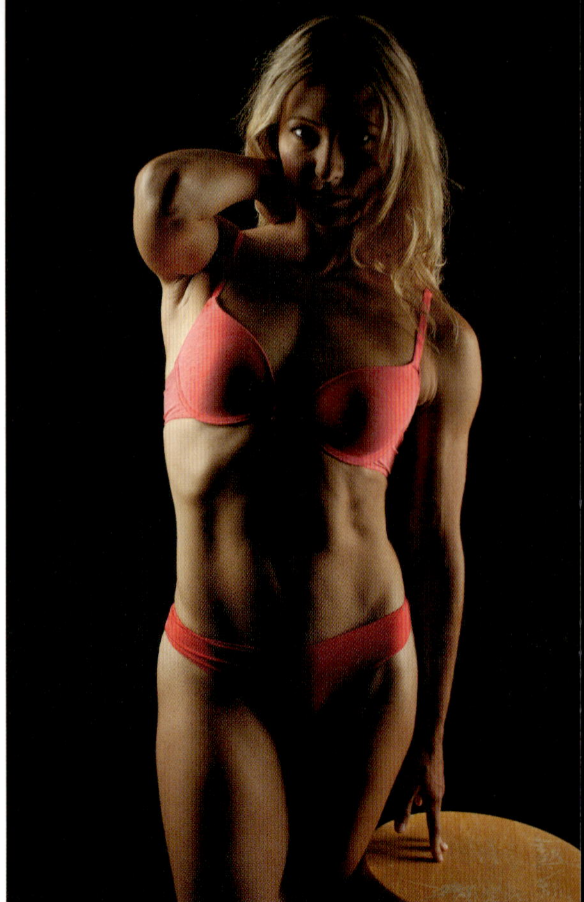

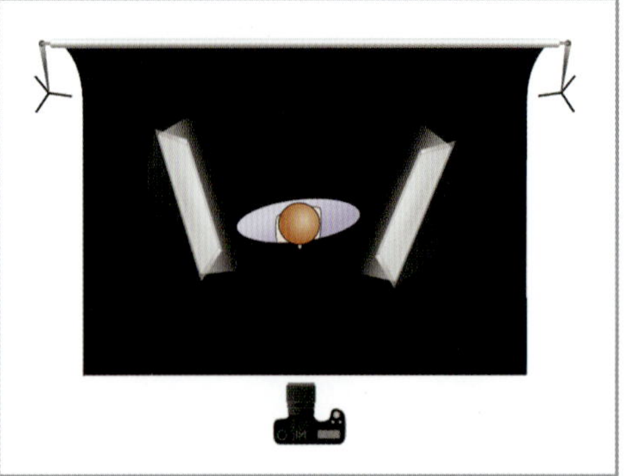

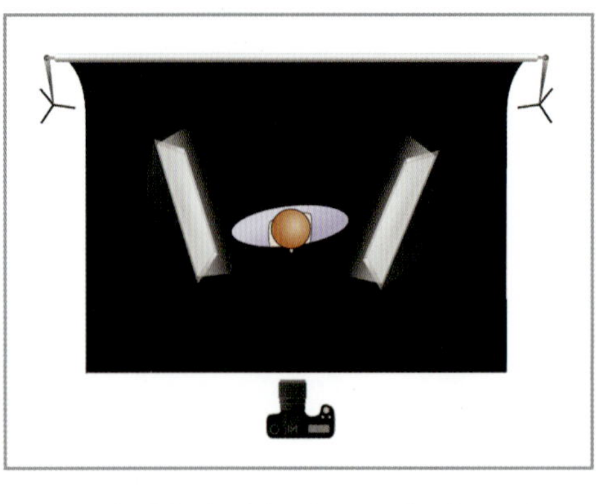

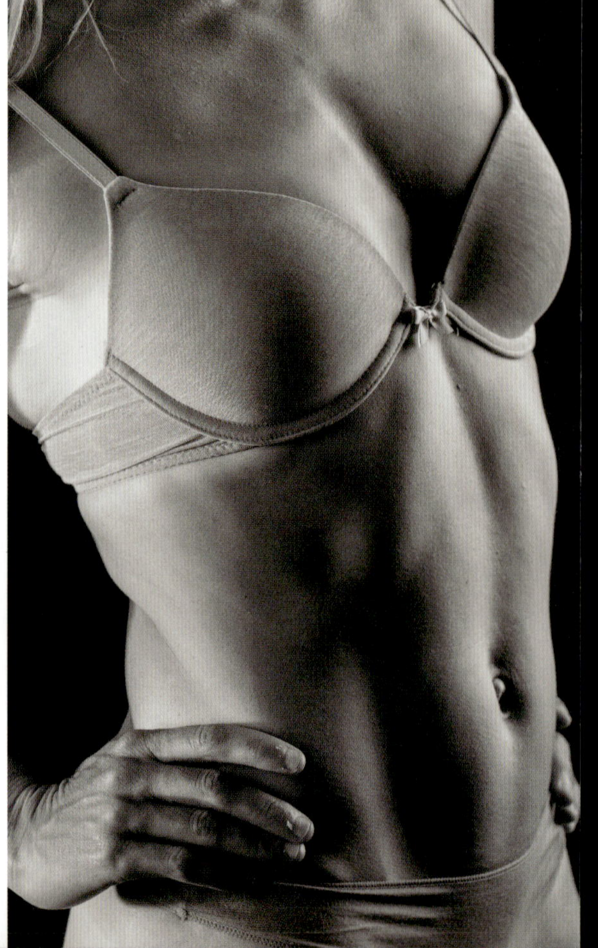

▲ Top, left and right: Feathering the lights back (as shown in the diagram) creates more shadow down the center of the body.

▶ Right: A detail photo shows how twisting the body toward one light or the other accentuates shadow in different areas.

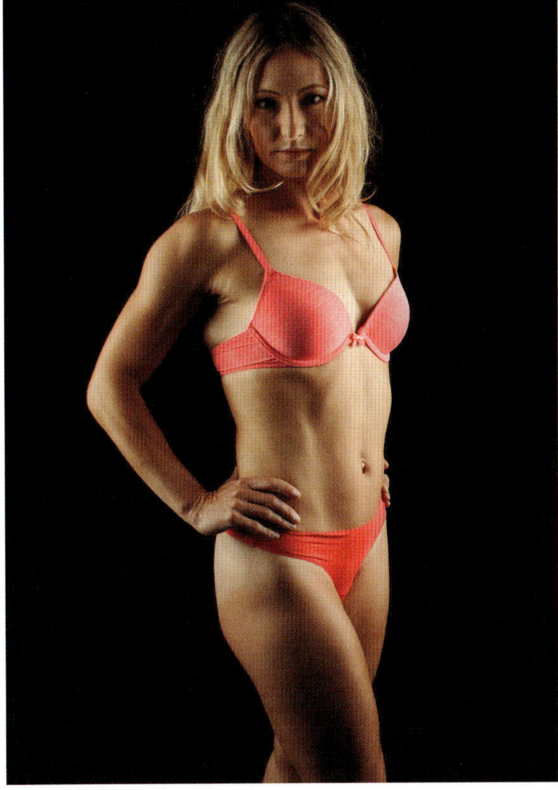

▲ With a slight turn of the hip, and a twist of the upper body, we have narrowed the waist line.

You can really play with this lighting setup and feather the softboxes, front or back, to get different effects. In the images on the facing page, you can see how feathering the lights back creates more shadow down the center of her body or on one side or the other. These shadows give even more definition to her muscles. Twisting the body toward one light or the other is another way to accentuate the shadows in different areas. The diagram shows how the model is positioned toward the front of the lights and the softboxes are feathered back toward the background.

Posing

Kristin is a professional triathlete with a rather flawless physique, so it's not hard to make her look good—but she is not used to posing for the camera, so knowing how to give direction

▼ What the legs and the feet do is equally important. The knee being bent and posed over the other leg creates a nice line and an appealing overall form.

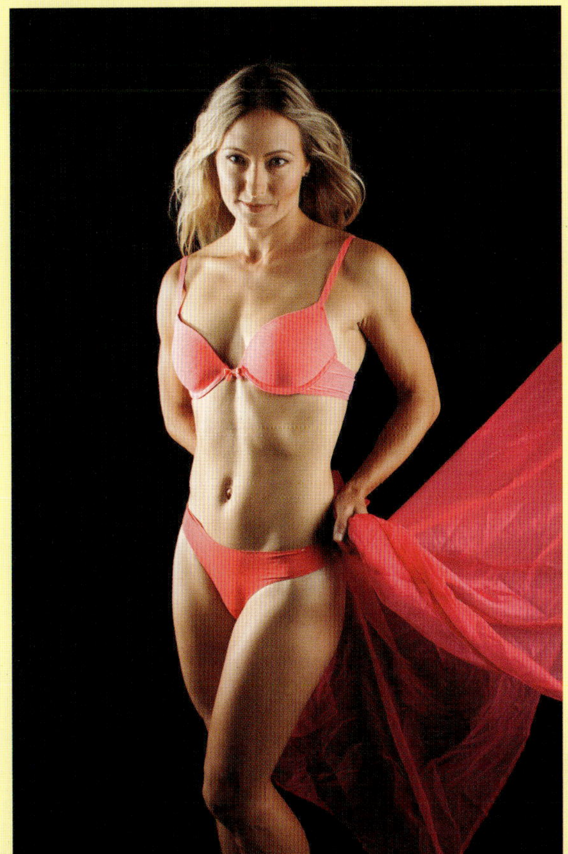

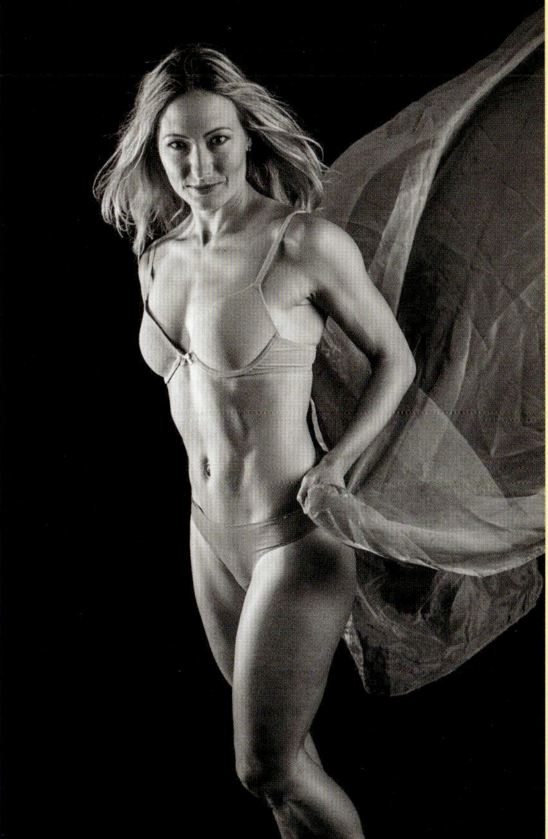

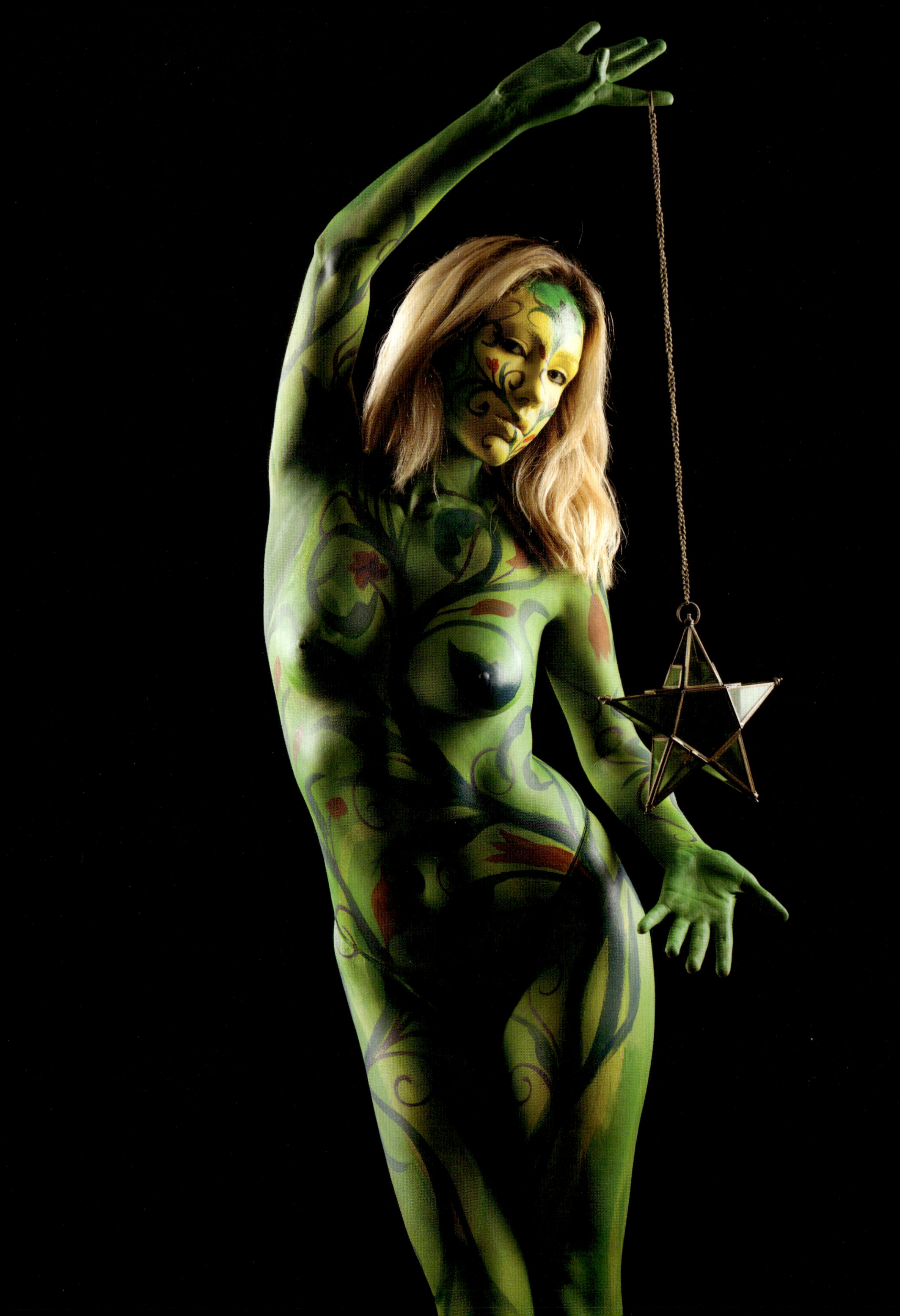

and help her pose correctly was essential. If she had just stood flat-footed and posed straight on, it would not have yielded the most appealing image. But with a slight turn of the hip, and a twist of the upper body, we narrowed the waist line. The pose was completed by experimenting with the positions of her legs and feet.

A Lookbook Test Shoot

These images (facing page, right, and next page) for a mock product "lookbook" are from a test shoot I did with a college class I teach. A lookbook is a collection of photographs used to show off the style of a particular designer or model. Here, I used models in body paint with lighting that sculpted their forms. The body painting was done to complement the product they were posing with: a line of glass lamps. (*Note:* body painting is done with a special makeup made for skin. Don't go out and buy regular paint to put on a model.) Very minor retouching was done on these photos. It's all sideways clamshell lighting, beautiful posing, and creative makeup. Dancers are a great choice for models when doing body shoots, because they naturally move into these flattering positions and often have long, lean bodies. The casting call I did for this "painted ladies" shoot asked for "dancers who move well."

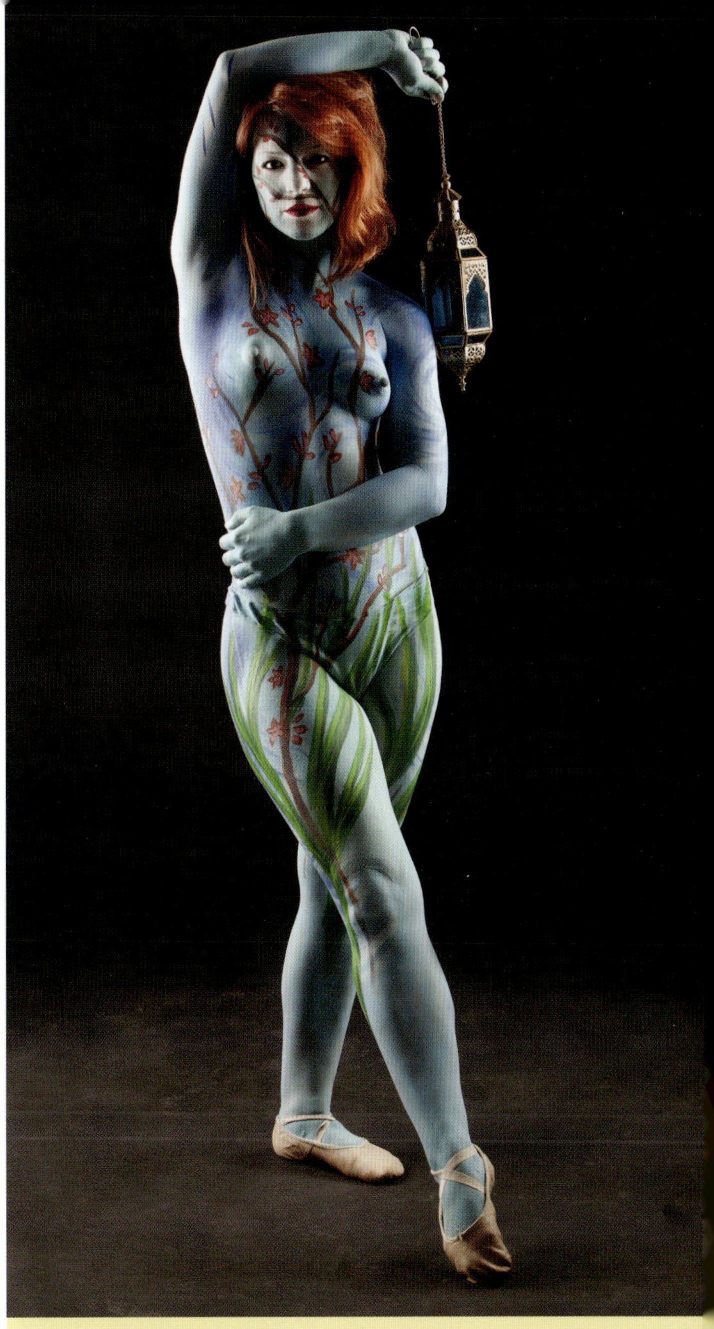

◄ Facing page: *Body paint by Carlos Nieto III. Model: Tahia Rivara.*

► Top right: *Body paint by Carlos Nieto III.*

► Bottom right: *Body paint by Cici Anderson and Caitlyn Brisbin.*

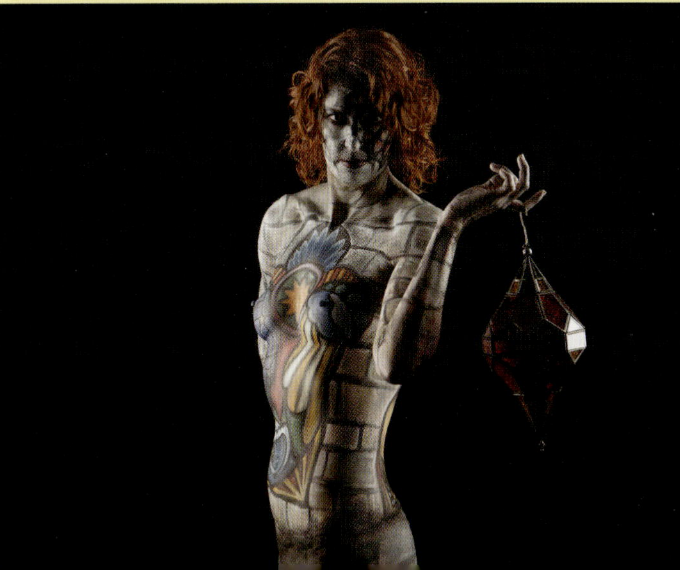

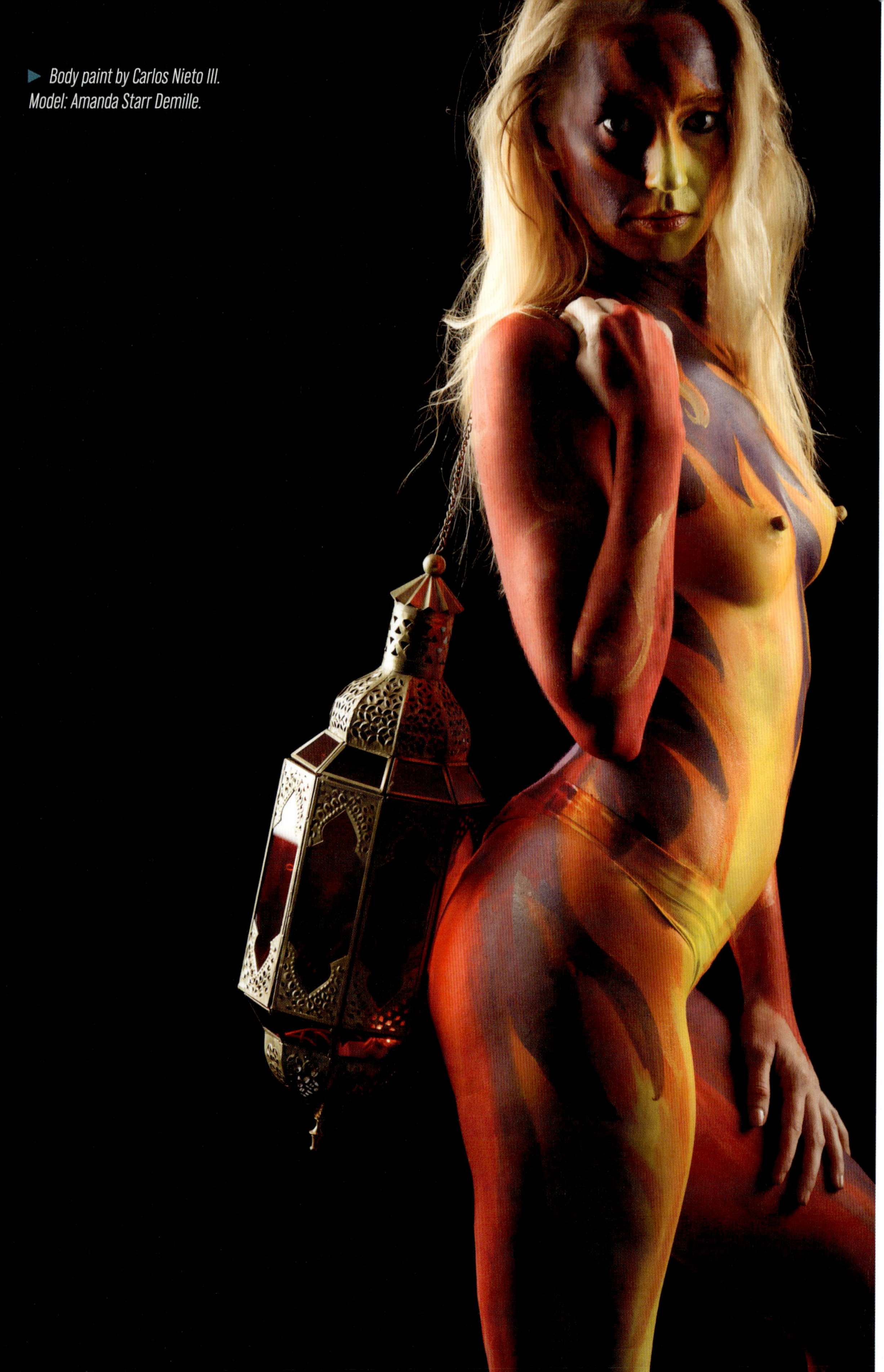

Body paint by Carlos Nieto III.
Model: Amanda Starr Demille.

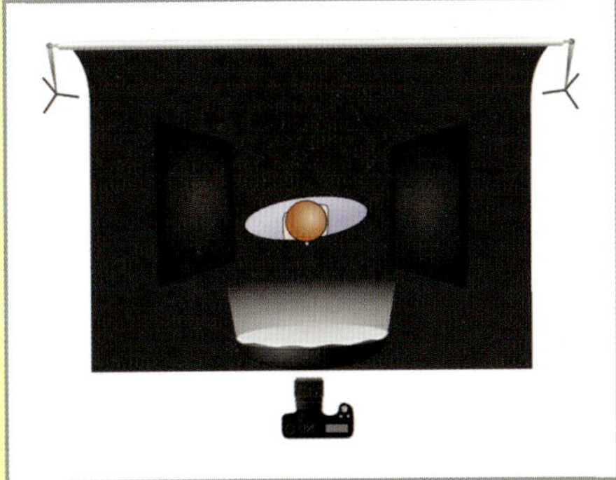

► The main light was one large beauty dish with diffusion. Black flags were added on either side of the model. *Setup image by Preston Perkins. (Specs: f/8.0, 1/160, ISO 100, 50mm f/1.2L lens)*

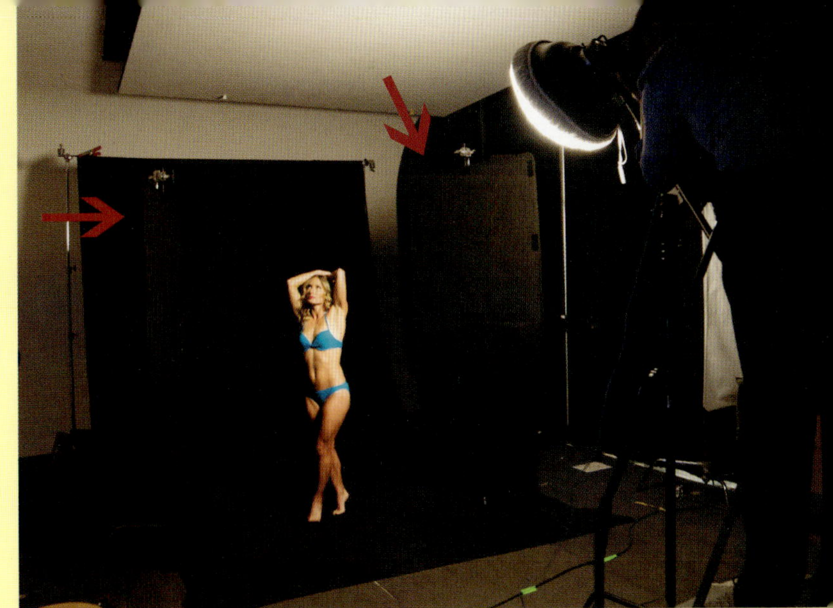

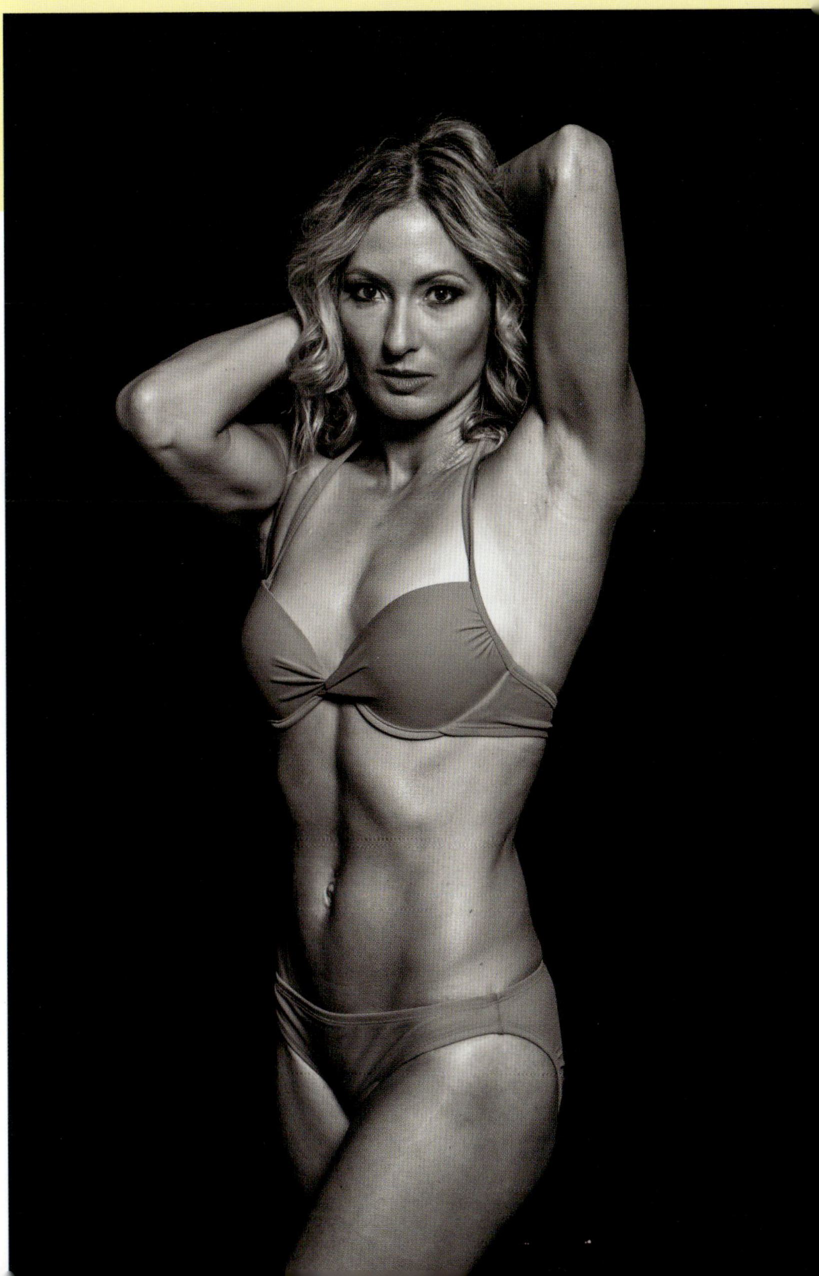

Contouring with Negative Fill
Against a Black Backdrop

Our next setup is basically the opposite of the clamshell approach; it utilizes negative fill. To create this sequence of images, I used one large beauty dish with a diffusion sock. The model was posed on a black seamless cloth backdrop. Then, I added two large black flags, placed vertically, that were long enough to span the length of the model's body. The key to this shot is positioning the flags. The closer you get the panels to the model, the more they suck up the light and the more shadow you will see forming on the sides of the model's body.

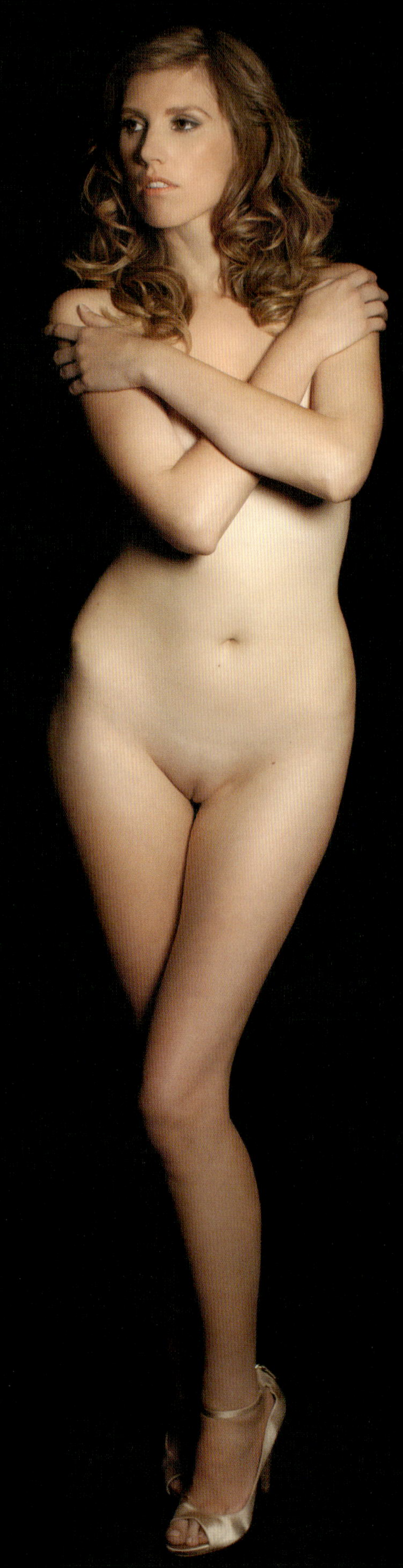

► Negative fill is very flattering, cutting into the body for a slimming effect. *(Specs: f/8.0, 1/200, ISO 100, 50mm f/1.2L lens)*

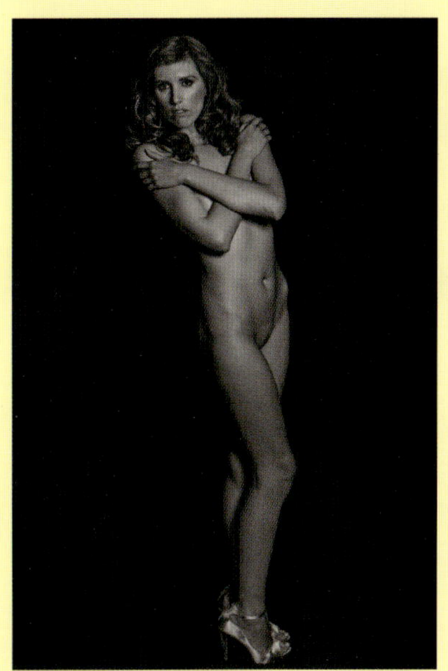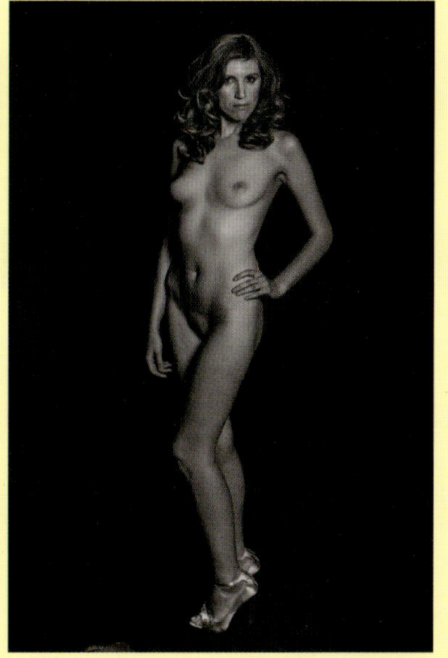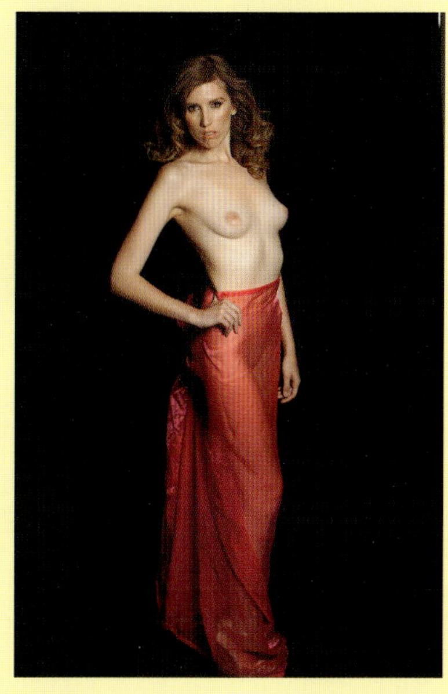

▲ Posing variations and the addition of fabric as a prop. *(Specs: f/8.0, 1/250, ISO 100, 50mm f/1.2L lens)*

Posing and a Prop

Posing nudes can be tricky, even if you have someone with a very nice figure. I suggest having your model move her body into different positions and taking a photo for every change in her pose. This will help you figure out what looks best for her unique figure. The images above show slight differences in posing and the addition of fabric as a prop. The arms up, the hand on a hip . . . what looks best? We also want to be thinking about what the face is doing. Does she look better with her chin up or down? Or her face turned one way or the other? The mouth closed or open? For the final image, I added a fan to get some movement in her hair and the fabric. This is a great way to bring some life and energy in your photos.

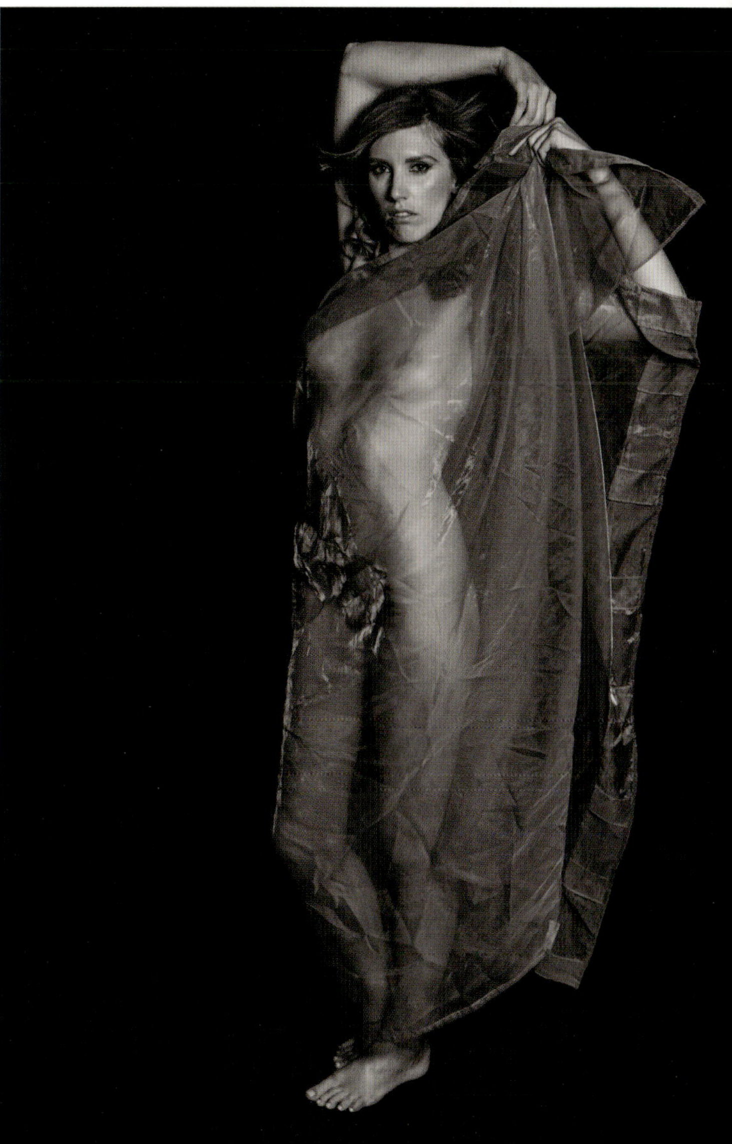

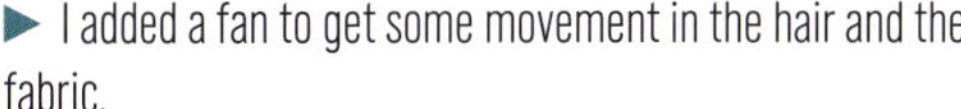

▶ I added a fan to get some movement in the hair and the fabric.

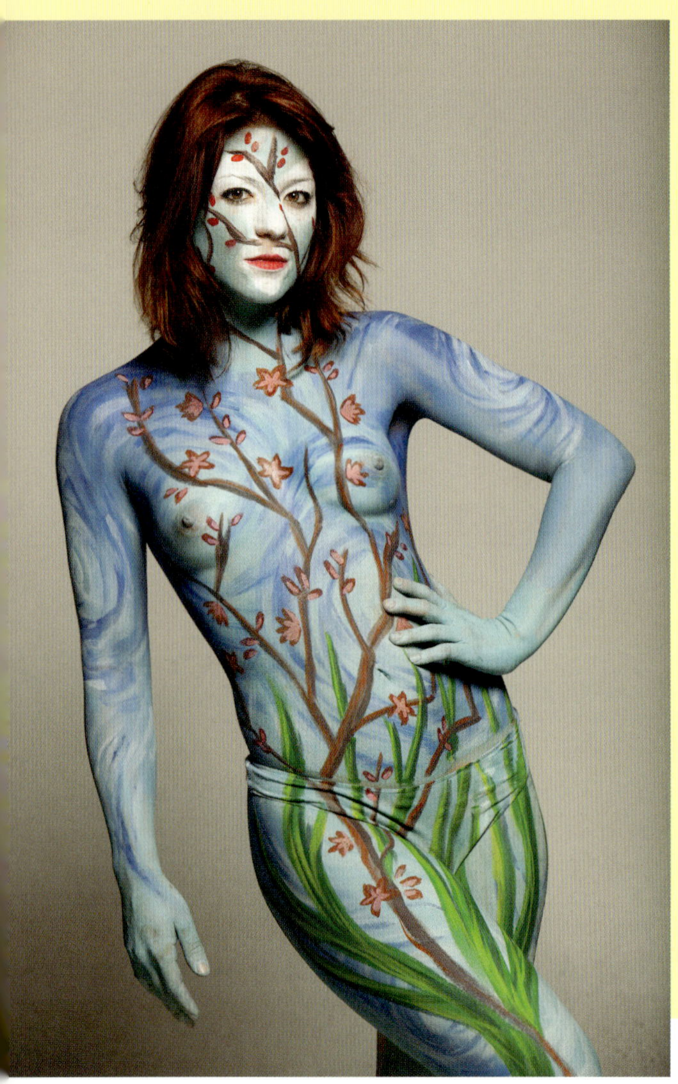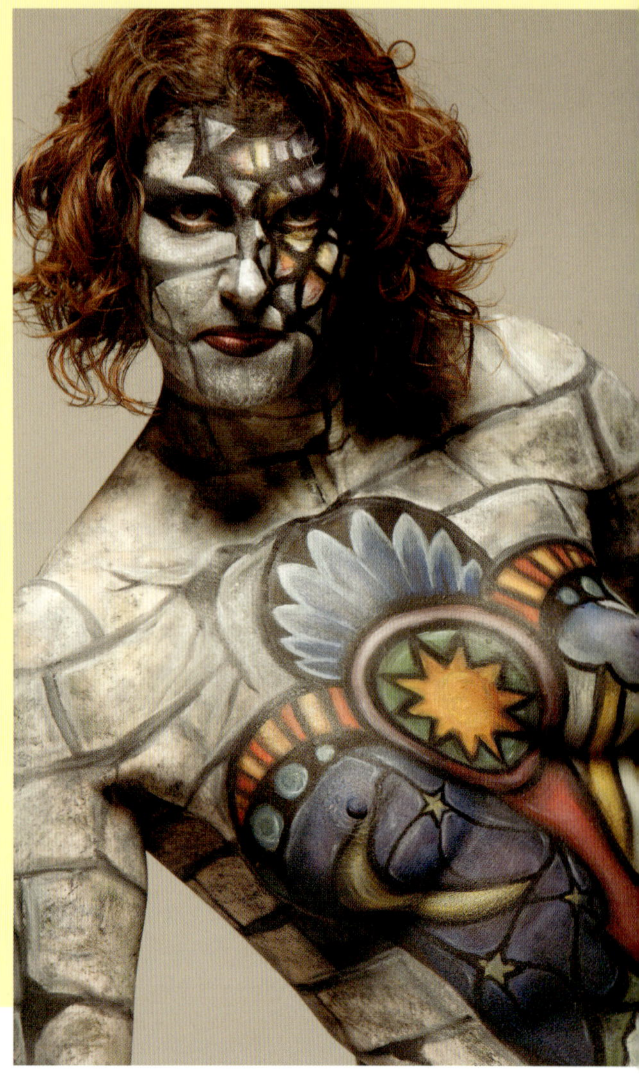

Switching to a White Backdrop

Let's look at this same lighting setup again—but going back to the painted ladies against a white background. As you can see in the diagram on the facing page, the only difference is that the background is white. Because it was not lit, however, the background recorded as gray. (Remember what we talked about when considering high-key lighting? If you want the background to be white, you need to light it with separate strobes—or make sure your front light source is big enough and close enough to light both your subject and your background.)

For the final image in the sequence (facing page, right), the model was backed away from the key light a little, so you will notice that the bottom half of her body is a bit darker and in more shadow. Moving your model closer to or farther from the key in a one-light setup like this will noticeably change where the light drops off.

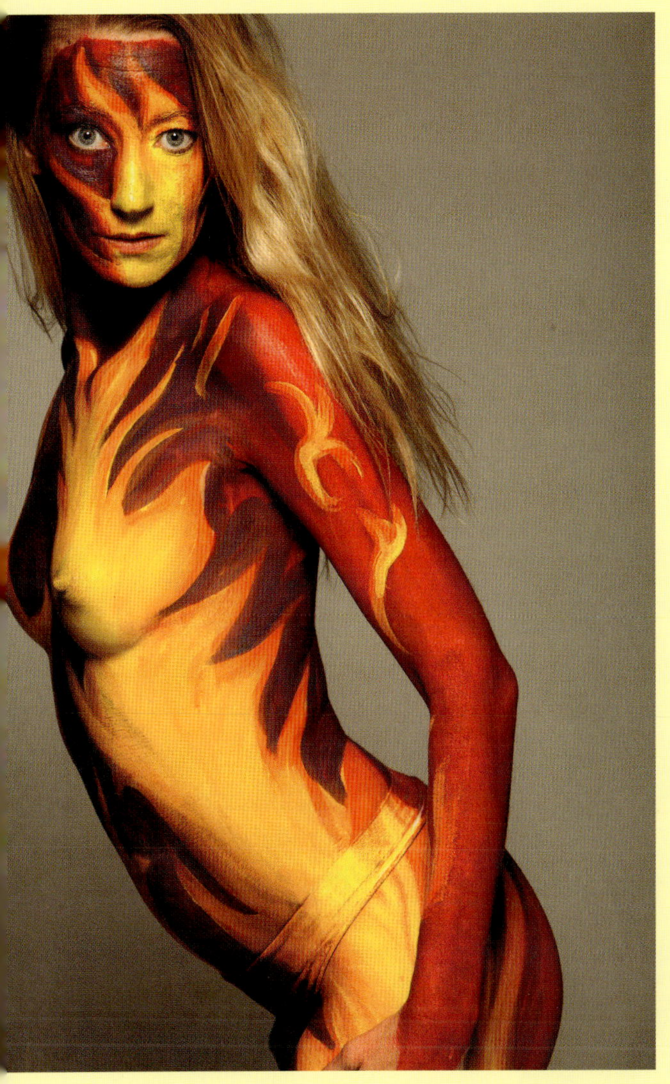

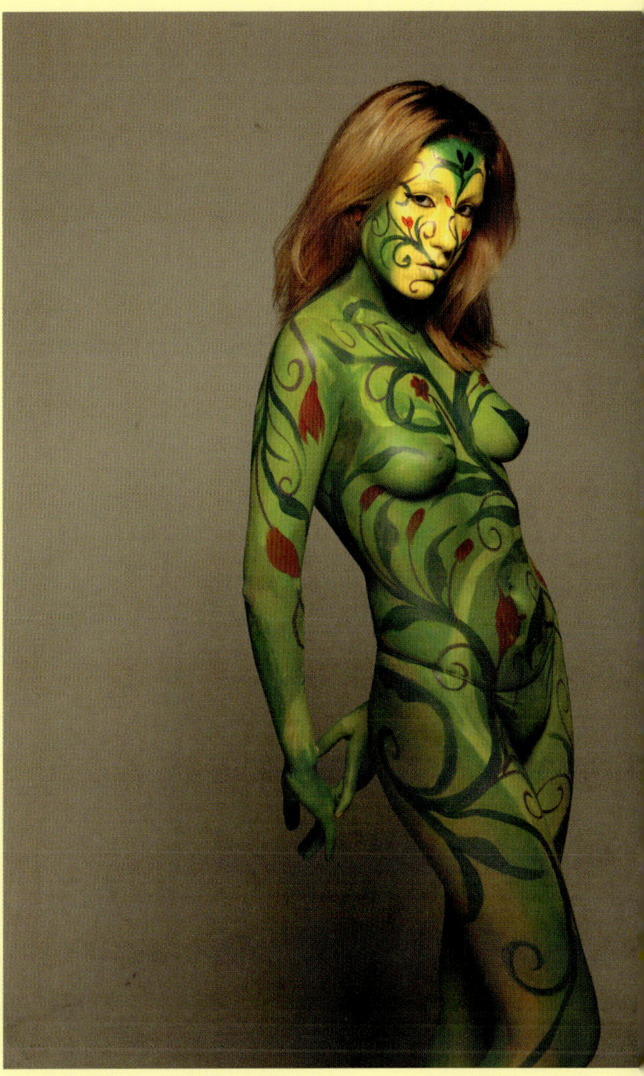

◄◄ ▲ Facing page and above: A beauty dish with diffusion was the only light. Black flags were added on either side of the model. For the first image (facing page, left), I asked the model to push back her front arm, bending it at the elbow to create separation and make a more pleasing pose. For the final image (above, right), the model was moved back away from the key light, creating more shadow on the lower half of the body. *Model: Tahia Rivara. (Specs: f/8.0, 1/200, ISO 100, 70-200mm f/2.8 lens)*

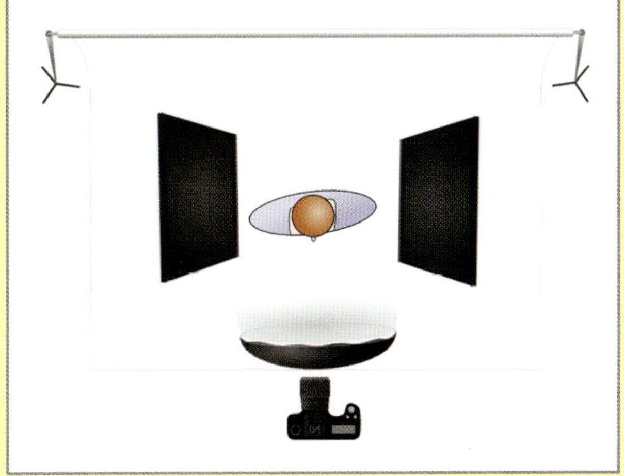

A Little About Gobos

There are a lot of uses for gobos (also called cookies, from the term "cucoloris"). A sort-of acronym for "goes before optics" or "go between," a gobo is placed between the light and the subject in order to cast shadows—often, shadows with a distinctive shape. I want to touch on this briefly here because we have just talked about using shadow to sculpt the body. Using gobos is another great way to play with shadow and light as you depict the human form.

There are many kinds of gobos available—and you can even make your own, if you like. A snoot, for example, is technically a gobo. Basically, you are looking for something that lets only some light through and creates patterns. The most recognizable example of a gobo may be the film noir look where strips of light fall on the subject, emulating the look of light coming through Venetian blinds. You can create this same effect simply by cutting long, thin lines in a piece of cardboard or foam-core board.

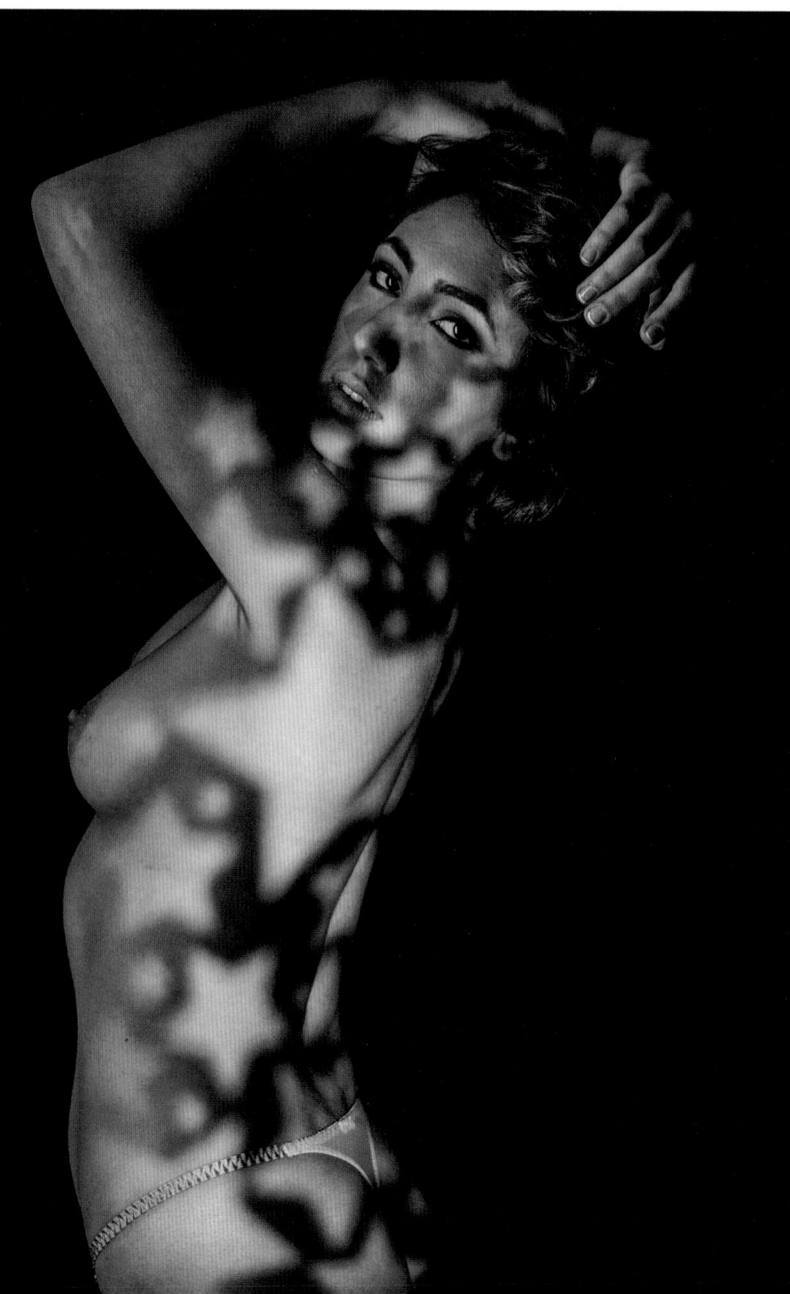

The image to the left was produced using a fantastic light modifier called a Light Blaster, which is designed to work with speedlights. From the Light Blaster set, I chose a gobo that looks like a small, metal slide with star cutouts which the light shines through. The flash goes in one end of the unit, the gobo goes in the middle, and a camera lens is placed on the front so that the unit acts like a projector and you can focus the light.

I created a different look with the Light Blaster by using a color slide—one normally used for backdrop projections—as a gobo on the main light (facing page). For a little fill, I added a strip light opposite the model and slightly in front of her. I shot this against a black background so nothing would distract from the gobo patterns on the model.

I had a lot of fun using the Light Blaster on these nudes and creat-

◀ I used gobo lighting with the Light Blaster for this image of model Tahia Rivara.

ed some fantastic looks with both the metal gobos and the colored slides. You could easily use an actual projector, with any slide, to create this effect as well. Another easy way to use gobos is to shoot with hot lights instead of strobes. With a continuous light source, you can move your gobo around and watch the effect on your model in real time.

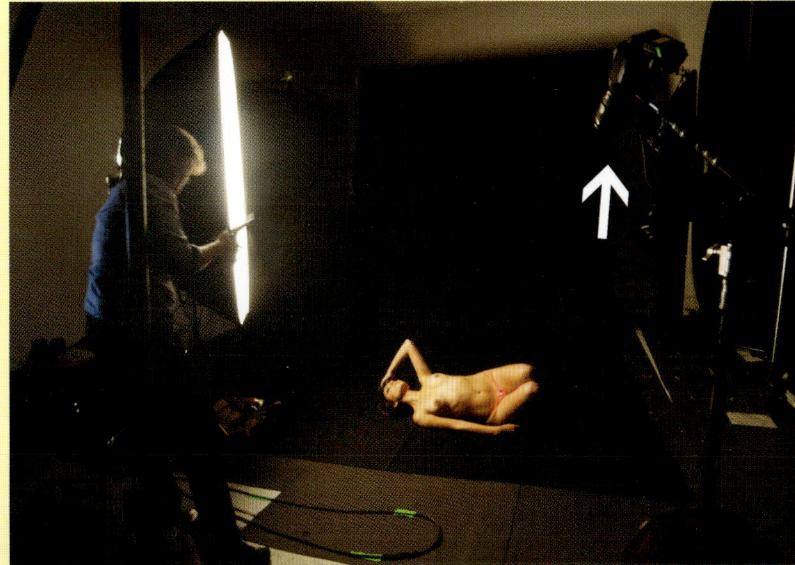

▶ The key light was the Light Blaster with a gobo. A little fill was added from a strip light. *Image by Preston Perkins.*

▼ I used a colored slide gobo to create this image of model Tahia Rivara. *(Specs: f/5.6, 1/100, ISO 200)*

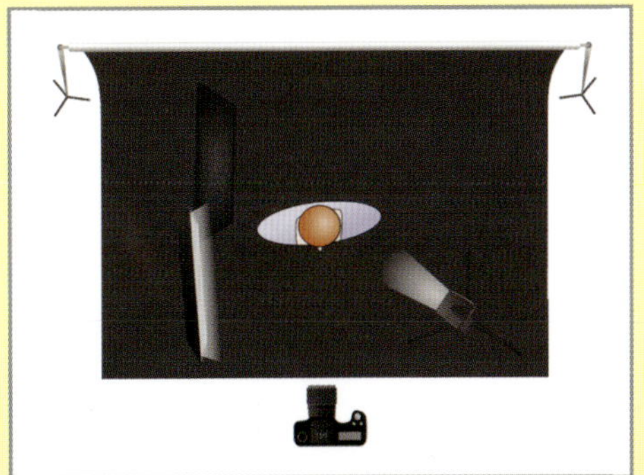

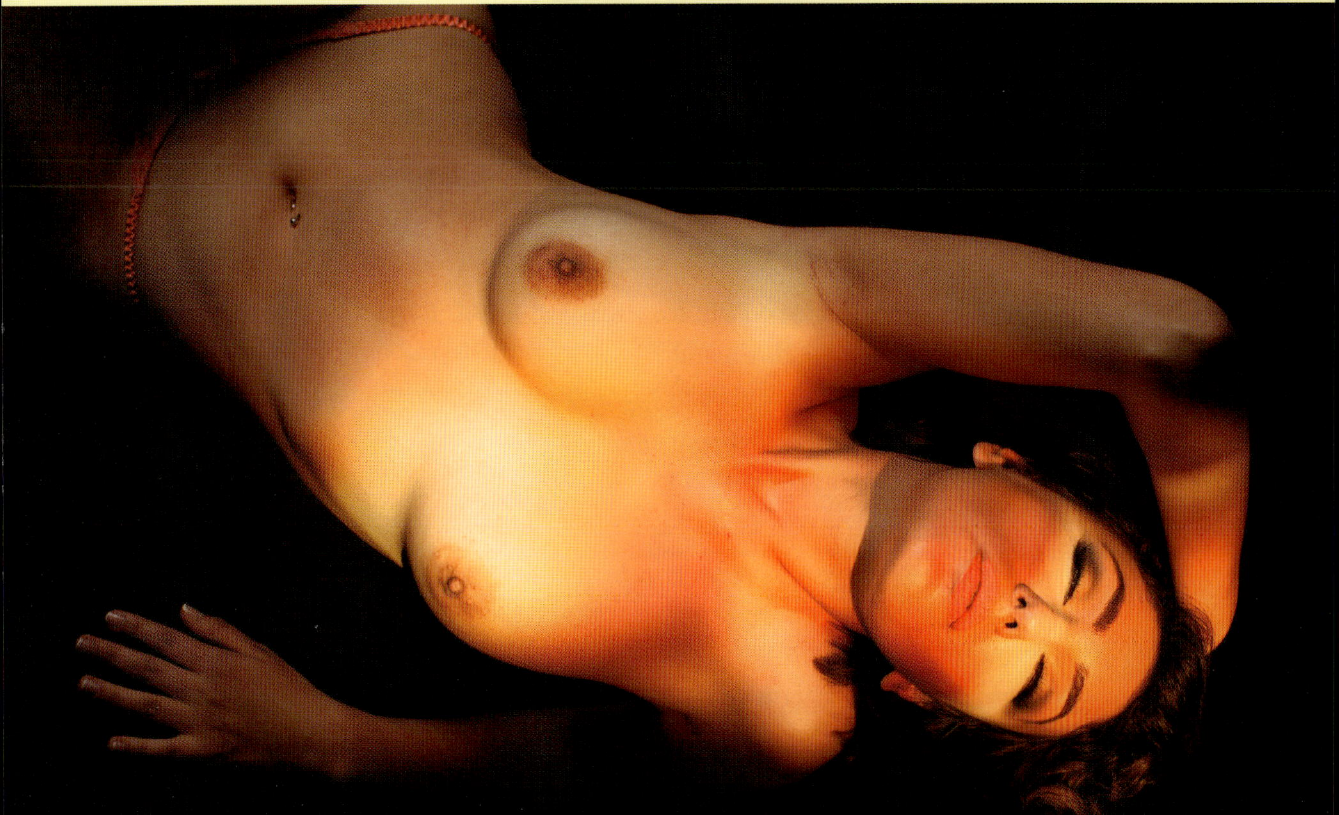

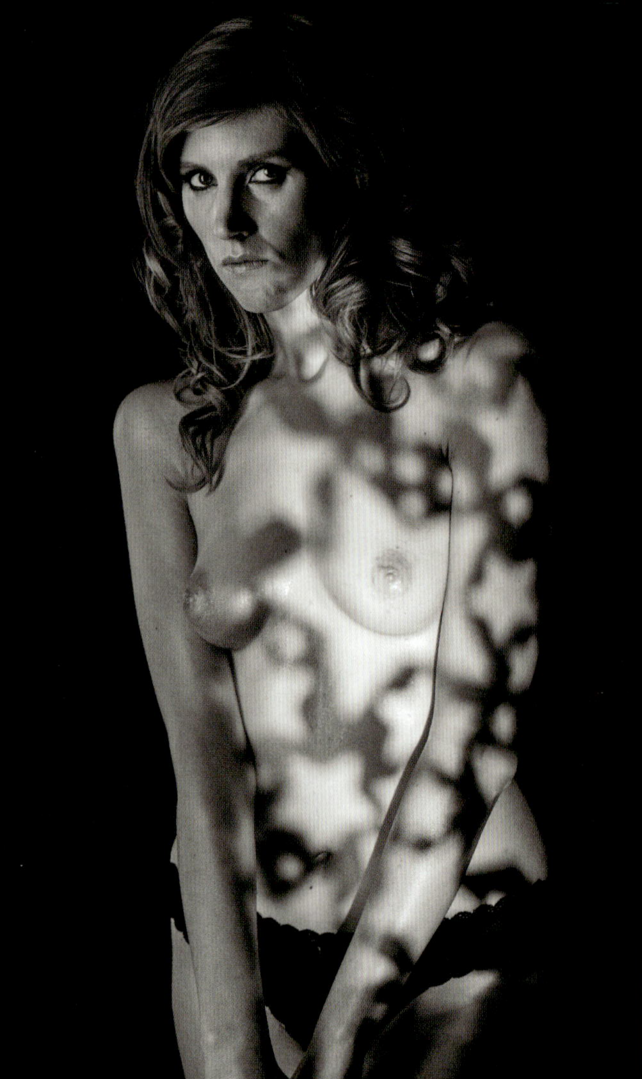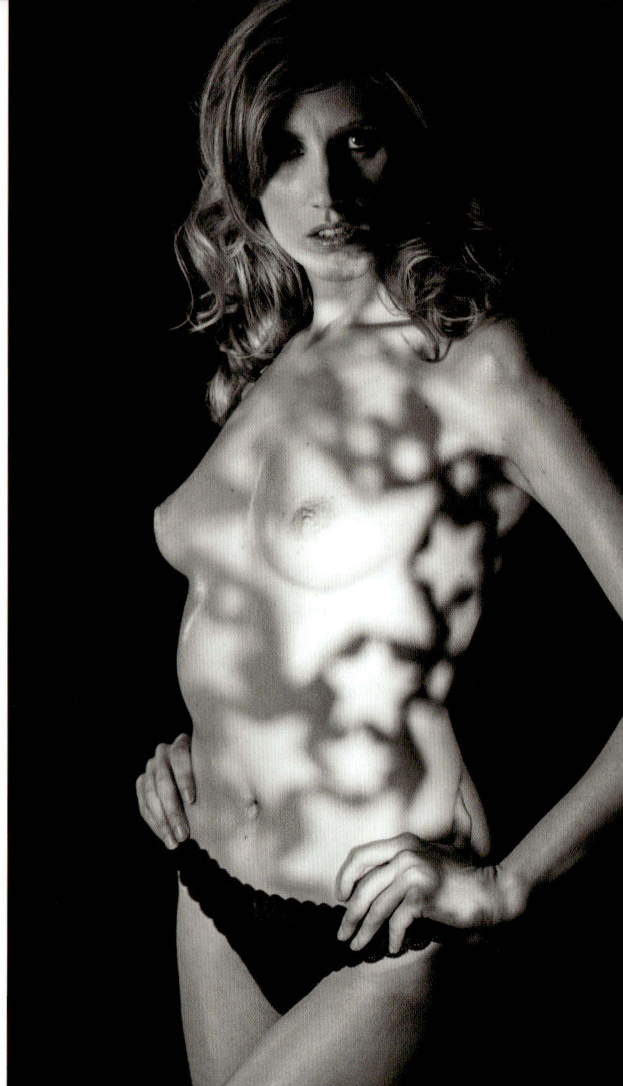

▲▶ Above and facing page: Several different poses, both lying down and standing, that incorporate different gobos.

Posing with Gobos

In the images on these two pages, you can see several different poses (both lying down and standing) that incorporate different gobos. What you like in a pose may change depending on how the gobo's pattern is hitting the body. Without having the model move, you can also change the look of the image by changing your camera angle. Maybe the existing pose would look better with you up above the model, or maybe lower, or maybe straight on.

And how does the light pattern hit your model's body as her position changes? How does the pattern change if you move the light to a different position? In the images on page 96, look at the difference in where the stars land on the model's body depending on whether she is turned one way or the other. And what about where the light patterns hits her face? What do you think looks better?

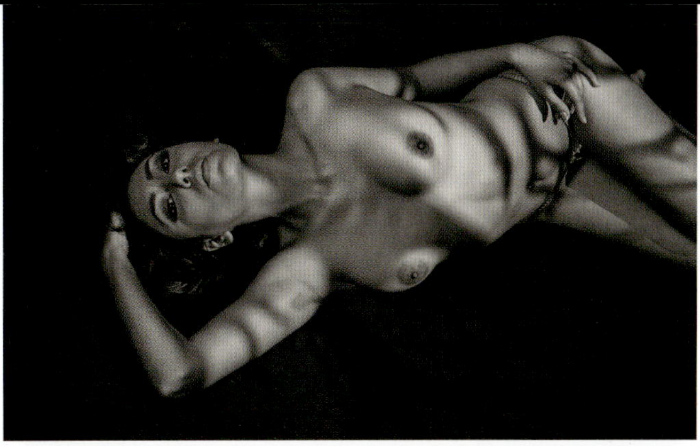

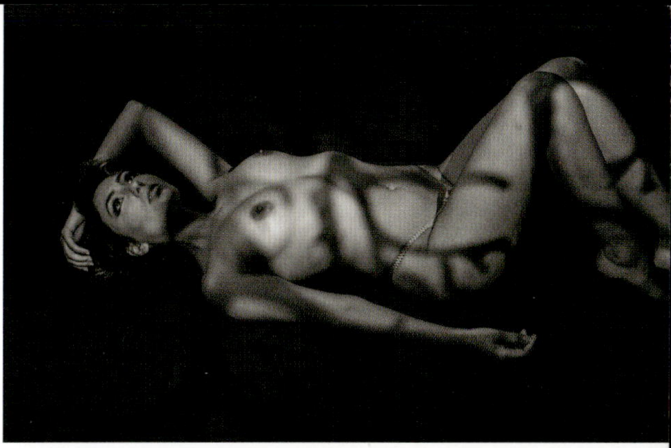

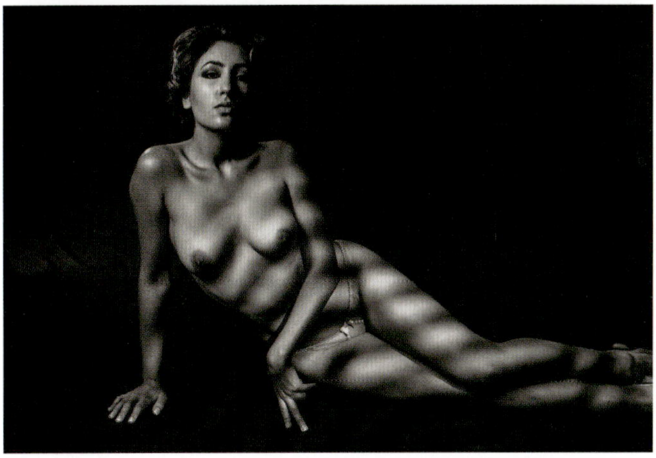

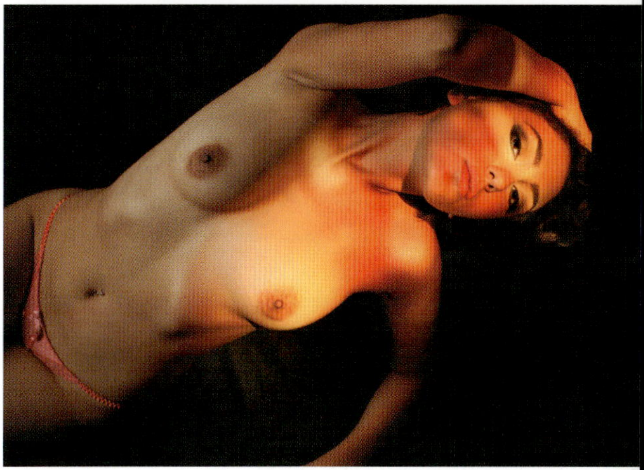

▼ For this variation, I moved over to the right and closer to the model's face.

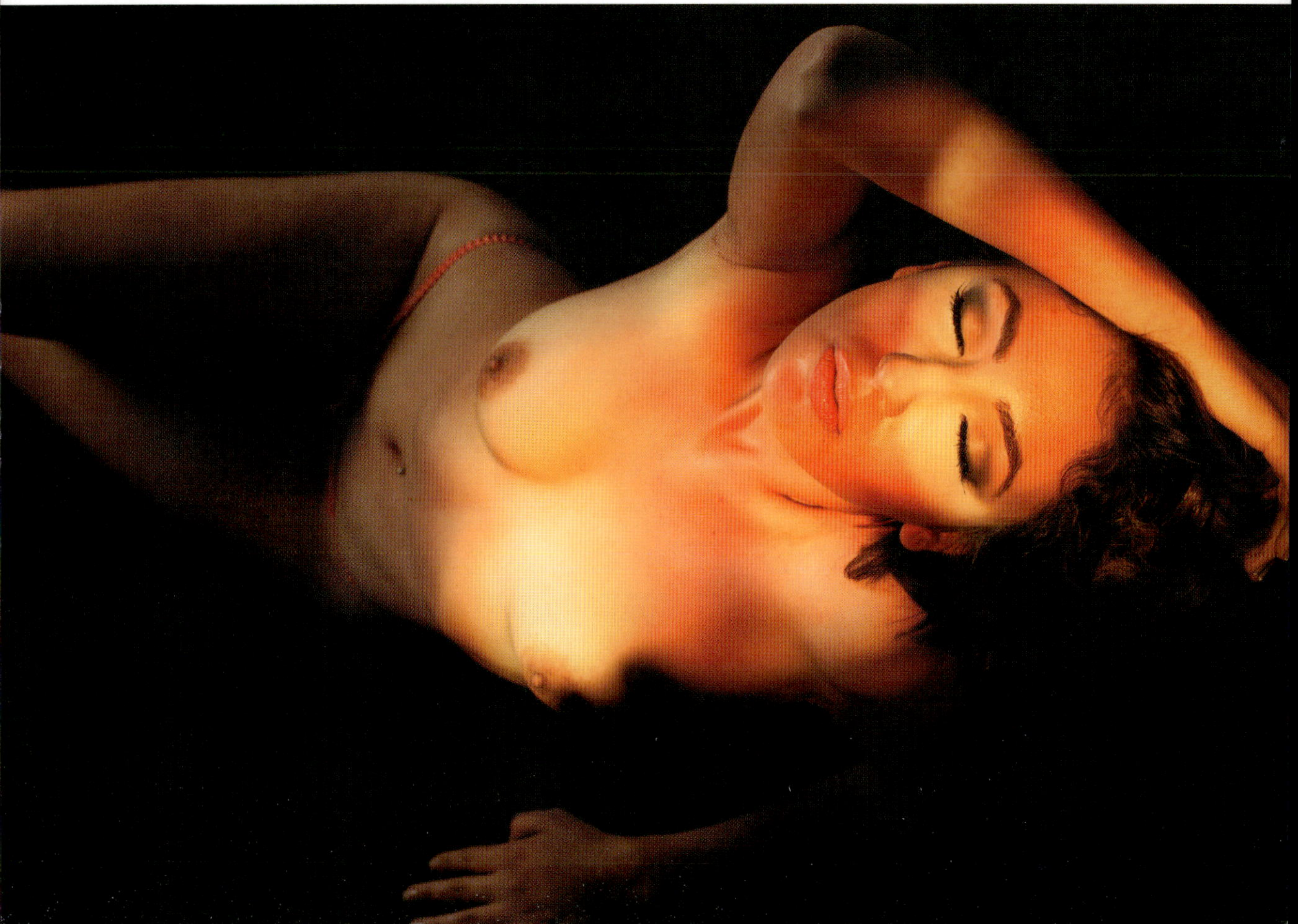

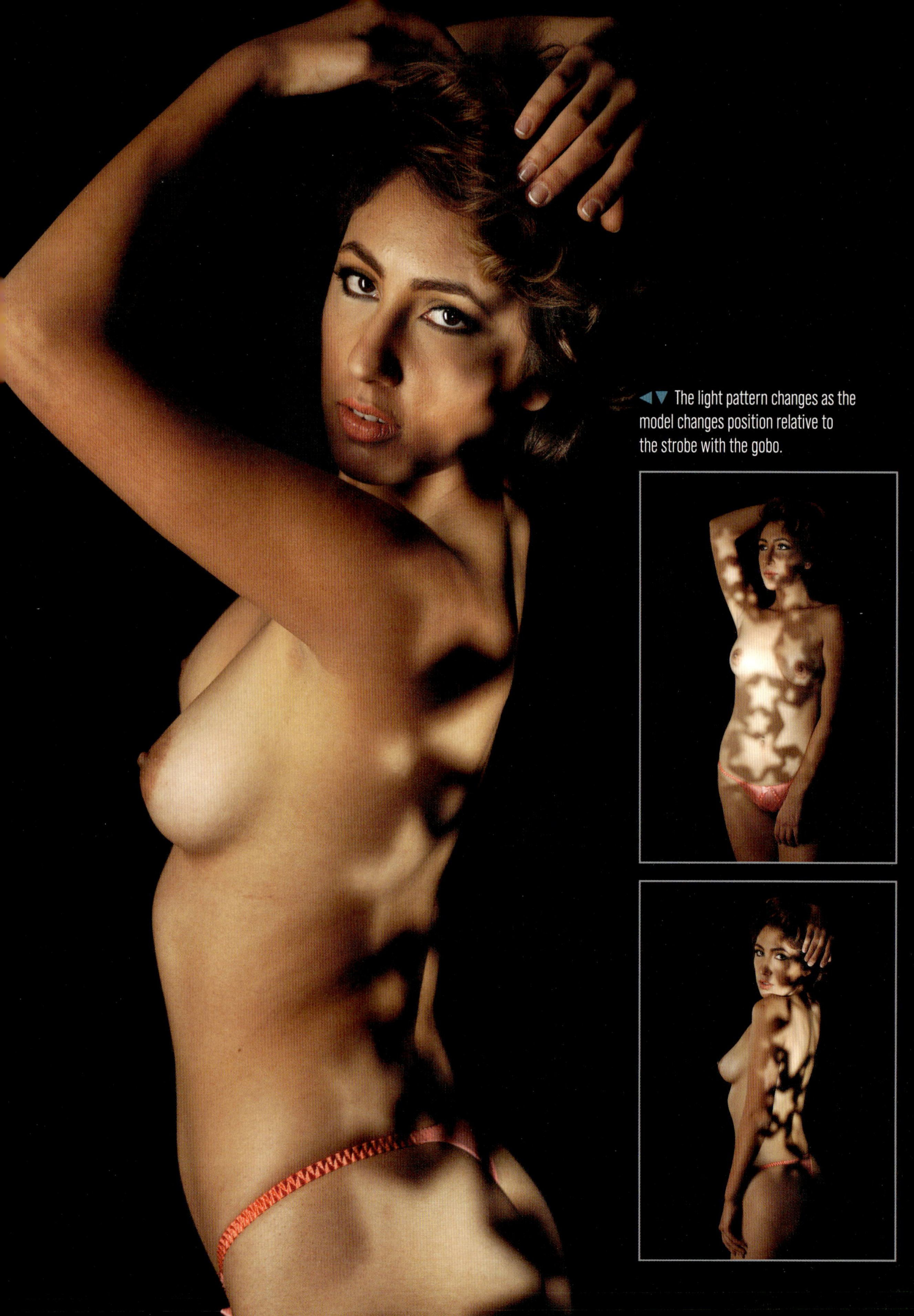

◀▼ The light pattern changes as the model changes position relative to the strobe with the gobo.

7. Speedlight Techniques

Key Techniques ▶ Off-camera flash; Dragging the shutter; Using snoots, bounce light, and modifiers

Application ▶ Fashion editorial

You don't always need strobes or hot lights to create professional lighting. When shooting on location, we often use small flashes to create beautiful lighting effects. Speedlights are portable and don't require power cords, so if you have multiple setups and locations to handle on a limited time schedule, speedlights are the way to go. I often find myself in this situation with smaller commercial jobs that require photography at several locations over just a three- to four-hour time period.

In this chapter, we'll look at how to shoot stylized editorial images using just speedlights and modifiers—and how to make the images look like you used some very high-end lighting. You can do a lot of this with just one speedlight and some creativity.

For most of the chapter, we'll be looking at a single editorial assignment: photographing a patriotic, pinup-girl theme for a story about handbags. As you will see, each model was posed with a different colored handbag—red, white, or blue—to coordinate with the Fourth of July theme.

Reflective Umbrellas
Even Lighting with Two Speedlights

For the first group of images (next page), I bounced two speedlights into umbrellas with white reflective interiors. These were positioned in front of the subject, to either side, and at an equal distance for very even lighting. A similar effect on the subject could be done with one umbrella centered behind the photographer, but using two umbrellas reduced the shadows on the background. (*Note:* There are also many speedlight modifiers, such as mini softboxes, that can help create this evenly spread lighting effect.)

It's important to note that, even when set at the same power, each flash may output a different amount of light. You should meter each light source, just as you would with strobes. If one flash outputs more than the other, turn it down or move it back.

> **❝** Speedlights are portable and don't require power cords, so if you have multiple setups and locations to handle on a limited time schedule, speedlights are the way to go. **❞**

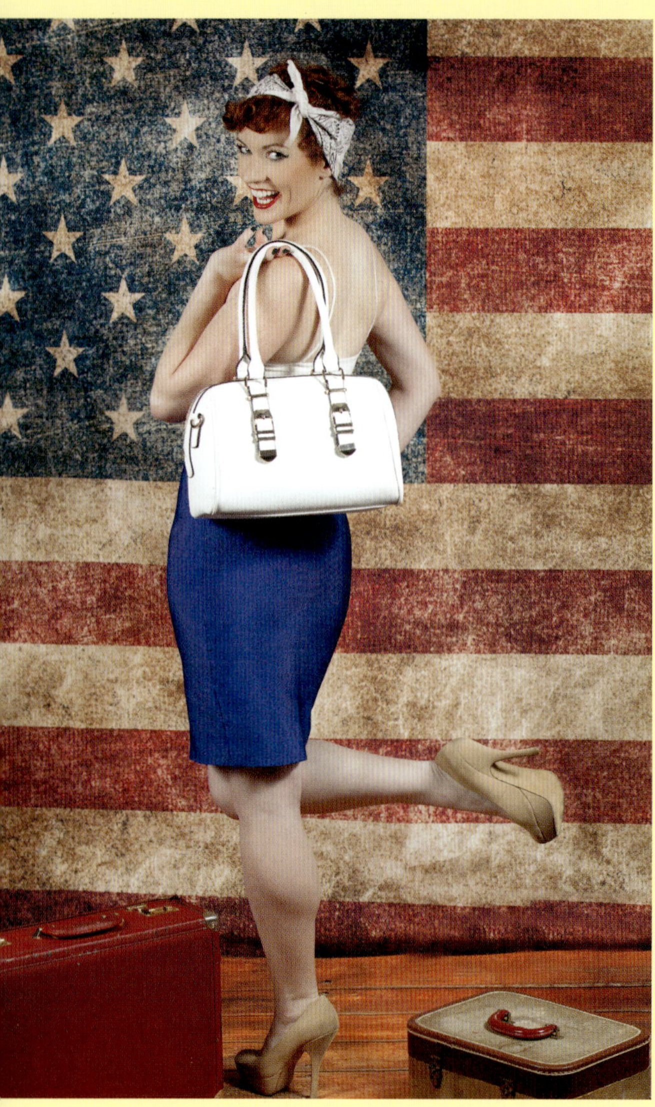

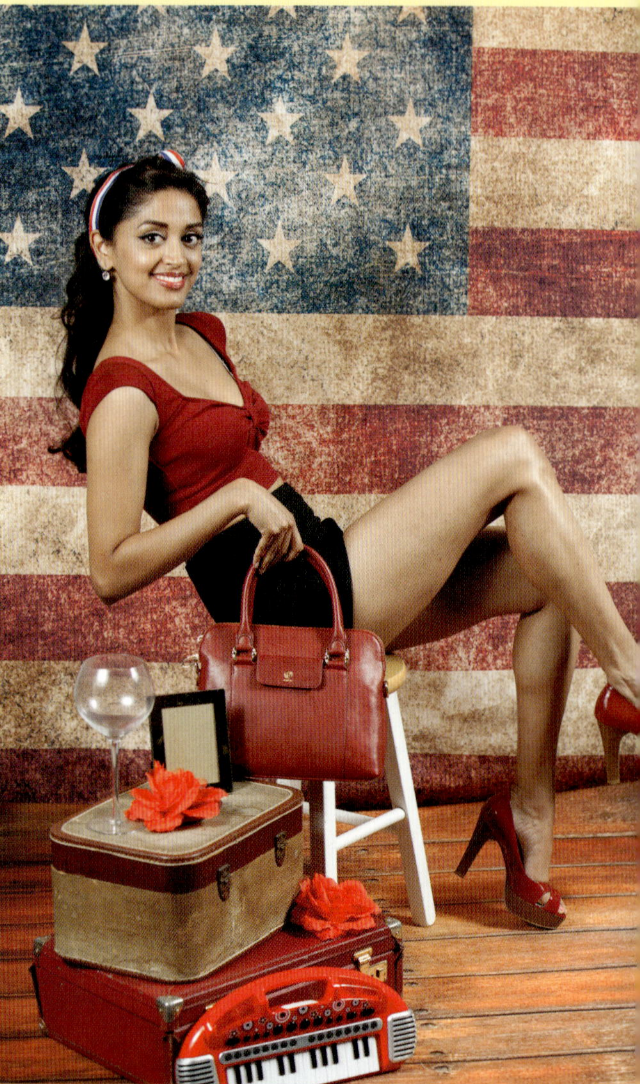

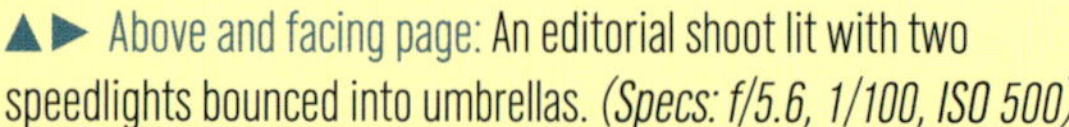

▲ ▶ *Above and facing page:* An editorial shoot lit with two speedlights bounced into umbrellas. *(Specs: f/5.6, 1/100, ISO 500)*

Notice that the model is very close to the backdrop, so the speedlights are lighting it as well. If the model were farther from the backdrop, and the lights were pushed farther away, the background would go darker. If you wanted your model farther from the backdrop, maybe to blur it out, you might need to use a third speedlight on the background.

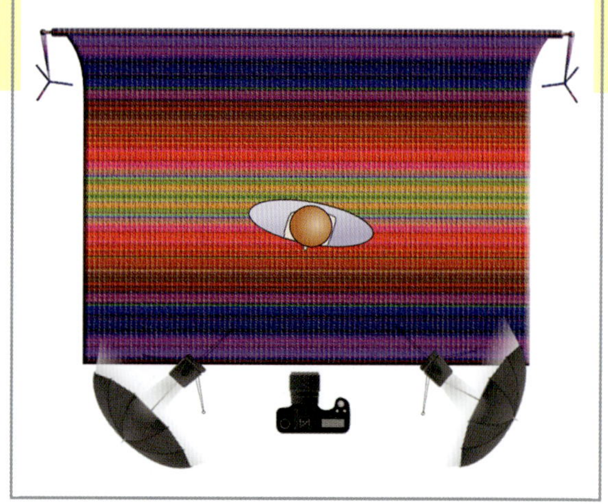

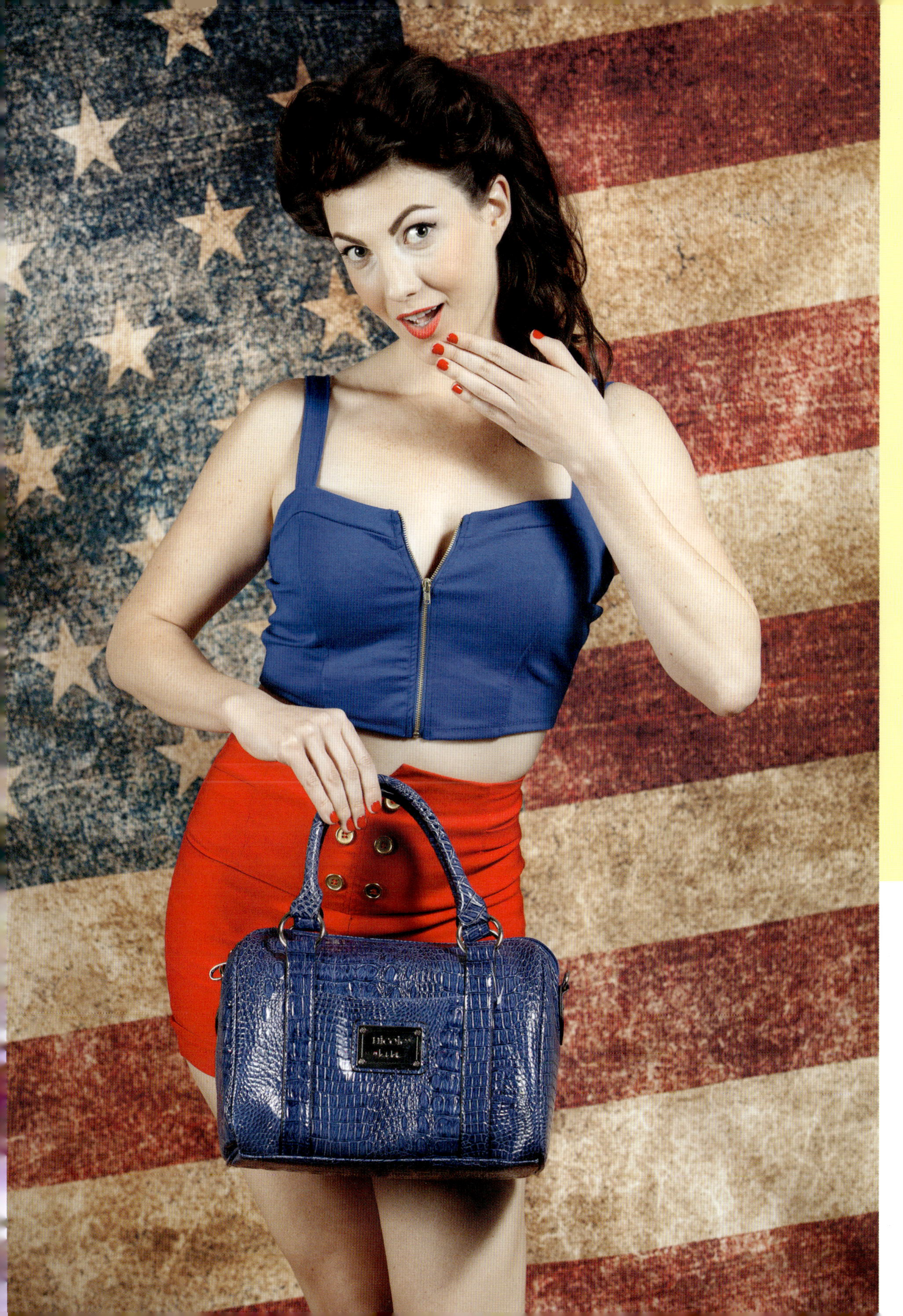

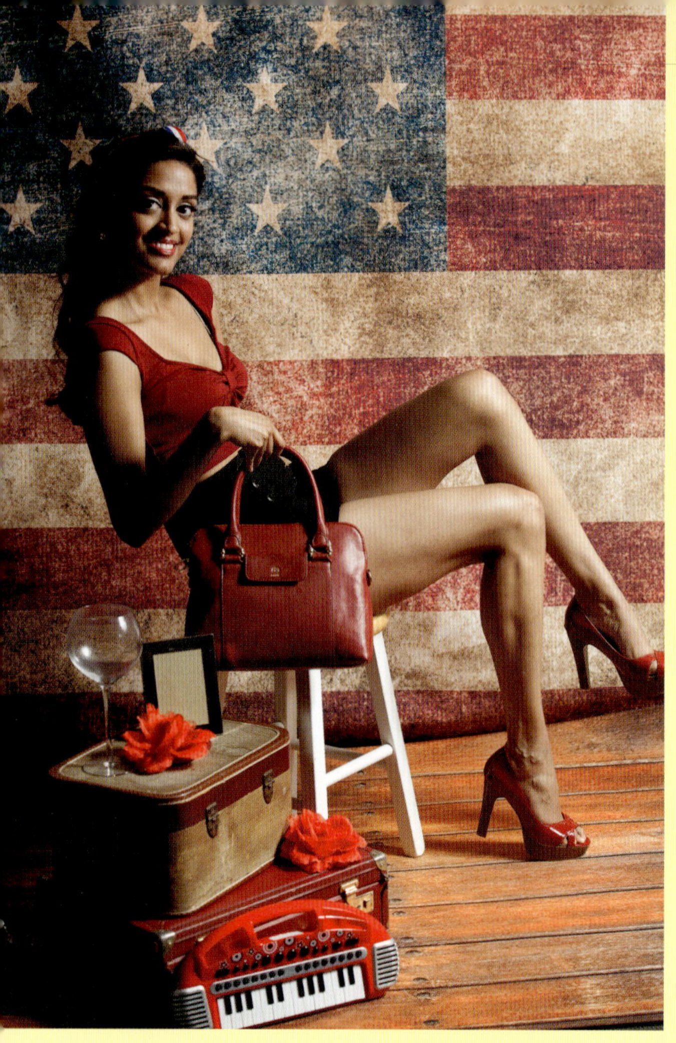

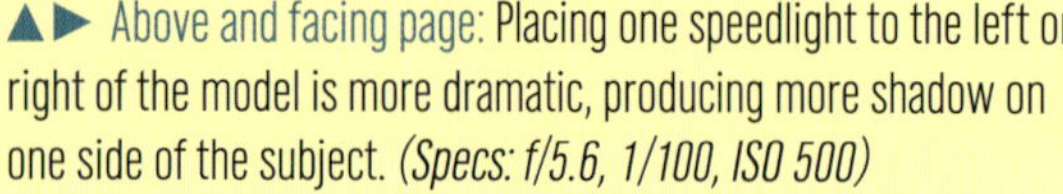

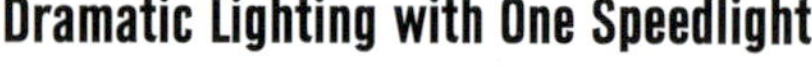

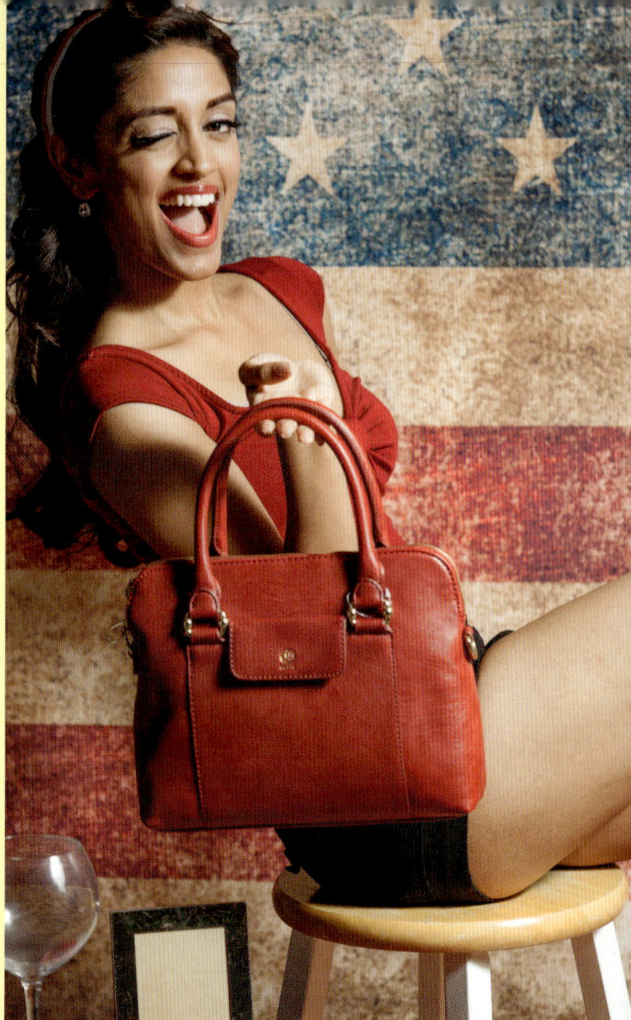

▲▶ Above and facing page: Placing one speedlight to the left or right of the model is more dramatic, producing more shadow on one side of the subject. (*Specs: f/5.6, 1/100, ISO 500*)

Dramatic Lighting with One Speedlight

As stated above, you can shoot with just one straight-on speedlight bouncing into an umbrella for an evenly lit look, but the images will be more dramatic if you position the light off center (relative to the subject). For the images above, I created some images using one speedlight in a reflective umbrella—and I didn't have to move anything I'd set up for the two-light images in the previous sequence.

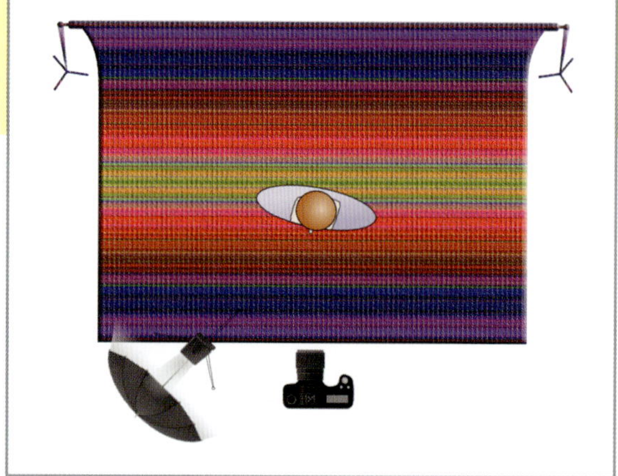

I simply turned one light off to get a more dramatic effect with more shadow on one side of the image.

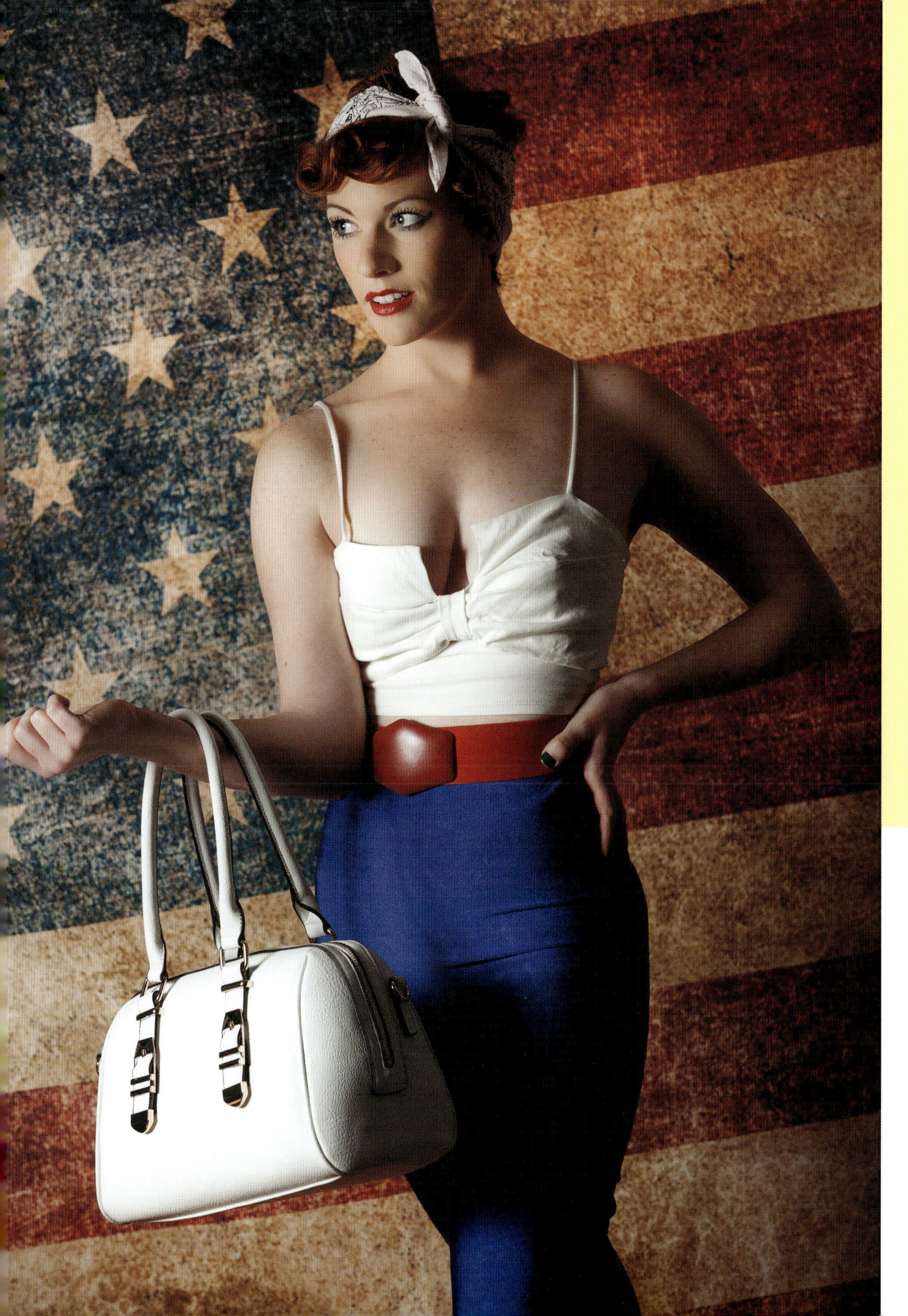

Adding a Snoot

There are a number of speedlight modifiers on the market designed to narrow the flash beam and produce a spotlight effect. For these images, I used a Rogue FlashBender by ExpoImaging. This device bends around the flash like a tube, restricting the output to a point of light. You can also make snoots out of Blackwrap foil—or, really, any material that can be formed into a long tube and attached to the front of your flash. The trick is to use something that makes the light directional and does not let light out of the sides.

In the image below, you can see that the snoot can be used to pinpoint and light one part of the subject. In this case, it was mostly the face. The closer the light is to the subject, the smaller the circle of light will be and the less area it will cover. The farther away it is, the more the light will spread and cover a wider area of the subject and the set.

Once you have it set up, experiment with repositioning the light or the model to illu-

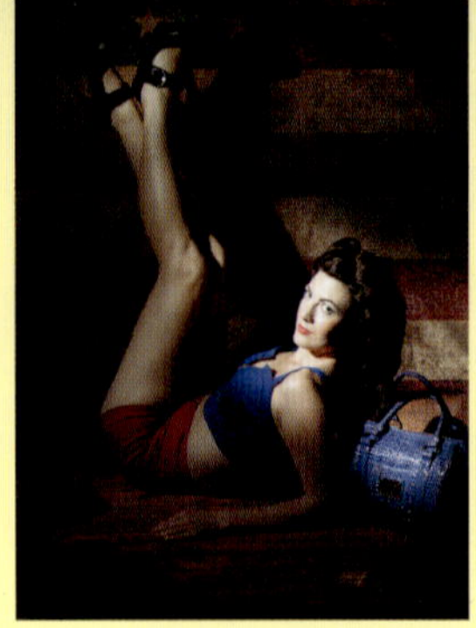
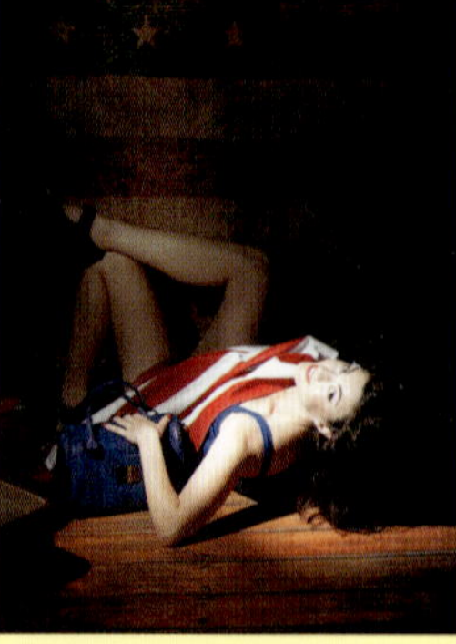
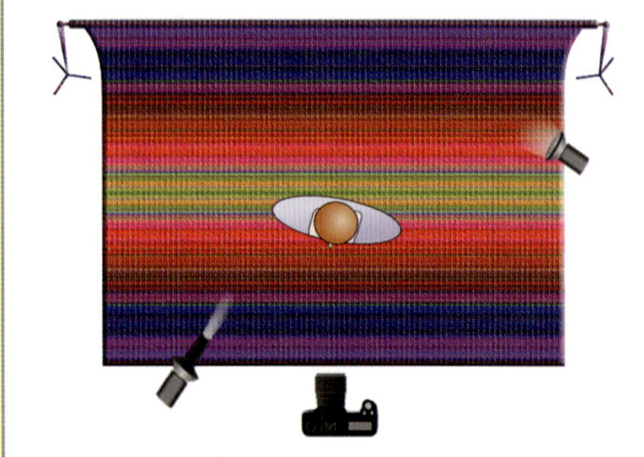

▲▶ Above and facing page: Moving either the snooted light or the model will illuminate different parts of the subject and the set. (Specs: f/7.1, 1/200, ISO 500)

minate different parts of the subject and set. For the images in this section, the snooted speedlight was placed about four feet from the subject to light only a small part of her. However, I also wanted to see the flag design on the backdrop just a bit more than was possible with the snoot light alone. To accomplish this, I added another flash with a circular grid, on a very low setting, close to the backdrop and off to camera right. It looks as if the snooted key light is bleeding onto the background and the model's legs, but this is actually the effect of the second light. While the background is still relatively dark, the patriotic feel of the images (important to an editorial image in telling the story) is still very apparent.

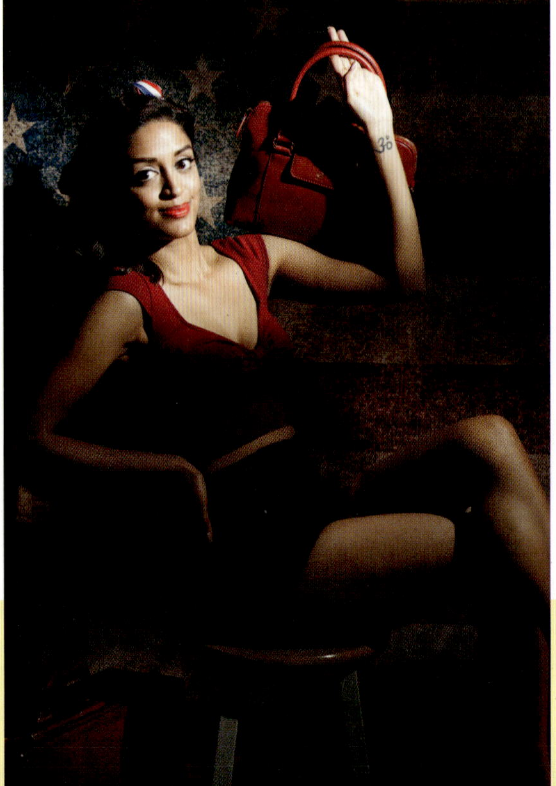

◀ Adding a snoot to the flash lets you pinpoint the light on one part of the subject.

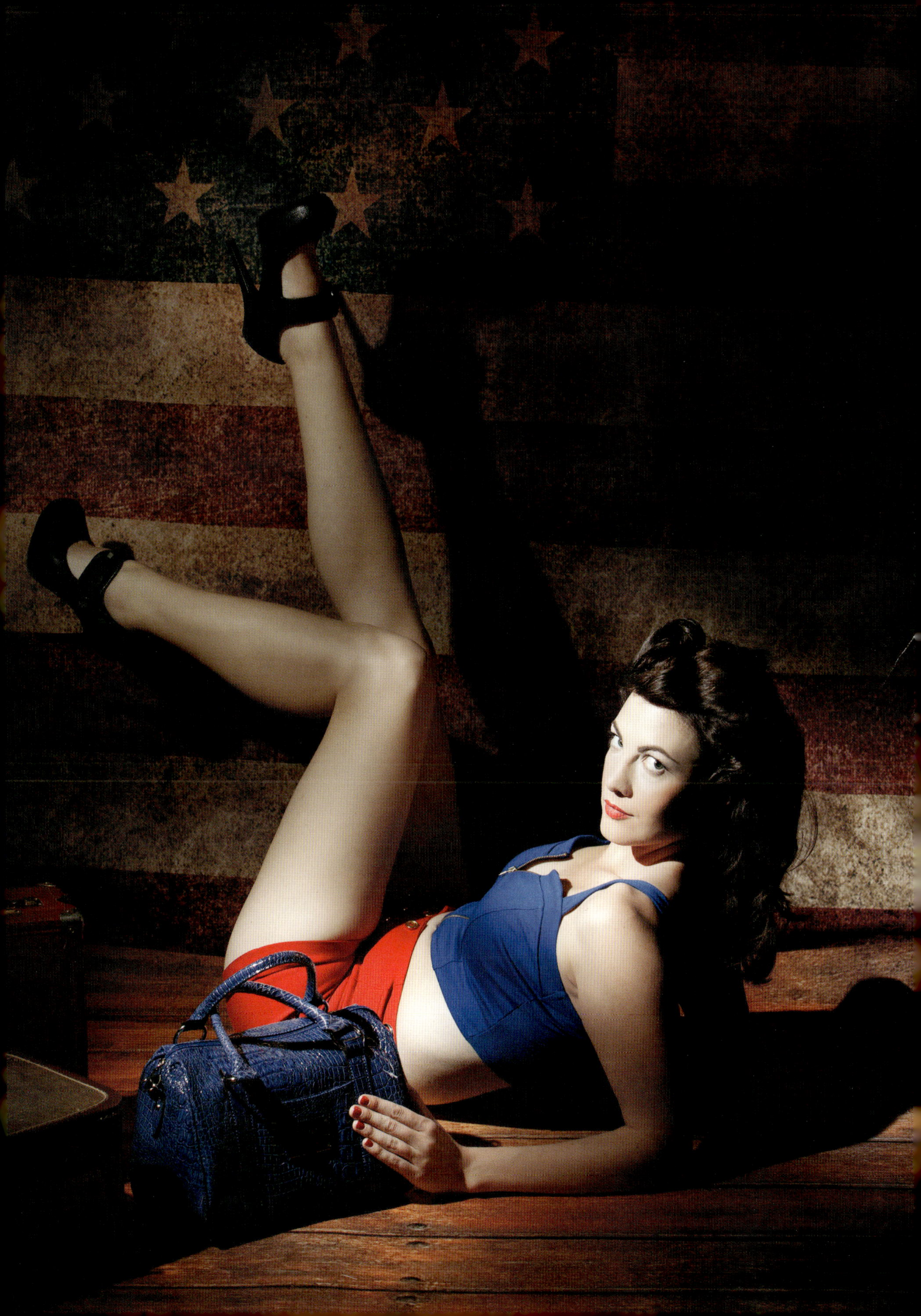

Backlighting

Yes, you can use your speedlights to backlight subjects for silhouettes or to improve the separation between the subject and the background.

Lighting Setup

The left image (below) shows the scene and model with only the backlight. The speedlight, fitted with a circular 40 degree Rogue Grid by ExpoImaging, was placed on the floor and pointed slightly up toward the model's lower back. The effect I wanted here was for the backlight to be the stronger light in the photo. The circle of light visible on the background is simply the result of light bouncing back from that speedlight through the circular grid.

To light the front of the model, I added another speedlight with a mini softbox modifier (bottom, right). This was dialed down so that it added just a bit of fill; I did not want it to overpower the backlight. The settings are the same for both images (the backlight was set at ½ power and the front fill was at ¼ power). The only thing that changed was the addition of a front fill light.

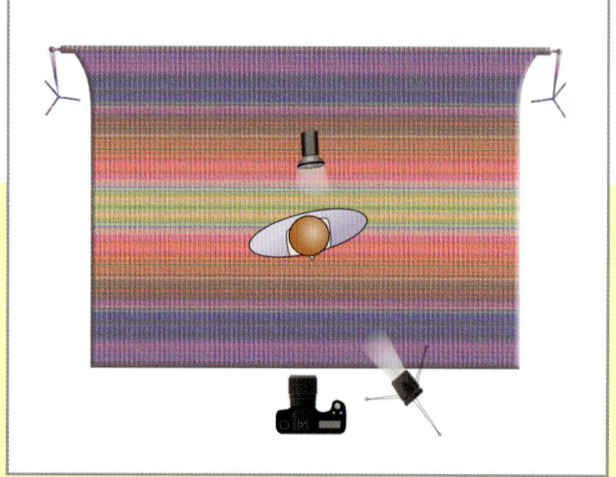

▼ Left: Here's the image with the backlight only. I used a Rogue Grid by ExpoImaging on my speedlight. *(Specs: f/5.0, 1/125, ISO 800)*

▼ Right: For this shot, I added a little fill light to the front. *Makeup by Andrea Yocky. (Specs: f/5.0, 1/125, ISO 800)*

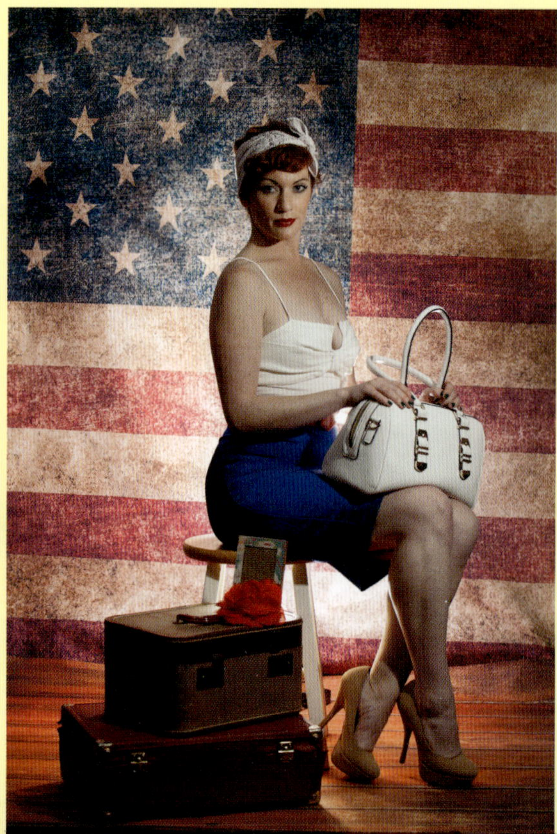

Posing and Composition Refinements

Let's talk about the pose. In the previous image, the bag on her lap (cutting through her midsection) and the sideways pose made her look a little wide in the hips. The cropping of the photos is dead-on and centered. This is okay, but it did not thrill me.

For a better look, I asked the model to turn her upper body more toward the camera and put the bag down so that it was not blocking her waist. I also asked her to cross her back leg over the front and keep that leg up a bit off the knee, so as not to squish her upper thigh. Finally, I had her lift the heel on her bottom foot. Better, right?

Once the pose was refined, I experimented with tilting the camera to create some movement and make the images more eye-catching. I also worked with some differences in her head tilt and cropping off the top of her head just a little. Cropping tight off the top brings the viewer's eye lower on the frame. Do you notice that the bag becomes more central to the image when the head is cropped? Along with the backlight shining through right next to the bag, it really

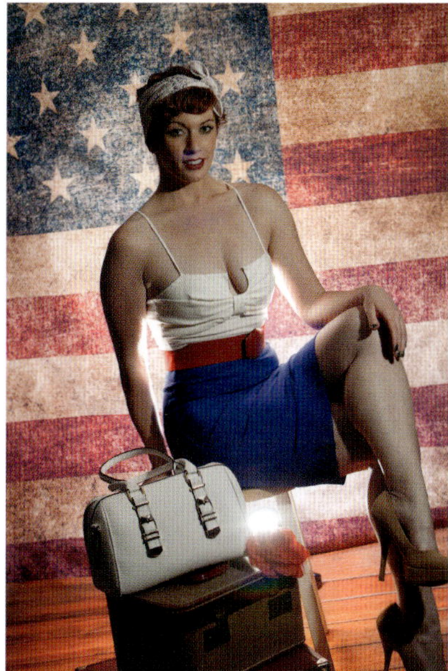
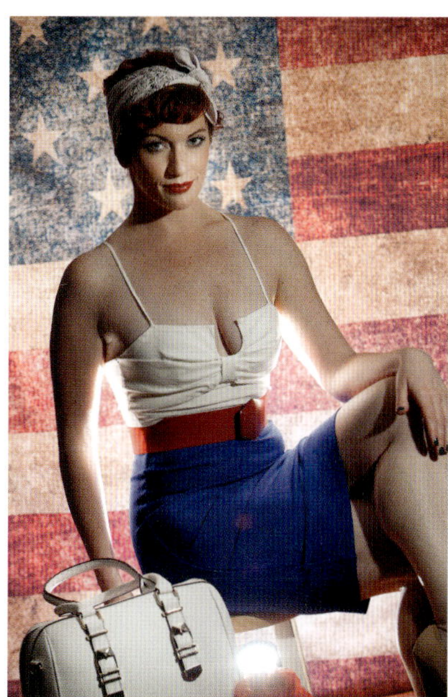

▲ Better posing that flatters the model—and a tilt of the camera for movement. *(Specs: f/5.0, 1/125, ISO 800)*

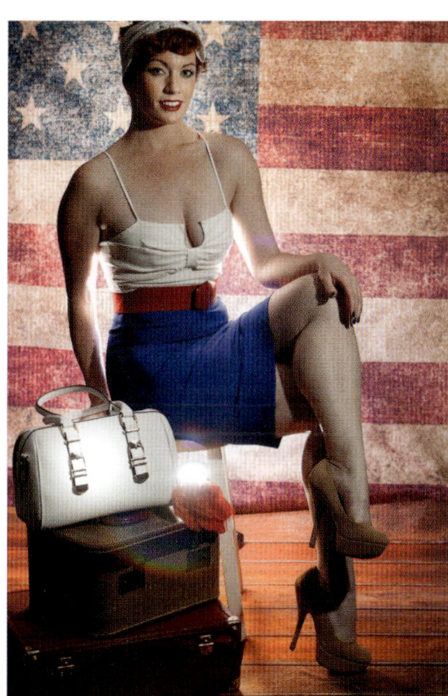
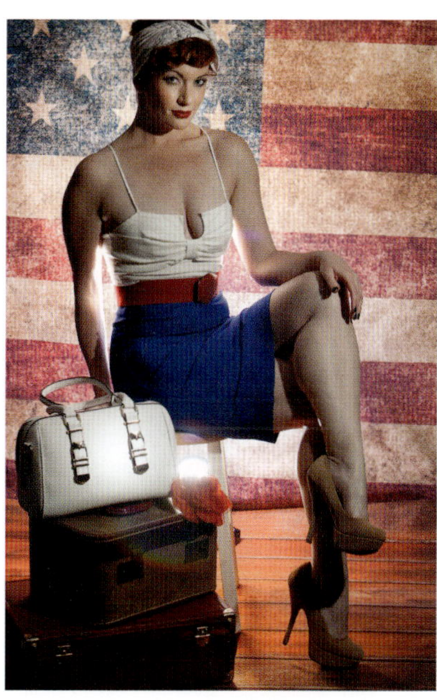

▲ Cropping tight off the top brings the viewer's eye lower on the frame. Do you notice the bag being more central to the image with the head cropped? *(Specs: f/5.0, 1/125, ISO 800)*

tells the story in an editorial way. (*Note:* Do be careful when copping off the top part of the head like this; it doesn't always work. A crop like this can easily become bad photography.)

Dragging the Shutter

Dragging the shutter means using a shutter speed that is *longer* than what is required to record the burst of light from your flash. During that extra time the shutter remains open, any continuous light sources in the scene will continue to record in the image. There are so many fun images that can be made by slowing down your shutter speed to create lighting effects. You can even keep your flash right on top of your camera and get these effects.

To create the image below, I began with the setup used at the start of the chapter; I had two flashes bouncing into umbrellas set in front of the subject, on either side. I then added extra twinkle lights (a continuous light source) to the background and shot at a shutter speed of $\frac{1}{6}$ second and f/5.6 at ISO 400. The wider f-stop helped bring in more of the ambient light from the twinkle lights, but the key here was the slow shutter speed. I had the model swing her purse around to show movement and I handheld the camera. Super-sharp clarity was not my intent, so a tripod was not needed. What I wanted was to show movement and a little blur. Looking closely at the blue skirt you can see a blurred shadow image of the purse.

> **Dragging the shutter means using a shutter speed that is *longer* than what is required to record the burst of light from your flash.**

For a second effect, check out the images on the facing page. Here, the shutter was slowed even further—to $\frac{1}{3}$ second—and I used the zoom on my lens during the exposure. Having additional lights in the photo, such as twinkle lights, is the key here. There needs to be a source visible in the frame of the photo to make those streams of light. To do this effect, zoom the barrel of your lens all the way out and manually focus on the subject. Then, at the same time as you press the shutter button (or just a heartbeat after, depending on your gear), quickly zoom the lens back to the wide position. It will take a little practice to get the timing right and to get the right shutter speed for your light settings. I find it usually works somewhere between $\frac{1}{2}$ and $\frac{1}{5}$ second. Note that doing this outside in the daylight is probably not going to work because there is too much ambient light.

▼ A wider f-stop helped bring in more ambient light from the twinkle lights, but the key here was a slow shutter speed.

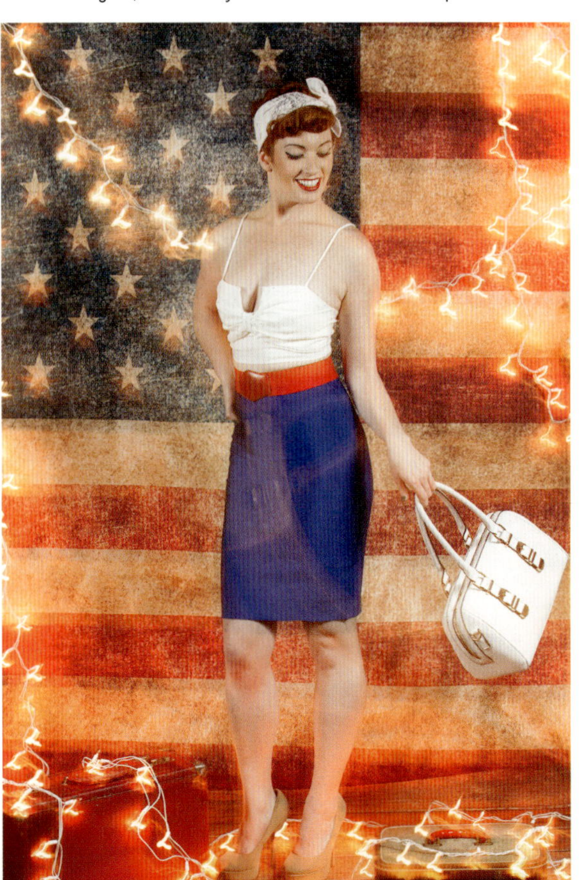

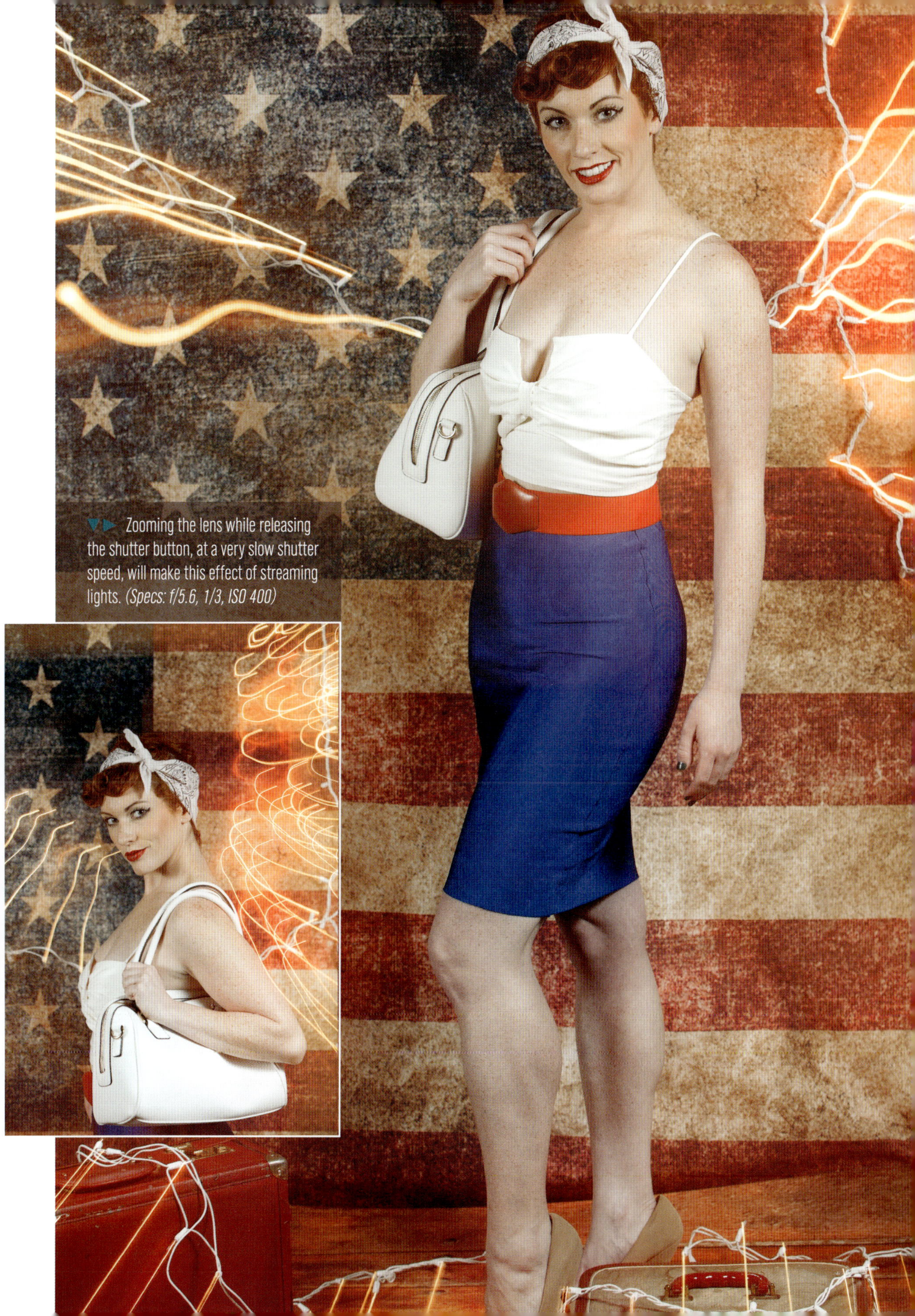

Zooming the lens while releasing
the shutter button, at a very slow shutter
speed, will make this effect of streaming
lights. (Specs: f/5.6, 1/3, ISO 400)

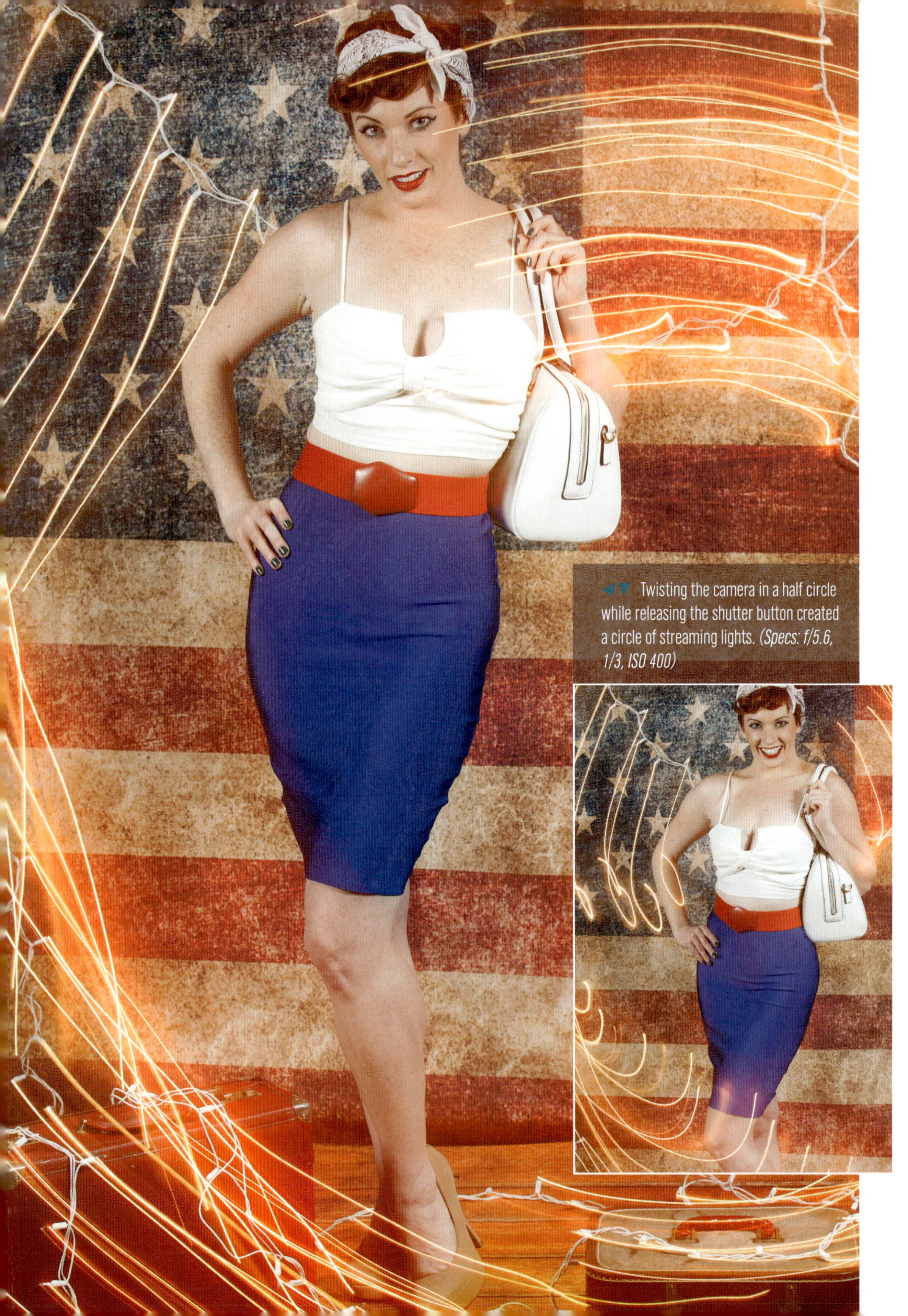

Twisting the camera in a half circle while releasing the shutter button created a circle of streaming lights. (Specs: f/5.6, 1/3, ISO 400)

The images on the facing page show another version using camera movement to create streams of light. The settings are the same—but instead of zooming the lens, I pressed the shutter button and quickly twisted the camera from a vertical position to just past horizontal. I kept the camera moving until I heard the shutter close. As in all these camera-movement examples, notice that your eye still goes to the handbag, so this look could work well in an editorial piece. Additionally, the streaks of twinkle lighting are reminiscent of fireworks and really ramp up the Fourth of July theme when paired with the American flag backdrop.

Location Lighting

Now that we have covered a number of effects that look like studio lighting with off-camera speedlights, let's look at how you can use speedlights in a similar fashion when shooting on location. (There's more on outdoor lighting in the next chapter, too.)

The images to the right and on the next page have a very high-fashion, dramatic look to them. These were shot on location at around 3:30PM in an area that is like a corridor. This exterior space only had natural light coming in from overhead and bouncing in from each end of the

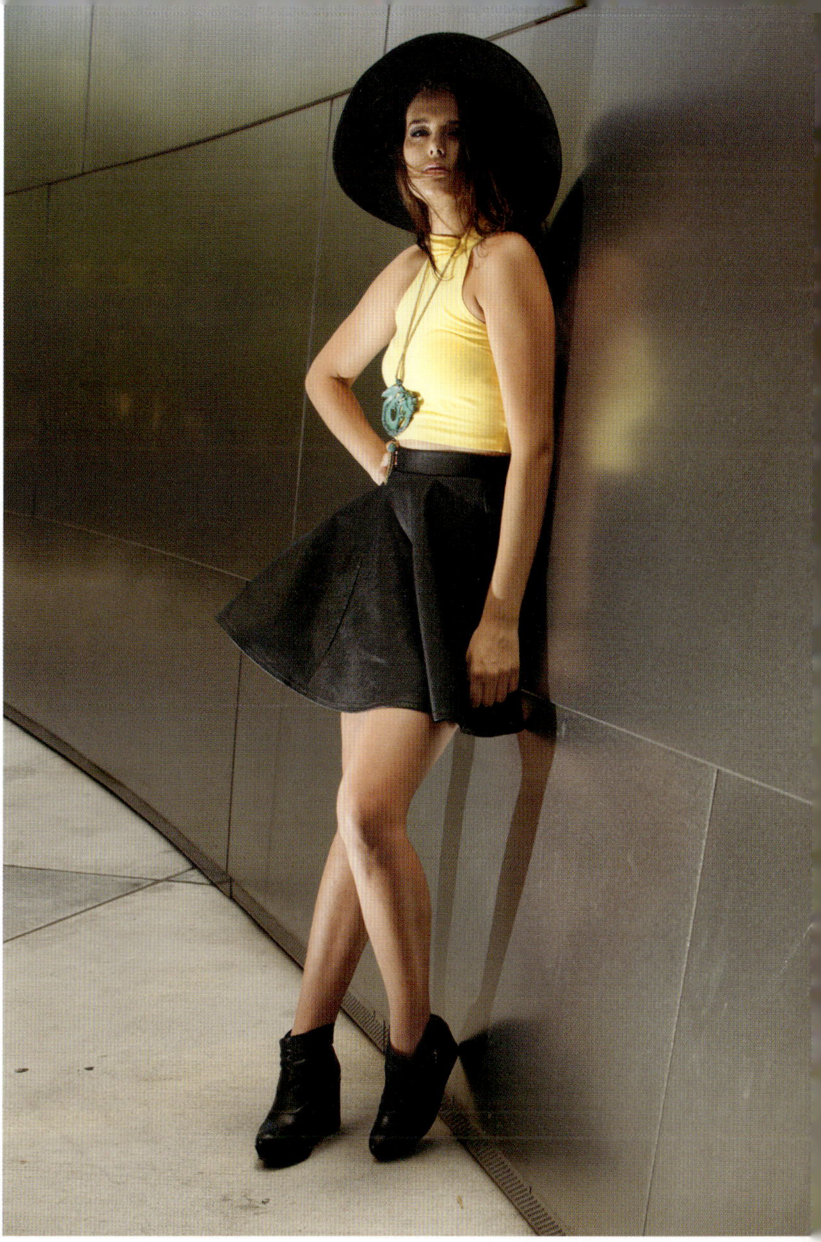

▶ Top: Shooting at an exterior location with off-camera flash at 1/4 power. *(Specs: f/6.3, 1/160, ISO 160)*

▶ Bottom: The speedlight setup for these images.

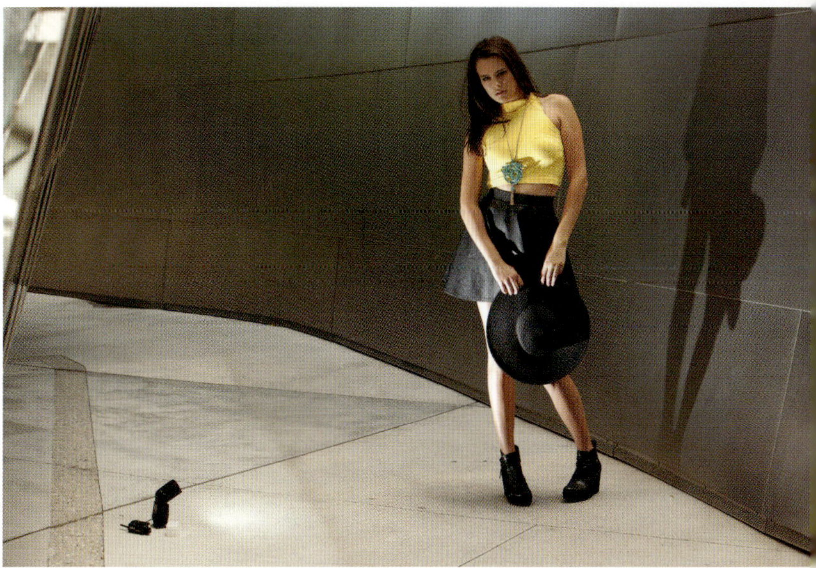

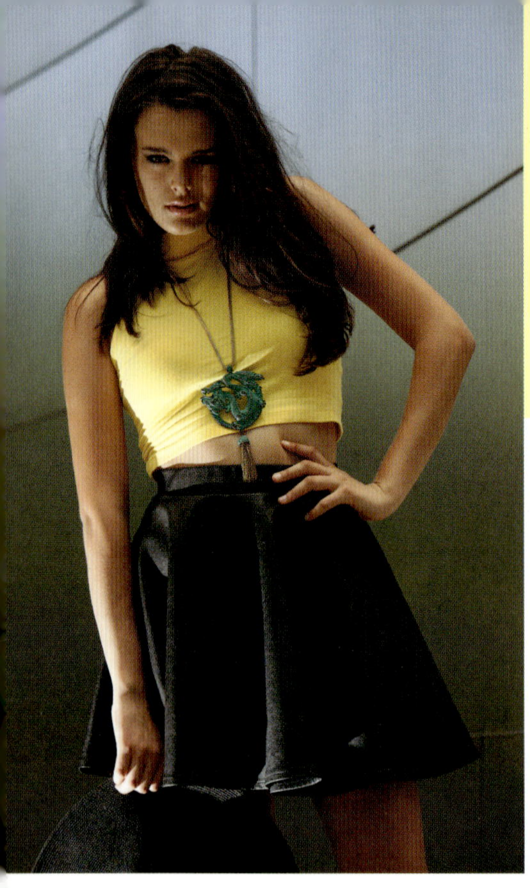

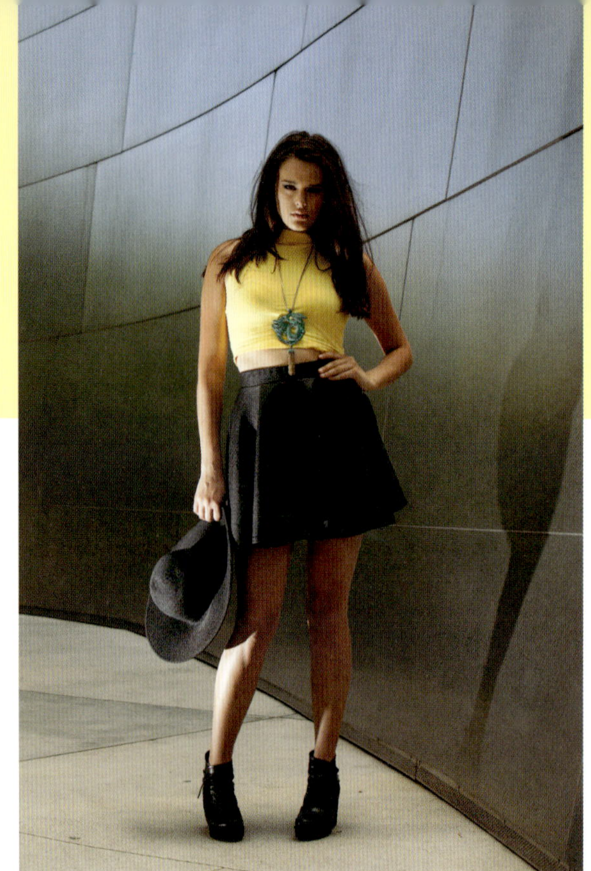

corridor. So, mostly, we were in shadow—in the even, diffused light that was bouncing off the reflective sides of the building. It was pretty, but it wasn't very dramatic. To pump it up, I added a speedlight on the ground, directing it up toward the model. I triggered it with my radio slaves for quite a different look—and one that is much more editorial.

For a few more images (one example is on the facing page), I wanted the light to be directed into the model's face from eye level, rather than from below. I simply had one of the other models hold the flash up as if it were on a light stand.

Need More Power?

The possibilities are really endless when it comes to using speedlights. If you need more power, you can group two or three flashes together on a bracket and bounce them into one umbrella. The most common use is a three-way flash bracket that comes fashioned with an umbrella holder. You can also use the multiple flash brackets with softboxes made for speedlights. And, of course, you can use the speedlights bare.

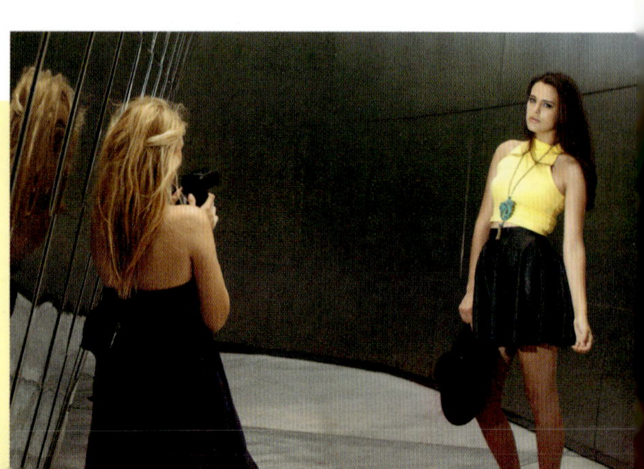

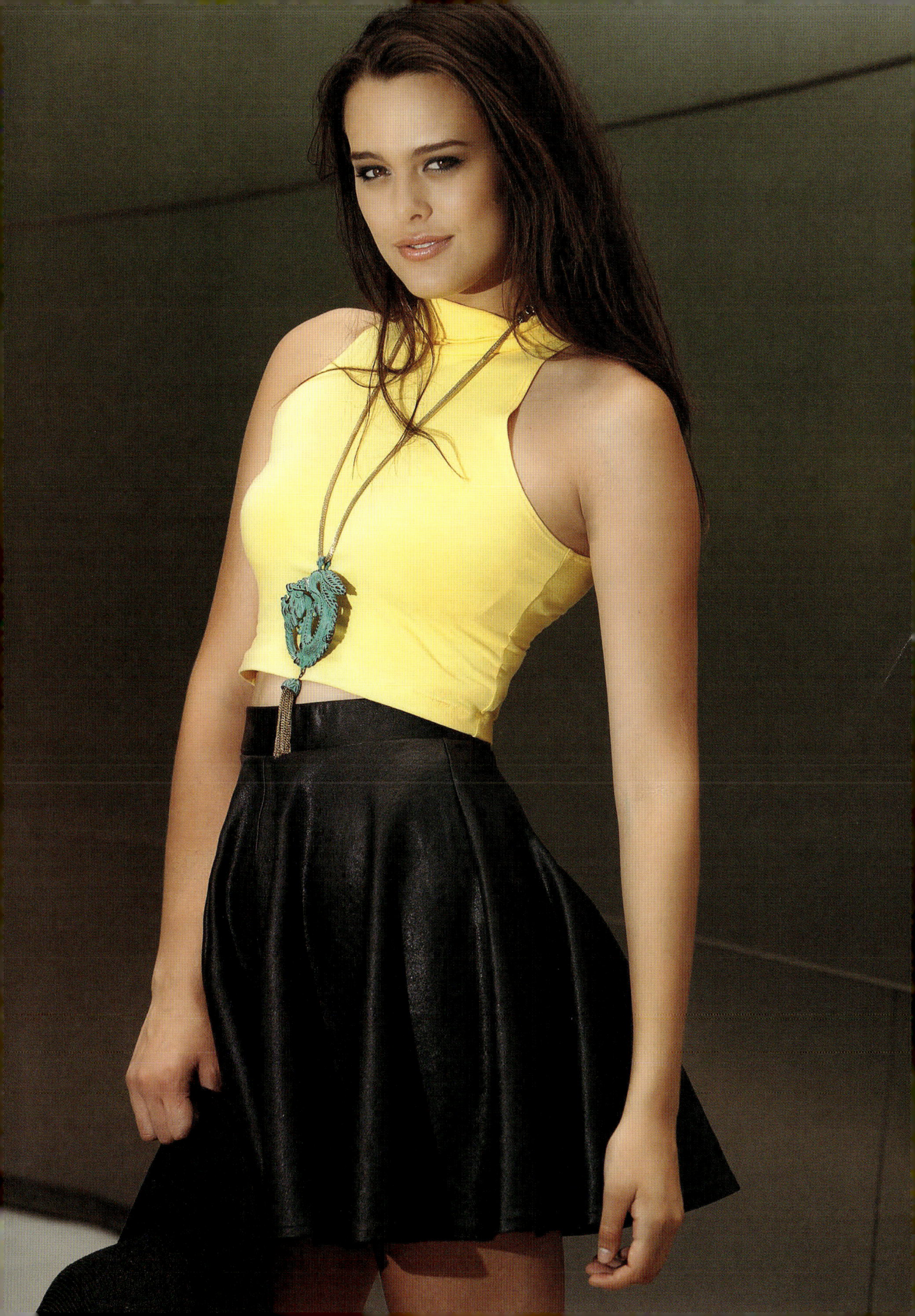

8. Outdoor Images

Very often, photographers find themselves shooting outside on location during daylight hours. There are many factors to deal with on a location commercial shoot, such as the existing light from the sun, shadows, wind, rain and other environmental factors—not to mention city permits. I'm not going to go into the logistics of permits; I will assume you are doing a small-budget shoot at a location where you have permission to be. Keep in mind, however, that if you are performing a commercial photography shoot for monetary gain, most public and private areas *will* require a shooting permit. Consulting the property owner well in advance of the shoot is the best way to ensure you have the right permissions and any needed documents.

Plan—But Be Prepared to Improvise

A major thing to remember is that the longer you are shooting, the more the lighting will change. The sun will move from lower in the sky to higher and then down again for sunset. Clouds can form and move across the sky. Shadow positions and intensities will change. Therefore, it's advisable to plan a test shoot at the location, during the time of day you anticipate scheduling your session. Even so,

you must also be prepared to make lighting adjustments on the fly.

Overpowering the Sun
Ferris Wheel Fashion

The idea of overpowering the sun is to balance the light on the subject with the light on the background. This does *not* mean placing the subject with the sun hitting their face. That would result in both the subject and background being lit by the sun. (Of course, you can take a photo like this, but often it creates harsh shadows on the face and is not flatter-

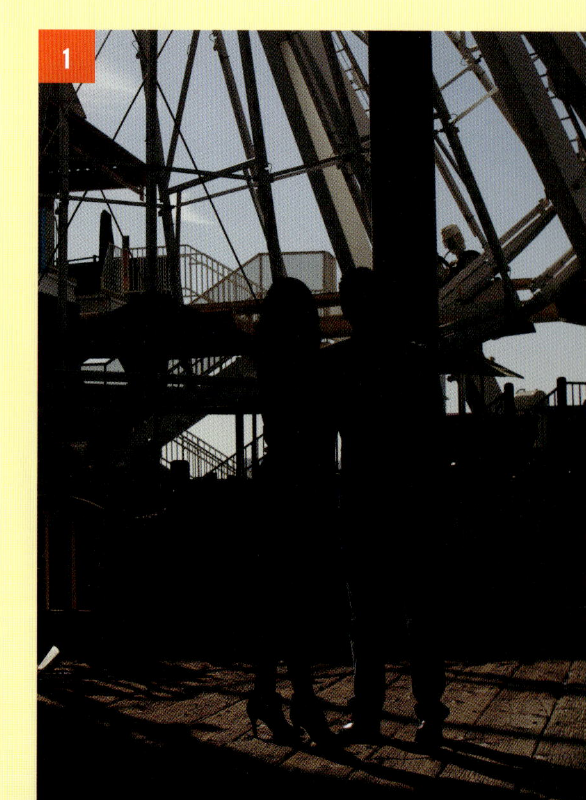

ing.) Instead, what you want is the sun above and behind your subject—so your background is hot and the face of your subject is in shadow.

In this setup, if you took the photo using only the existing sunlight from behind your subject, without adding any light to the front of the subject, you would get one of two results. Result one: If you expose for the background's bright light, the background will be perfectly exposed but the subject will go dark—and your models, in their fabulous designer clothing, will be nothing but silhouettes. Result two: If you expose for your subject's face, your subject will be perfectly exposed, but your background will be overexposed. (Yes, we can see the Ferris wheel in the sample image, but the sky has gone white.)

So what do you do? Put enough light on your subject to match the natural light in the background. You can use this technique with portable strobes, but for the final image in this sequence I used a speedlight held off-camera. To get enough light on the subjects to balance them against the morning sunlight, I pumped up the flash as high as possible (1/1). I also shot with the lowest ISO and smallest aperture and fastest shutter settings I could use without exceeding the camera's flash-sync speed. The

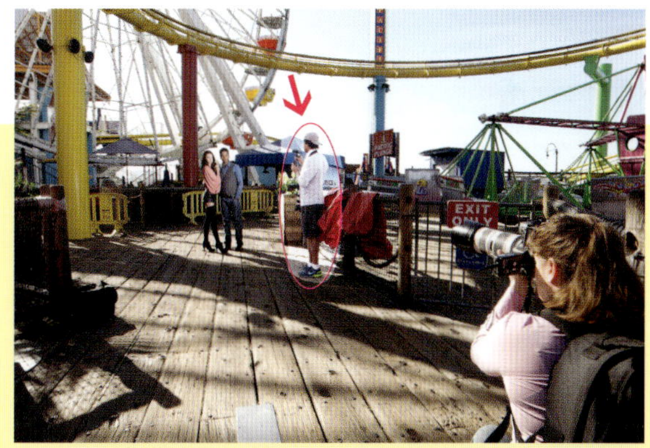

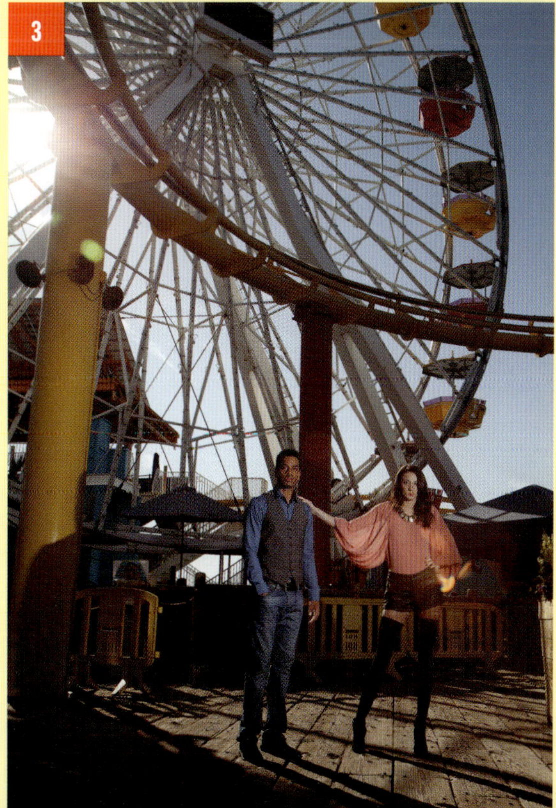

result is a well-balanced photo. Closing down as much as possible minimized the ambient light entering the camera. If I had let more light in, I would have needed more light output from the flash, but it was already maxed out. (*Note:* While most current pro-level flash units have a high-speed sync mode that allows you to close down your shutter more, many strobes do not have this feature and you may only be able to sync at around $\frac{1}{200}$ second.)

Nuts and Bolts

Think about this as if you were shooting in a studio. The first thing you would do is take a light meter reading. So, if you spot-metered for your sunlit background, your reading might be ISO 100 and $\frac{1}{1000}$ second at f/22. If you had a camera and light that would sync at $\frac{1}{1000}$ second, you would be fine—you would just add that much light. Most likely, though, you don't have that much artificial light output. So, here's the cheat. Go ahead and spot meter your background and see what you get so you know where you stand. If the shutter speed you get is over $\frac{1}{200}$ or $\frac{1}{250}$, you know you don't have the sync ability (unless you have a high-speed sync setting on your light). So pump up your artificial light source as high as you can, then take a light reading

of the strobe with the settings on your camera closed down as far as you can get them. That would be something like setting your meter to 100 ISO and $\frac{1}{250}$ second and seeing what f-stop it gives you. We will say it's f/22. Now, set your camera at those settings, turn on your light at full power, and (in most cases) you will be overpowering the sun and you will be able to get that background to pop.

Adding an ND Filter

The image below is another good example of overpowering the sun on the beach. The sky was a little hazy, but I achieved good color and definition in the background by adding light.

▼ I achieved good color and definition in the background by adding light. (*Specs: f/11, 1/200, ISO 100, flash at 1/1 power*)

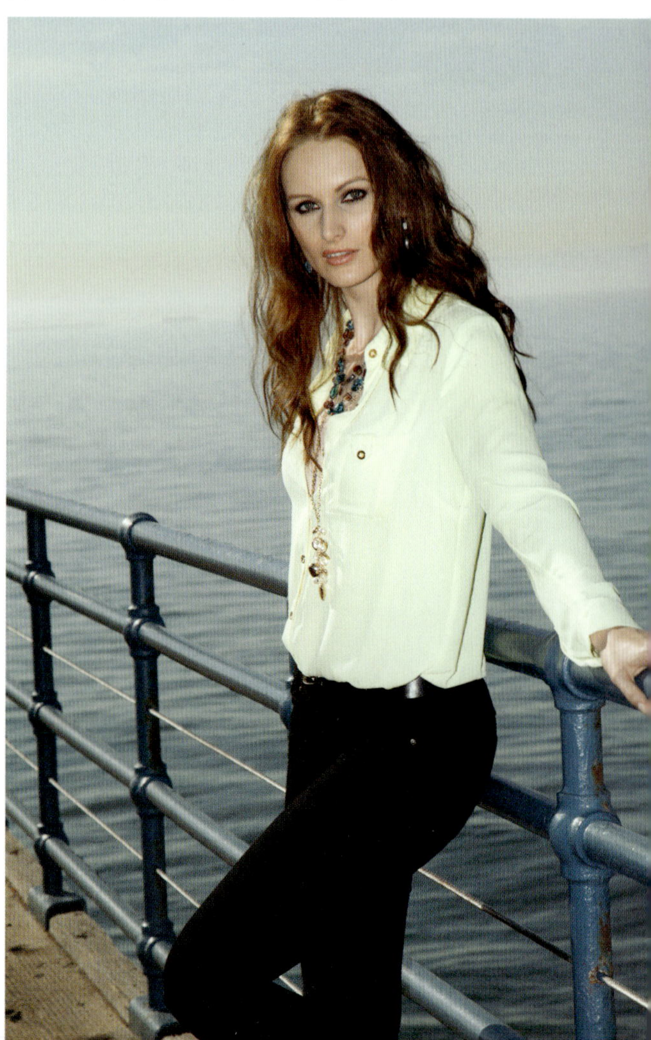

The next image (below) was shot at the same location just a few minutes later—but the settings are quite different. Adding a neutral density filter enabled me to use a lot less

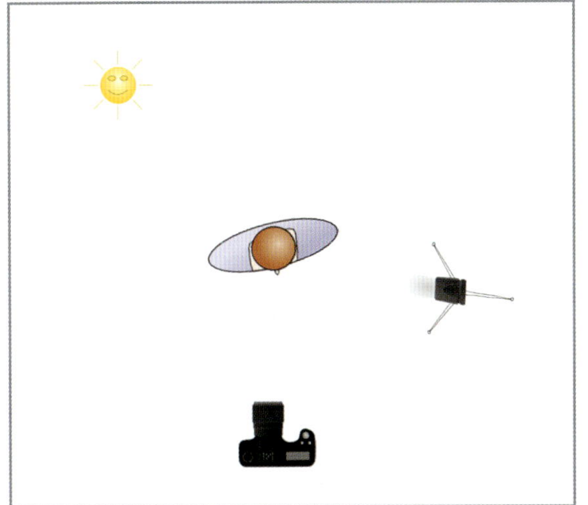

flash to overpower the sun in the photo. Why would I want to do this? Because I wanted to blur out my background and create more compression in the photo by being able to shoot at f/6.3 instead of f/11. (Lower depth of field, with better compression, is often used in fashion photography.) ND filters are designed to cut down the amount of light that comes into the camera, without affecting the color. Depending on the strength of the ND filter, you will lose from 1 to 10 stops. I like what is called an ND8, which gives me a 3-stop loss.

The same technique can be handy if you want some motion blur in your photo. Let's say you want your model to walk by in full sunlight, but you want her blurred without overexposing the image. If your regular read-

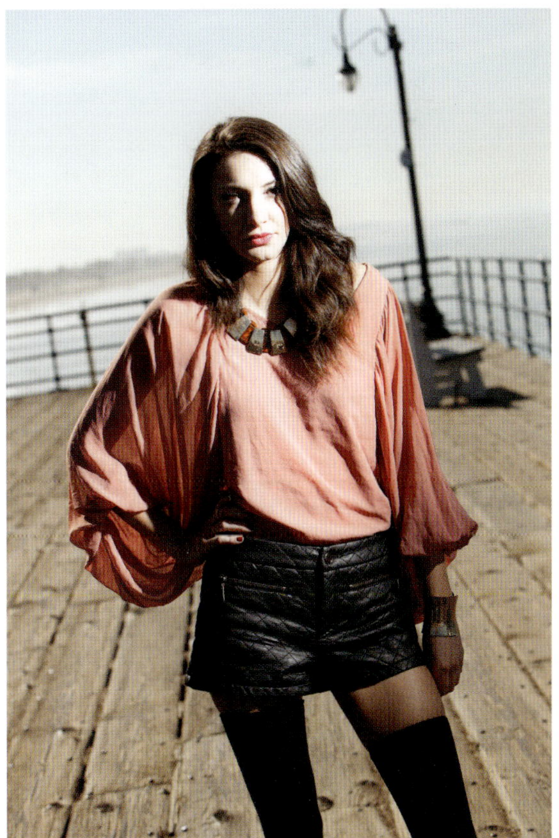

ing without the ND8 filter was at $\frac{1}{250}$ second, adding the ND8 filter would let you shoot at $\frac{1}{30}$ second and capture that motion blur. (If you opened up to $\frac{1}{30}$ second *without* the ND filter, you would seriously overexpose the image and lose a lot of detail.)

If it confuses you, don't get too worried about the math—just know that, for fashion photography at exterior full sun locations, an ND filter is something you can use to create photos with settings that are more wide open, for lower depth of field or motion blur. Yay!

Adding Fill Light

Simply finding a place with white cement and placing your model on top of it can give you fill on location. For the purpose of this exercise, however, we want to look at adding fill ourselves—so we'll again be talking about your subject's face being in shadow with the sun behind or to the side. The best way to add fill is to bounce the sunlight into the subject's face. To do this, you can use a commercially made reflector, a piece of white foam-core board, or any kind of homemade reflector; as long as it reflects the sun, it will work. Be sure to consider the color of the reflector—usually white, silver, or gold. Each will provide a different color and amount of light. Gold is warmer and reflects more light than white. Silver will also reflect more than white, but with more neutral tones. Additionally, the bigger the reflector, the more area it will fill.

The sample photos to the left show the models placed in full shade and the use of a gold reflector to harness the sunlight and bounce it back onto them. The sun was above and slightly to the right and behind the subjects, making it easy to reflect. Simply hold the reflector, pointing up and slightly toward the subject, and adjust it until you can see it reflecting on them. (*Note:* This will not work

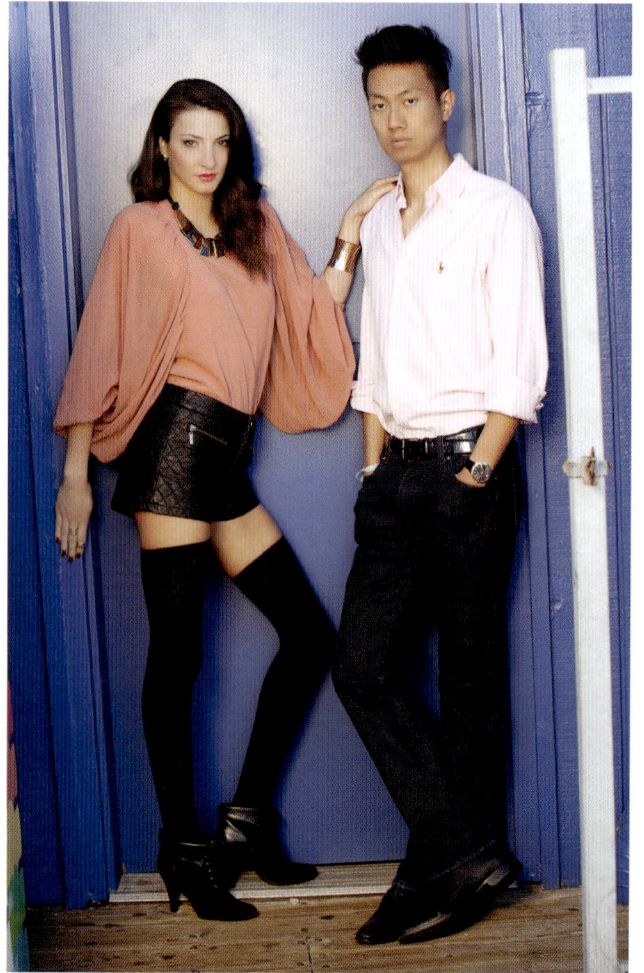

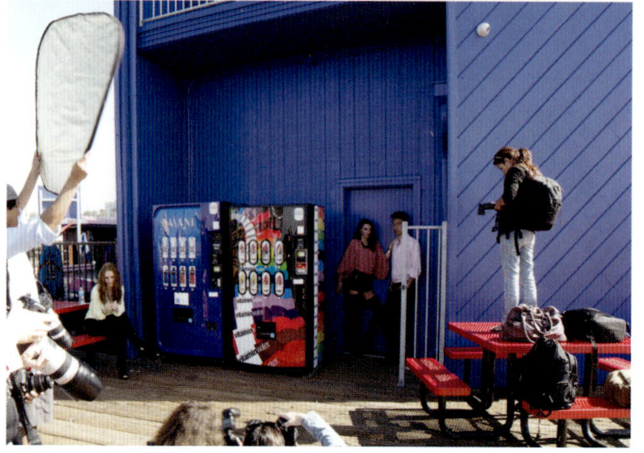

◀ I used a gold reflector for warm fill. Hold the reflector pointing up and slightly toward the subject and adjust it until you can see the light reflecting on them. (*Specs: f/5.6, 1/320, ISO 400) Image by Preston Perkins.*

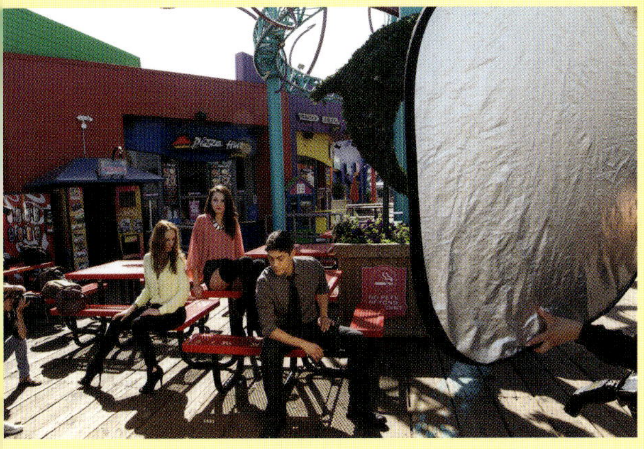 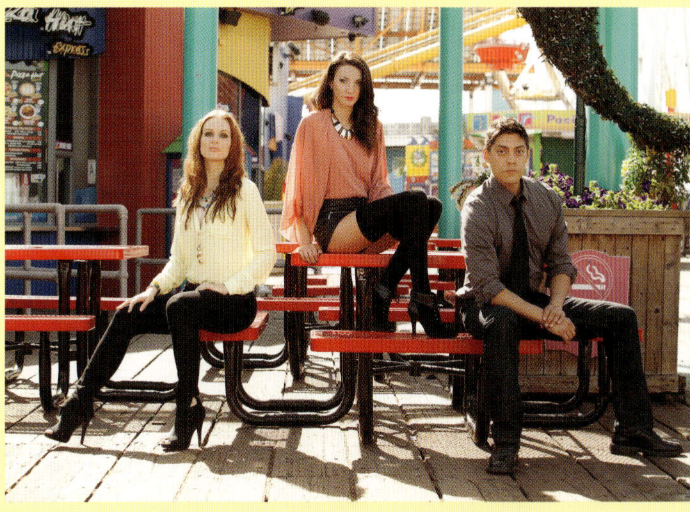

▲▶ Top, left and right: Using reflected fill. *(Specs: f/5.6, 1/500, ISO 400) Setup shot by Preston Perkins.*

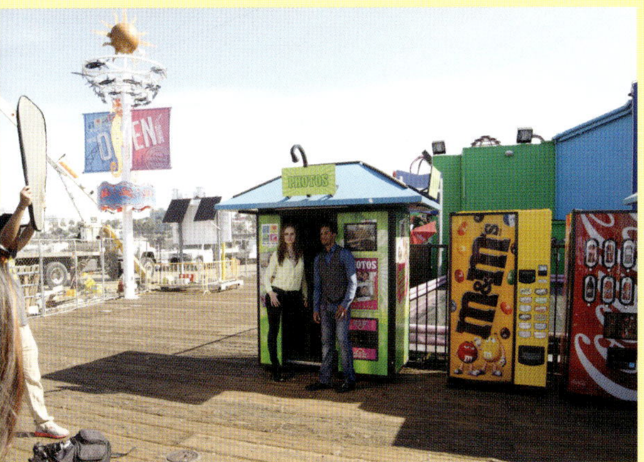 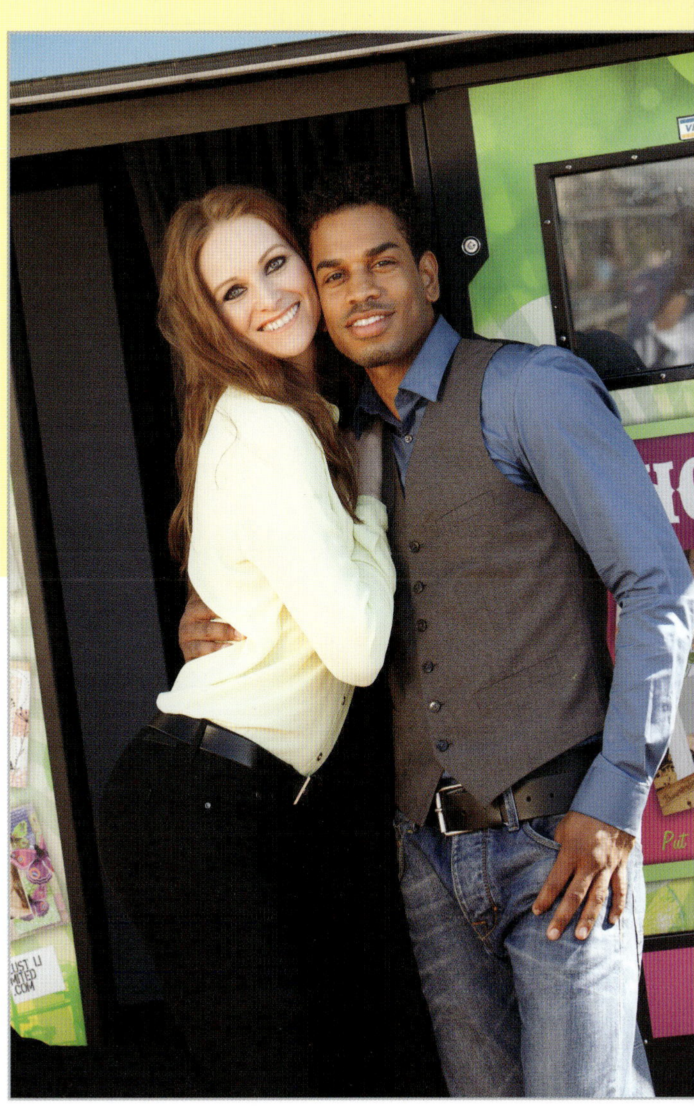

▲▶ Above and right: Using reflected fill. *(Specs: f/5.6, 1/320, ISO 400) Setup shot by Preston Perkins.*

if the sun is behind you, the photographer, because you can't direct your reflector in the correct direction toward the subjects.)

The images on this page are a couple more examples of lighting with a reflector for fill. You can see how the reflector was held in the setup shots that accompany the final images.

In addition to using reflected fill, you can use artificial light to add fill to your images. A diffused flash works great for this purpose. The trick is to not overdo it and create hotspots on the subjects' skin. You just want to fill in a bit.

Using Lens Flare

Lens flare (sometimes called "sun flare") has become a very popular style in lifestyle editori-

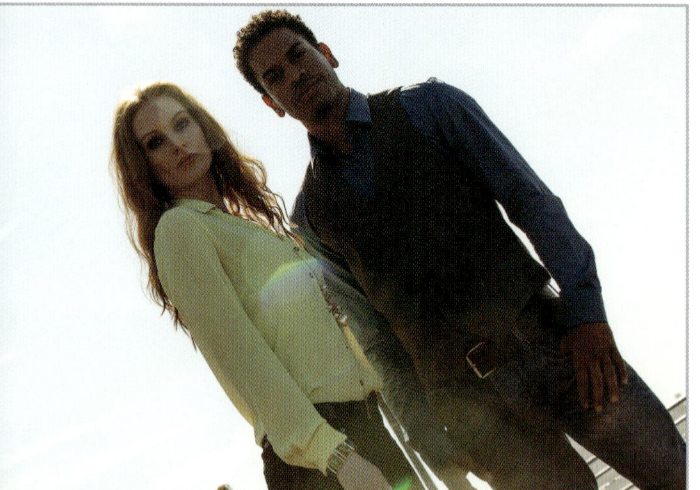

als and even weddings and retail photography. It used to be considered bad photography when the sun ripped across your lens and created flare—but when it's done correctly and intentionally, it can be a really beautiful and artistic style. Still, you should use it sparingly; unless you and your client have discussed *only* having images with this effect, make sure you shoot plenty of images without flare, as well.

The Basics

Lens flare is easy to create and there are no real rules. But here are a couple of hints on getting it to look like you want. First, take off your lens hood. You don't want to shield your lens from the sun; to create flare, you need the sun to be right in your face (oh joy!) and entering your lens directly—meaning it will be behind or a bit to the side and behind your subject. The lower it is in the sky, the easier it is to create this effect. If the sun is high in the sky, you will need to get yourself low and point your camera up toward the sun and your subject. Look for the sun hitting your lens and you will see what pattern it's making. In some cases, you will see little sun-flare circles. If you move your camera more sideways to the sun it may change the effect. The effect will also be different depending on the lens you use.

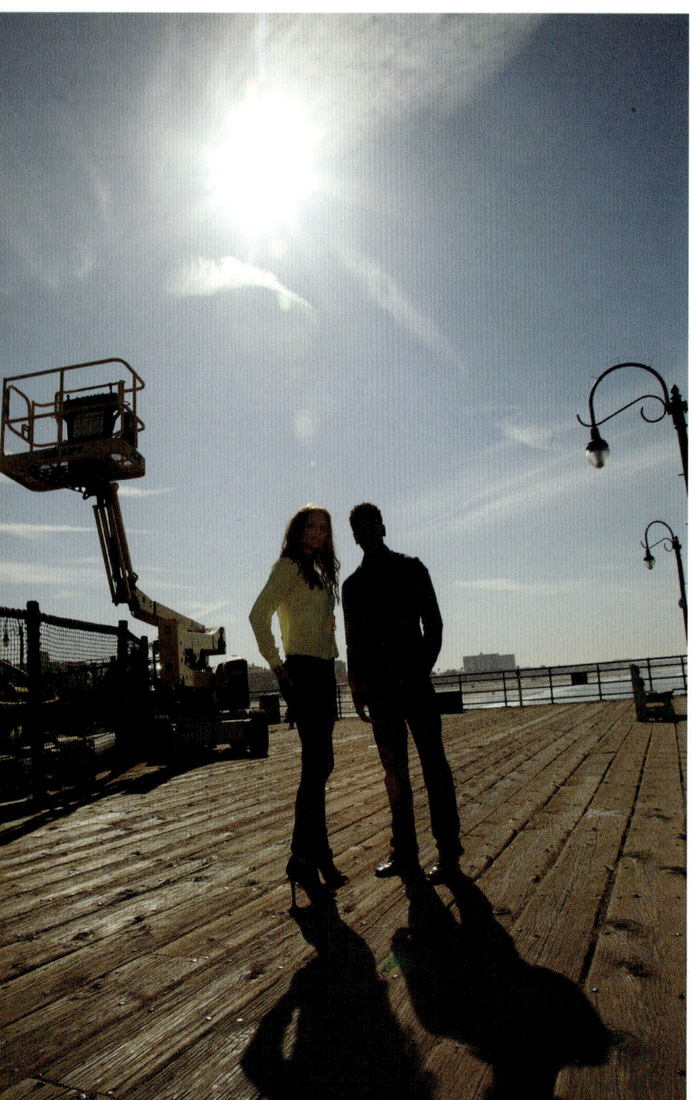

◄ Top: Using a 70–200mm lens, I crouched down low on the ground to get this effect. The sun was very high in the sky and behind my subjects. (Specs: f/10, 1/1000, ISO 400)

◄ Bottom: Here, we are getting more of this spotlight or star effect with the subject silhouetted. (Specs: f/16, 1/200, ISO 100)

Exposure and Camera Position

Exposure will also create different effects. The more you close down, the more your subject will be in shadow and the more of a spotlight effect the sun will make, streaming through toward the lens. For the first image in the sequence on the facing page, I shot at f/10 and $^{1}/_{1000}$ second at 400 ISO and got more of a blown-out, hazy look to the image. For the next image, the settings were f/16 and $^{1}/_{200}$ second at ISO 100, giving me more of a spotlight or star effect with the subject silhouetted.

The next two images (below) show how changing the camera position impacts the effect. The sun did not move down between the couple's faces; I moved so that the sun was directed differently into the lens.

Decisions, Decisions, Decisions . . .

So how do you decide how to expose your lens-flare images? Try it a couple of ways and see what you come up with.

First, expose for your subject without any added flash or reflected light. Take a meter reading for your subject's face in shadow and set your camera for that. This will keep your subject exposed and create more of the hazy or blown-out effect. The flare on the lens will

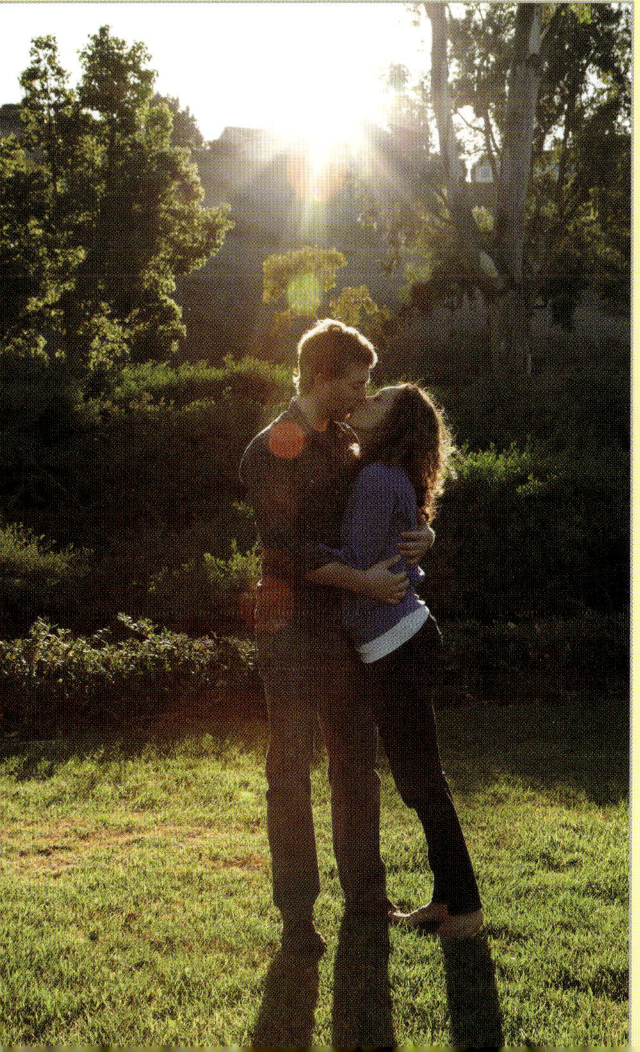

▼ Shooting with the sun higher in the sky, relative to the couple, creates one look. *(Specs: f/11, 1/400, ISO 400)*

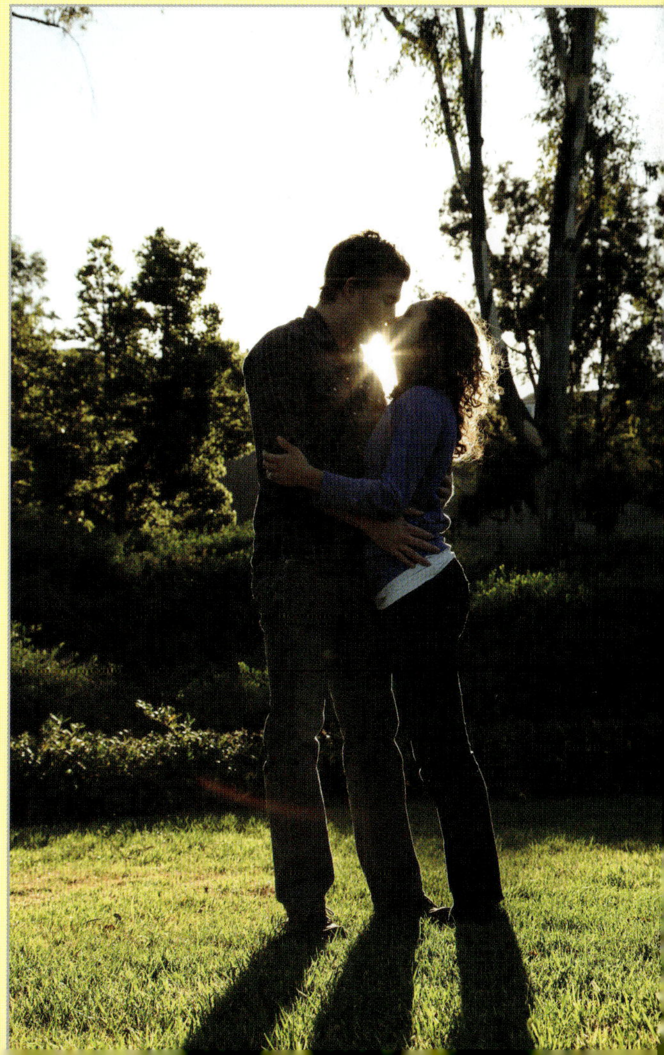

▼ Bending down lower to position the sun between the couple's faces produced an entirely different look. *(Specs: f/8, 1/400, ISO 400)*

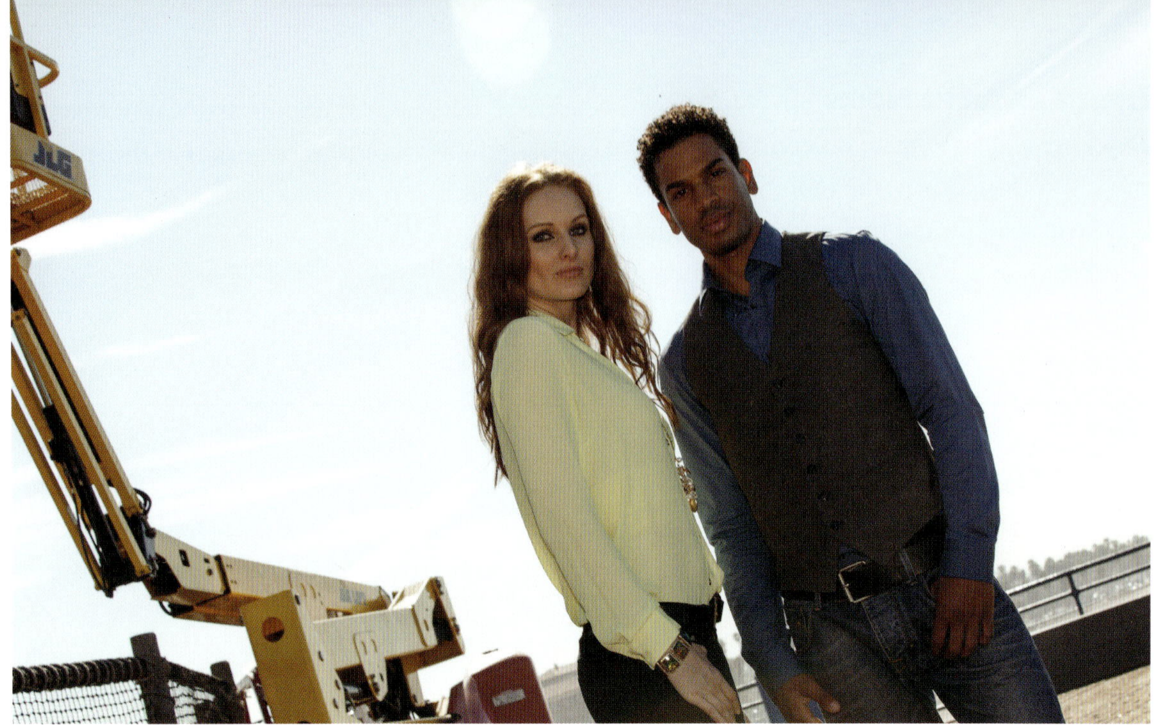

▲ Using flare in combination with flash to overpower the sun. (*Specs: f/11, 1/200, ISO 100, flash at 1/4 power*)

depend on how you angle the camera and how far you are zoomed out. Your lens being set wider will give you a different effect than if it is zoomed out.

Next, try exposing for the sun or stopping down so your subject is in shadow. Take a reading of the background light and set your camera for that. Frame your photos with the sun coming directly into the lens. This will create a look where the subject is in more silhouette, giving you that spotlight or star effect.

Finally, try adding some fill—flash or strobe—to both scenarios. This looks great, especially when you expose for the background. Basically, you are overpowering the sun (as described earlier in the chapter), but with the sun directed into your lens. It's the best of both worlds. Your subjects are exposed correctly, not in silhouette, and you still get that great flare.

Keep in mind that the sun isn't the only source you can use to create images with lens flare. In the next chapter, I'll show you some images I created using flare in the studio.

Sunset and the Golden Hour

In the movie business, we call the time just before sunset the "golden hour" or "magic hour." It's that time when the light is just perfect—golden, soft, and low in the sky so it falls from a flattering direction. The thing to remember about shooting at golden hour is that you have *very little time*. Once the sun is down, the sky may still be colorful but there is no sunlight left to shoot with. When someone

Golden Hour Flare

It is very easy to work on your sun-flare images when the sun is low in the sky like it is at the golden hour. You can easily achieve silhouetted images or hazy, blown-out effects – and work with these looks in combination with some fill light.

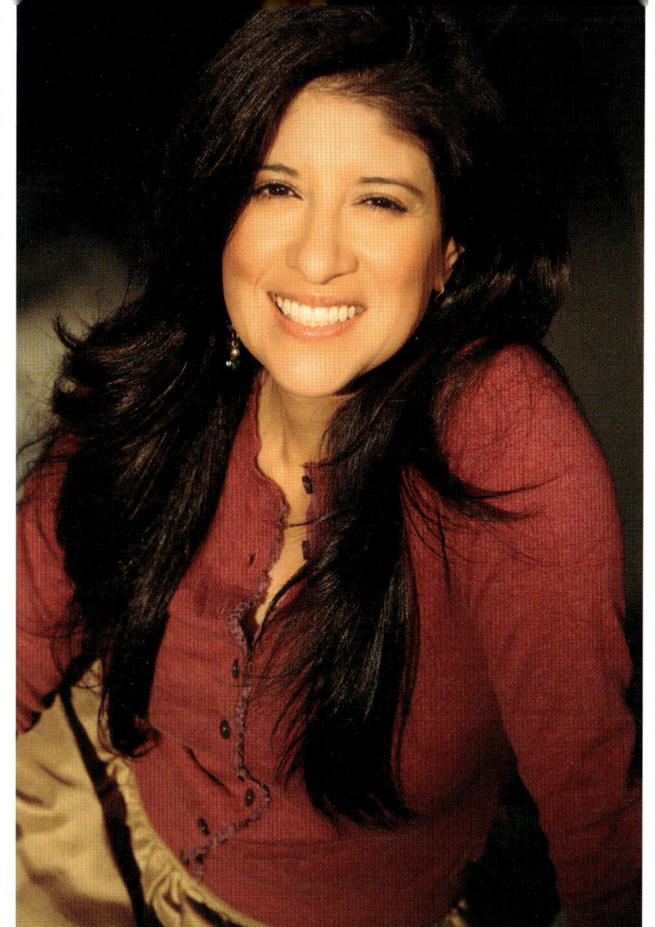

▶ Top: Beautiful golden hour sunlight directly on the face of the subject. *(Specs: f/7.1, 1/640, ISO 400)*

▶ Bottom: No additional light was needed here – just the golden-hour sun over the subject's shoulder. *(Specs: f/6.3, 1/200, ISO 400)*

asks for a sunset shoot, we often start preparing two hours before sunset. We set up and start some shooting well before we get into that short "golden hour" window. Once the sun is gone, it's gone. (I know some of you are thinking, "What about the sunrise golden hour?" Yes, it's the same thing in the opposite direction . . . if you want to get up that early!)

Lighting your subject with the sun directly in their face is incredible at the golden hour. It's the one time of day that the sun is so soft and perfect that you will be missing out if you don't try some images like this. Just put the sun at your back and let it shine on your subject's face. At any other time of day, this would be a big no-no—but it's the best way to shoot golden hour images. And now that your subject is lit with the sun, that means the background is equally lit. Shoot away!

Why is the sun softer and more golden at these times? Well, I don't want to get too technical here, but basically when the sun is positioned low in the sky like this, it has to travel through more of the atmosphere, meaning it's more diffused. It's like nature's own softbox. The image to the right (bottom) is a great example of that beautiful, golden light. There was no additional light needed; the golden hour sun came over the subject's shoulder and there was a little extra bounce from the side of a building.

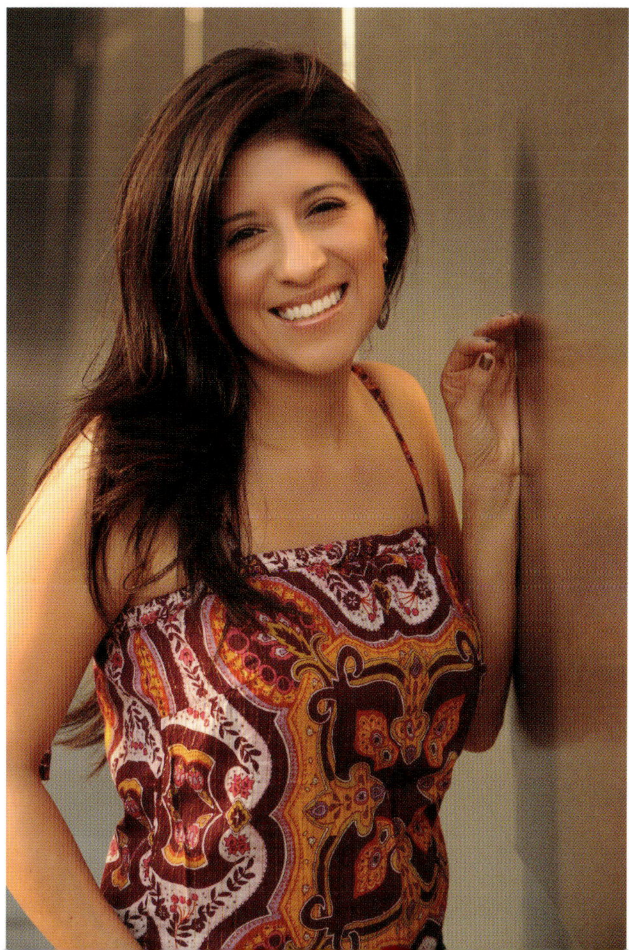

9. Putting It All Together

Key Techniques ▶ Multiple light setups with grids and other modifiers
Application ▶ Models with products; Catalogs

To wrap up the book, let's look at a fun lighting design that combines many of the elements we have discussed in the book—a conclusion to all the lighting designs discussed to keep your creative thoughts flowing. We will apply it to models working with products in such commercial settings as catalogs and lookbooks. This will be a brief chapter to illustrate how endless the potential lighting patterns can be and to draw on what you have learned throughout the book.

Concept

Lets start with the concept. The products for this shoot were a line of candles that come in different colors. I wanted to do something that really incorporated the models with the products, rather than just having them hold the candles. Therefore, I decided to have their hands painted with a latex body paint to make it look like the candle was melting onto their hands—or, perhaps, as though their hands were becoming part of the candles.

I decided I would gel the background light so that each model/candle was in a matching color scheme (so, red for the red candle; yellow for the yellow candle, etc.). I also had the makeup artist match each model's lipstick as closely as possible to the candle and painted hands.

Each of the models had the same makeup, with pale foundation on the skin and white eyelashes, so that it is obvious they go together. We also wrapped each model in sheer cloth of a different pattern, allowing the shoulders to show skin. This ensured that the wardrobe would not distract from the story of the product.

Lighting

This is a three light set-up, and every light has a different modifier. In a clamshell setup, a large beauty dish with a diffusion sock acted as the key light. This was set slightly off-center with a silver reflector underneath. I used silver, rather than gold, so the colors would not shift. The strobe lighting the background was bare, but fitted with a gel of the specific color needed to coordinate with the model and candle.

The hair light had a 40 degree grid. Looking at the photos in this chapter, you can see that I frequently changed the position and

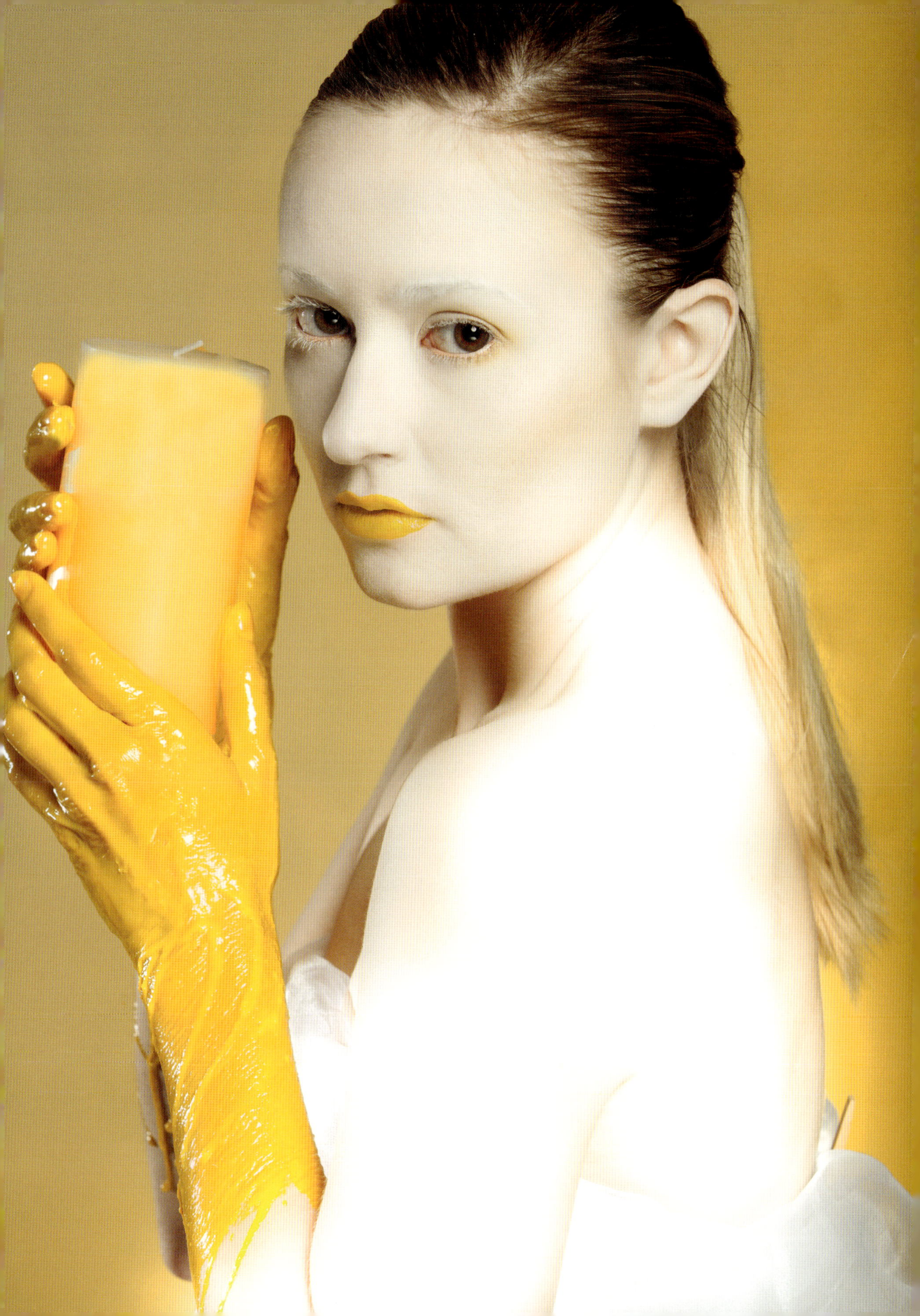

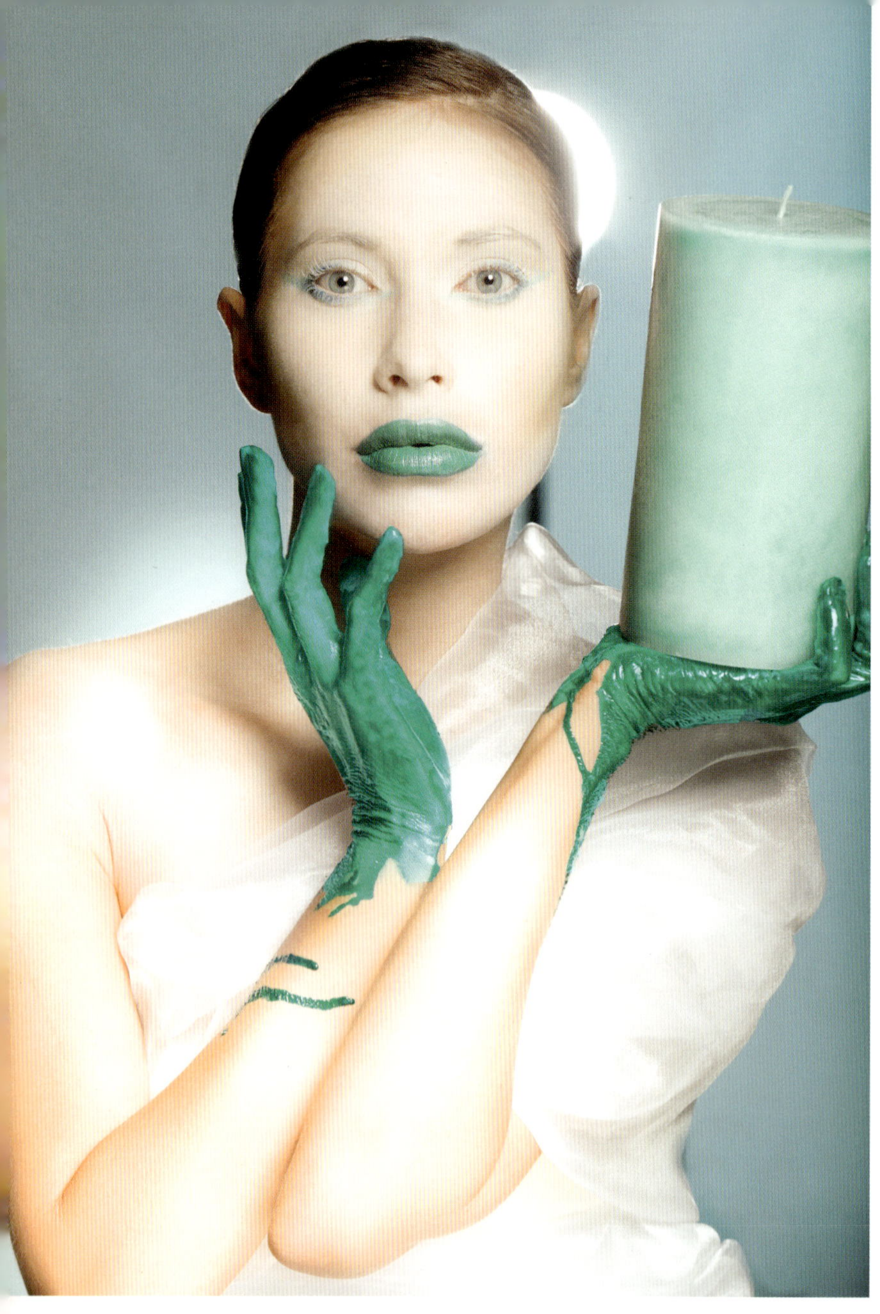

look by adjusting my camera position to allow only some of the light to flare through.

There are a couple of things to notice about these images. The key light beauty dish was slightly off center to camera right, so the left side of the model's face is a little darker, creating more shadow on that side of the face. I also added two large black flags, on either side of the model, to help add shadow and definition in the cheekbones (for more on negative fill, see chapter 6). The black flags also helped to prevent spill from the colored gel on the background. Although the flare from the backlight created a bit of a glow around the model, I added a bit more of a white glow to the skin in postproduction.

Final Thoughts

Lighting for commercial photography can be very creative. Even if your client comes to you with the idea for a basic clamshell lighting design, you may suggest adding a few elements that really take the images (and the advertising campaign) to another level. Something as

usage of that backlight. I started with it off to the far side of the set, and just used it to separate the model from the background. Next, I positioned it just over the shoulder of the model and used it to create a circular flare pattern with a rainbow coloration (that circle of light is not something I added in postproduction; it's straight out of camera). I got another

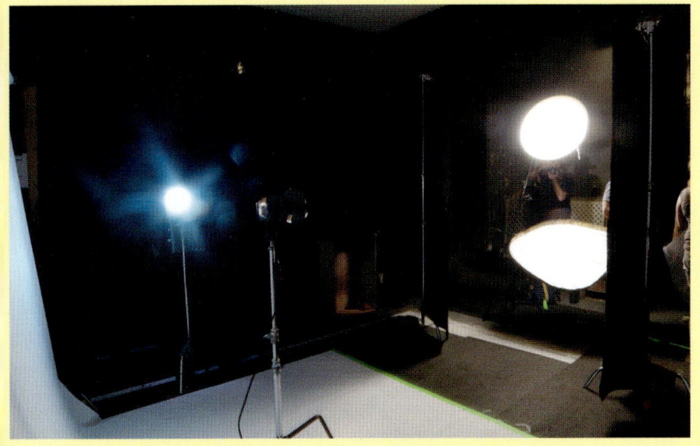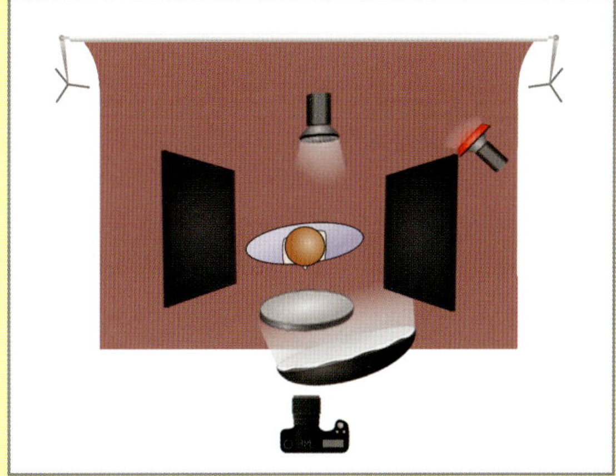

simple as adding a colored gel or snoot on the background, or maybe a strobe with a grid flaring back into the camera, can make the images really stand out. Always start with the lighting as the client asks, but then see if they might like to try some of your ideas, too. If they don't, you can stick with the basics—but chances are, they will appreciate your creativity. Now, get out there and make some photo magic!

▼ The backlight, a 40 degree grid on strobe, flared into the camera to create a rainbow circle of light. *Hair and makeup by Doniella Davy. (Specs: f/8.0, 1/200, ISO 100)*

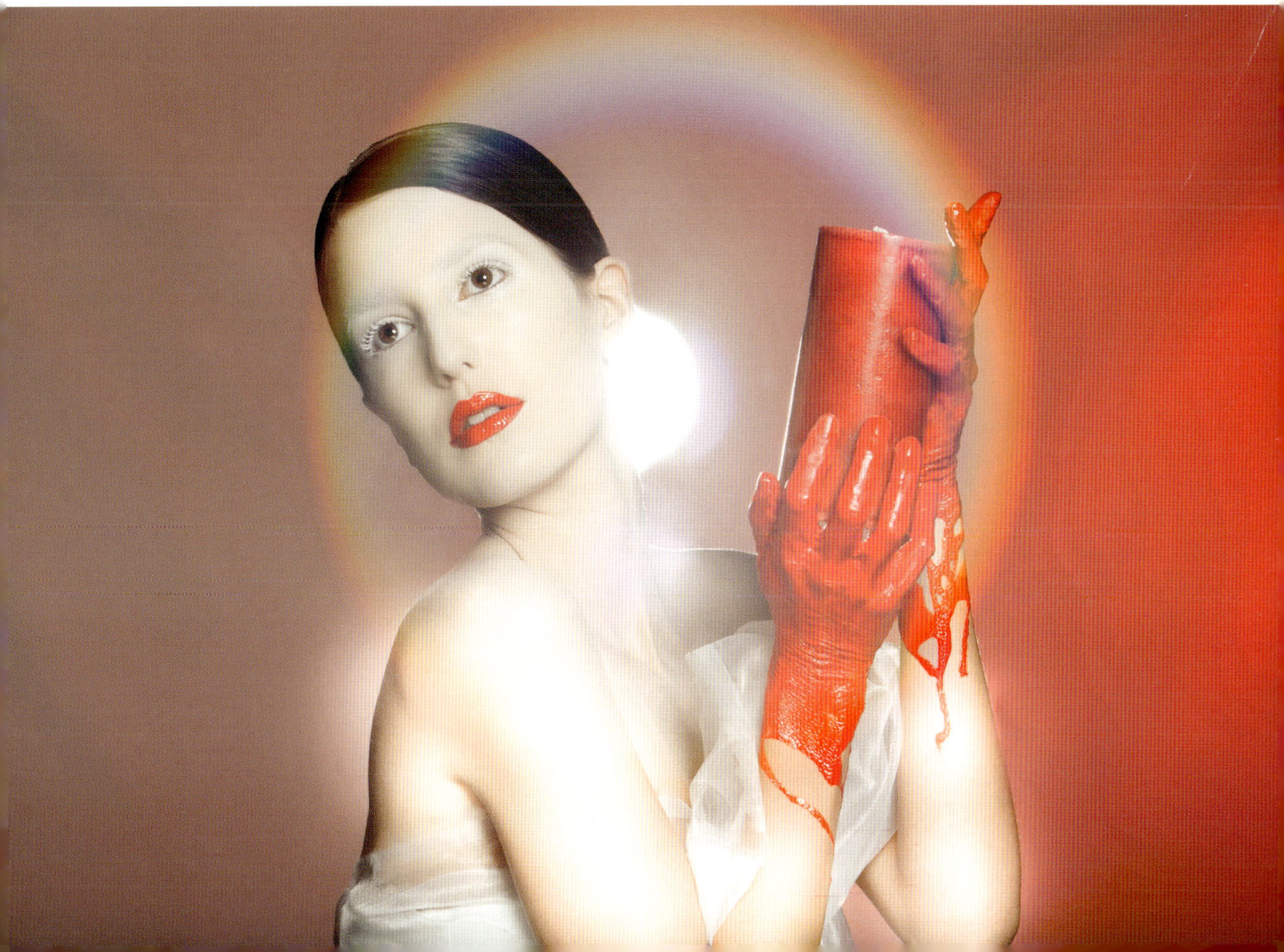

Index